Theme Town

THEME TOWN

A Geography of Landscape and Community in Flagstaff, Arizona

Thomas Wayne Paradis

iUniverse, Inc.
New York Lincoln Shanghai

Theme Town

A Geography of Landscape and Community in Flagstaff, Arizona

iUniverse, Inc.

For information address:
iUniverse, Inc.
2021 Pine Lake Road, Suite 100
Lincoln, NE 68512
www.iuniverse.com

ISBN: 0-595-27035-2

Printed in the United States of America

For Linda, Ken and Dee

Contents

Preface

My inspiration for this project can be traced to 1997 when I started teaching a series of world geography classes at Northern Arizona University in Flagstaff. With relatively large classes of 50 or more students representing the spectrum of majors and programs throughout the university, I found it difficult to organize any type of field trip that might be remotely manageable and effective. Clearly, the idea of trying to shout over the hustle and bustle of places like downtown Flagstaff to 50 students appeared quite unreasonable. Still, field trips are vitally important to provide geography students with some real-world experience outside the traditional classroom. My solution was to produce a written, self-guided tour that students could complete on their own time, answering various interpretive questions along the way. A short walk through part of Flagstaff would successfully introduce students to various important geographic trends taking place throughout the United States.

After 1998 I expanded the tour with each passing year as I learned more about the Flagstaff community. I soon found that my own research interests involving small-town change, downtown redevelopment, and America's railroad industry dovetailed well with the evolving walking tour through Flagstaff, and the tour itself soon became an important research project in its own right. Before I knew it I had collected more than enough material to write a lengthy book, and the challenge soon became one of containment and organization. I desired to compile these efforts into a book that might appeal to anyone—on or off campus—who might be interested in learning more about the world in which we live, or about a place called Flagstaff particularly. Thus, here in its final form, *Theme Town* operates on multiple levels—as an introductory geography textbook of sorts for NAU students, as an academic research project that investigates some of Flagstaff's geographical changes, and as a collection of local stories that provide an understanding of Flagstaff as a distinct place. The first four chapters focus on the geography of Flagstaff and its close link with the railroad industry, whereas the final four chapters consist of the aforementioned walking tour, which I refer to as *Flagstaff's America Tour*—or more simply, *the Tour.*

For this book I used a combination of research methods to study the process of downtown redevelopment and other changes affecting the human landscapes of Flagstaff. These methods consist of numerous open-ended interviews with various city leaders and other influential role players; content analysis of local and regional newspaper articles, editorials, and letters to the editor; visual landscape analysis of various local scenes; inspection of specific historical and city planning documents, maps, and city directories; and participant observation, consisting of my personal attendance at certain community forums, city meetings, and local discussions. All of these qualitative methods, when used together, provide for a rather thorough understanding of various local issues and changes taking place within and around the Flagstaff community. More specifically, my research involving the process of downtown redevelopment in Flagstaff continues beyond this book and will likely be the subject of future publications.

The writing of this book would not have been possible without the support, contributions, and cooperation of numerous individuals. First, I am indebted to my colleagues within the Department of Geography and Public Planning at Northern Arizona University, all of whom have enthusiastically supported my teaching and research efforts since my becoming a new assistant professor in 1997. This is truly a faculty dedicated to higher education, community service, and—especially—to the future success of our students. I continue to thoroughly enjoy working and teaching with my current academic family: Samantha Arundel, Lenn Berlin, Robert Clark, Carolyn Daugherty, Lee Dexter, Dawn Hawley, Tina Kennedy, Alan Lew, and Deborah Martin. Other individuals associated with our Department have either retired, sought opportunities elsewhere, or taught occasional classes with us; nonetheless, I have benefited in appreciable ways from their knowledge and strong support, namely Tom Conger, Frank Hanna, Joy Mast, Pete McCormick, Stan Swartz, and George Van Otten.

Research for this book was facilitated more directly by the Intramural Grant Program at Northern Arizona University, which provided funding for my research during the summers of 2000 and 2001. The results of the research conducted during these times appear throughout this book.

Also on campus, the friendly staff of the Special Collections Room at Cline Library was especially helpful with tracking down specific historical materials and city directories. Instructive feedback from my own students further improved the quality of this work as they completed earlier versions of the inclusive walking tour. It was vitally important to obtain constructive opinions and information from the students themselves, many of them geography or planning majors studying within our department. Although they are too numerous to mention here individually, I fully appreciate their enthusiasm for the project and their collective interest in helping to make it better.

One particular individual, Louella Holter, spent numerous hours thoroughly reviewing and editing a draft of the book, for which I am especially grateful. As editor for NAU's Bilby Research Center, Louella offered many helpful suggestions and comments. I also thank Randy Wilson, editor of the Flagstaff *Daily Sun*, who read the entire book and personally approved the use of information extracted from numerous issues of that newspaper. Local artist Gary McAllister assisted with the book cover design and supplied the graphic from his own painting entitled "Mainline Flagstaff".

I owe similar gratitude to numerous community members who donated their time to provide important information and local perspectives. Specifically, I wish to thank Paul Babbitt, Jim Babbitt, Rick Barrett, Sergeant Gerry Blair, Kent Burnes, Kim Gavigan, Pamela (Sam) Green, Maury Herman, Charles Hoffman, Michael Kerski, Don Leamon, Michael McCallister, Al Richmond, Henry Taylor, Steve Vanlandingham, Harold Watkins, David Wilcox, Susan Wilcox, and Mark Young for sharing their knowledge of the community. Discussions with these individuals proved to be one of the most rewarding aspects of this project. Further, I am indebted to certain individuals who have already enlightened the Flagstaff community with their own publications related to Flagstaff. The research and writing of Platt Cline, Marie Jackson, Richard and Sherry Mangum, James Woodward, and J. Lawrence Walkup proved instrumental in providing a solid base of information for my own work here. I also thank the helpful staffs of the city of Flagstaff, the Flagstaff Public Library, and the Pioneers Museum for their assistance in locating specific sources of information and new leads for research.

One of the prominent themes of this book is the historical development and influence of the railroad industry in and around Flagstaff. It would therefore be an oversight not to recognize my fellow members and friends of the Flagstaff Model Railroad Club, with its impressive model railroad layout located at the Coconino County Fairgrounds. Spending time with fellow railroad enthusiasts is clearly one of the best ways to learn about the industry and its heritage in Flagstaff and elsewhere. I am continuously grateful for their willingness to share their own knowledge with me and with the community.

The superb and tireless employees of Flagstaff's *Daily Sun* deserve special accolades. Much of the research and information presented throughout this book is due to the efforts of numerous reporters, editorial staff members, and all other employees and community members who work to provide one of the most important sources of information to Flagstaff and northern Arizona every day. Information and perspectives found in literally hundreds of news articles, editorials, and letters to the editor between 1987 and 2002 provided the basis of research for this project. In addition, I am grateful to the *Flagstaff Tea Party* and its editor, Dan Frazier, for publishing an excerpt of this book in a previous issue of that newspaper.

I am also indebted to all the professors who collectively contributed to my own education in geography. Specifically, it was Professor Peirce Lewis at the Pennsylvania State University who designed a similar type of walking tour in State College, Pennsylvania. No other assignment during my undergraduate years contributed more to my understanding of human landscapes and small-town growth and development. As I continued my education as a graduate student at the University of Illinois, Urbana, Professor John Jakle greatly enhanced my knowledge of small towns and American landscapes, often through rather impromptu road expeditions through Midwestern farm communities.

Last, and most important, I am very fortunate to have the continuous encouragement of my entire family in this and all endeavors—above all, from my wife, Linda. She often fed me with new ideas and thoughts that helped to improve this work in immeasurable ways. She also accompanied me on a trial walk of the inclusive Tour, adding her own observations and perspectives. And, as always, I am ever grateful to my parents, Kenneth Wayne Paradis and Doris (Dee) Tshudy Paradis, who have always encouraged me to explore the world and to seek new opportunities. These fine parents have nurtured within me a strong interest in, and appreciation for, local community and cultural diversity. Without these fundamental interests I imagine this book would never have been written.

Introduction

A Place Called Flagstaff

Nestled within the ponderosa pine forest of northern Arizona is a seemingly ordinary place called Flagstaff. Not the biggest of cities or the smallest of towns, Flagstaff is probably known best for its proximity to the Grand Canyon, some 80 miles to the north. Visitors from around the world are familiar with Flagstaff as a gateway to the Canyon or to other popular attractions in the region. Others merely patronize various roadside services along Interstate 40 through town, most of them passing through on their way to somewhere else. Folks from "the Valley," or the Phoenix metropolitan area, drive to Flagstaff for weekend trips either to cool off in the summer or to enjoy the snow and its various entertainment values in the winter. Although many people have "been through" Flagstaff, however, it is likely that few people outside of the community actually know the place well. Flagstaff's location on the scenic and culturally diverse Colorado Plateau makes it famous. Still, the town of Flagstaff and its growing community of 52,894 residents as of the 2000 U.S. Census are in many ways not unlike other lesser-known places. Although some may perceive Flagstaff as a place overrun with tourists, many characteristics of its community and the way it functions are not all that different from any other place.

What may be easy to lose sight of is that underneath Flagstaff's thick veneer of tourism is a living, breathing community that calls Flagstaff home. For those who have lived and pursued their dreams here—newcomers and old-timers alike—Flagstaff is perhaps the most special place in the world. In many ways, however, Flagstaff and its community are not all that unique, instead maintaining much in common with other places of its size. To learn something about a place called Flagstaff, then, is to learn about America—and Americans—as a whole. This book investigates beyond Flagstaff's tourism economy to understand something about an all-American community and its own human landscapes. Although the focus here is on Flagstaff itself, the geographical story presented herein is actually about America, and about all Americans who have ever lived their lives and participated in communities of some form.

Ours was for generations a nation of small towns. Only recently in the developmental history of the United States have Americans become accustomed to suburbs, exurbs, or edge cities—our sprawling urban areas referred to by Peirce Lewis as the "galactic metropolis," the lights of which can be imagined as star-filled galaxies from airplane windows at night (Lewis 1979).

Prior to America's march to the cities and suburbs during the twentieth century, America's dominant culture was largely a product of its small towns. In 1880, during the time of Flagstaff's initial settlement, a full 70 percent of Americans lived in rural areas or in towns of less than 2,500 people (Jakle 1999). Nearly half of the labor force was engaged in farming (42%) at that time, and only 25 percent of all Americans lived in so-called urban places with more than 25,000 people.

Today's booming western cities, for instance, barely made the maps in 1880. With its 234,000 residents in that year, San Francisco served as the commanding urban metropolis of the West. With its deep, natural bay and access to California's interior valleys, this was America's true gateway to the Pacific Rim well into the twentieth century. The next largest city was Oakland, just across San Francisco Bay, with 88,000 people. Los Angeles hosted only 11,000 residents in 1880—a fifth of Flagstaff's population today. At that time, Phoenix had barely been thought of. Settled as one of numerous agricultural villages in the central deserts of Arizona, Phoenix finally registered some 3,000 people by 1890. Even in that year, following a decade of extraordinary growth in the American West, no city west of the Rockies—except for San Francisco and Oakland—exceeded 50,000 people. Of course, all of that changed very rapidly. By 1920 the population of Los Angeles had grown to more than half a million people, with no end to the growth in sight (Hornbeck 1990a). Likewise, there are still people alive who could remember today's Phoenix as a very different place, with a mere 29,000 residents in 1920.

Like their metropolitan counterparts, smaller towns and cities are never static, but instead are dynamic places, always changing with the times. Having once thrived as regional trade centers scattered from coast to coast, America's small towns had collectively descended into an era of economic and social depression by the 1970s (Lewis 1972). Business districts withered, young people moved out to take advantage of perceived opportunities in the metropolis, and local economies based on agriculture or manufacturing gave way to competition elsewhere around the globe. Small towns generally found themselves struggling to deal with new economic realities over which they had little control. No longer could communities and their small-town landscapes rely on the industrial, manufacturing, or extractive activities (e.g. mining, logging) that had previously supported them, and provided a generally reliable job base. By the 1980s America—both urban and rural—had entered a vague postindustrial era in which the service sector, tourism, and high-tech industries reigned supreme. America's new economy would be based primarily on consumption, not production.

The initial reaction of small-town residents to this national economic shift, for lack of any better idea, often consisted of tearing down buildings perceived as obsolete (Lewis 1972). Although Americans are generally familiar with the era of "urban renewal," which effectively wiped out entire swaths of perfectly fine urban fabric, few are aware that this same philosophy was also alive and well in America's ailing small towns—at least in those that could afford the high costs of destroying older buildings and infrastructure. For towns not able to absorb the costs of demolition by the acre, their old buildings just sat there, undergoing a process known as *benign neglect.* In no small twist of irony, by the end of the twentieth century it was these towns that would eventually attract throngs of visitors and new residents to see and experience their surviving "historic" building stock (Figure 1).

Figure 1. Derelict commercial buildings in Las Vegas, New Mexico. These buildings patiently await some attention from historic preservation enthusiasts. Many older structures like these have sat for decades, neglected by both investors and the wrecking ball. (Photo: Author's collection)

Consequently, those abandoned commercial buildings, courthouses, and train depots dismissed as antiquated and obsolete in the 1970s are now absolutely cherished by their communities. Flagstaff is no exception. A good number of urban folks, now falling out of love with the city, are even attempting to return to America's small towns in search of a different way of life long forgotten by many. This process of *counterurbanization* has not been lost on the media. In a *Time Magazine* cover story entitled "The Great Escape," Eric Pooley announced to a national readership that "Americans are fleeing suburbia for small towns" (Pooley 1997). Though "fleeing" may be a bit overstated, there is some truth to it. For instance, between 1990 and 1992, 64 percent of nonmetropolitan counties (those not considered metropolitan by the U.S. Census Bureau) showed an increase in their populations.

The recent revival of interest in America's smaller communities has given rise to new types of developments and human landscapes not previously seen. Replacing traditional downtown trade centers, for instance, is what Donald Getz (1993) has called the *tourism business district*, or TBD. Except in rare circumstances, Main Street no longer serves as a community's primary center of local businesses and services. Especially since the 1960s, traditional businesses have braved new locations at the edge of town, typically lined up along a commercial strip, within a regional shopping mall, or near the ubiquitous Wal-Mart shopping center. Most agree that America's downtowns will never return to their former economic vibrancy as local trade centers. Typically, small-town business districts have either been abandoned, as evidenced by rows of boarded-up commercial buildings, or they have been transformed into tourist attractions, such as what has occurred relatively recently in downtown Flagstaff.

According to Getz, tourism business districts can be described simply as concentrations of visitor-oriented attractions and services located in older downtown areas large and small (Getz 1993). In Europe as well as in America, these evolving TBDs most often coincide with local heritage areas and can be the subject of intense planning and regulation efforts by their communities. Since downtown redevelopment efforts began in the late 1980s, Flagstaff's own business district has been largely transformed into a TBD, with businesses oriented more toward leisure, entertainment, and specialty goods than to the general needs of the local population.

As the overall function of *main street*—the generic but symbolic term describing small-town business districts—has changed since the 1970s, so too has its appearance. This fact alone has encouraged many a community discussion between those who lament the loss of traditional downtown commerce and those who celebrate the revival of downtown in its new guise as cultural and entertainment hub. In such places, main street now comes complete with rows of "olde" street lights pretending to be antiques, immaculately restored historic brick buildings with pastel-colored trim, quaint-looking business signs advertising up-scale antique and gift shops, and pedestrian-friendly sidewalks complete with benches, trees (usually protected heavily by six-foot iron fences), and tasteful brick pavers. And for those who still may be unsure of where they are, celebratory banners are often found at regular intervals announcing one's location within a "historic district" or "downtown" (Figure 2). By and large, this is the look of America's reinvented main streets. As we will see, this does not happen by accident.

Figure 2. Historic downtown Hemet, California. Indications of recent redevelopment efforts are everywhere, including tree planters, flowers, new sidewalks and lampposts, stylish signs, and a banner announcing "Hemet Downtown." (Photo: Author's collection)

The transformation of small-town business districts into tourist attractions is often associated with some form of image making. That is, small towns are being "themed" with some predetermined identity to encourage local consumption by visitors and to enhance the community's sense of place. The recent rise of *theme towns* has been the result, whereby community leaders often decide by committee the dominant identity of their town. Then, they more or less plaster the prescribed identity throughout the historic downtown area, where the theme is most commonly applied to the visible landscape. Most often, a given theme will not be totally fictitious or created out of thin air, but will purposely exaggerate some aspect of local heritage. Various authors have identified a variety of general themes commonly used by smaller communities, including western–gold rush, ethnic–cultural, old town–historic preservation, industrial–mining, waterfront–wharf, and many others (Lew 1989; Engler 1994). The historic architecture of many small town business districts often becomes its own theme through the process of historic preservation and renovation.

Reflecting an all-American trend in theme development, the Southwest region is home to an increasing number of theme towns, including Boulder City, Nevada (Hoover Dam theme), Roswell, New Mexico (UFOs and aliens), Jerome, Arizona (arts and crafts), Holbrook, Arizona (Route 66 and the Petrified Forest), Calico, California (western, mining), Santa Fe, New Mexico (Indian Pueblo and Spanish culture), Silverton, Colorado (Victorian town) and Kanab, Utah (Utah's "Little Hollywood"). Of course, the adoption of any theme to represent a community's dominant identity is always subject to the complicated issue of authenticity. For example, which theme would serve as the most authentic representation of Roswell, New Mexico: One focusing on the legends and lore of the Wild West, or one that revives the legends and lore of a mysterious UFO "crash" on the New Mexico plains in 1947? Both themes are rooted in the overall heritage of the Roswell community and carry with them questionable levels of truth (Paradis 2002a). This is precisely the community discussion that has been taking place in Roswell since 1996 when the first friendly aliens began appearing in storefront windows, and model flying saucers began to adorn rooftops downtown. Should the dominant identity for any given place be specifically crafted or invented, or should the whole idea of image making be left alone? These are issues that scholars and community leaders have only begun to investigate.

Although it may appear that all smaller communities are enjoying an equal chance to jump on the tourism and theming bandwagon, this is hardly the case. A town's success in transforming its local economy from one based on traditional industries to one dominated by tourism and amenities lies partly with the energy and perseverance of its community leaders, and mostly with its geographic location. Although many towns have made the leap to tourism development to sustain their ailing economies, many others are still characterized by their diminishing populations and boarded-up storefronts.

A variety of recent studies have demonstrated the criteria necessary for small-town growth (see Booth 1999). Generally, the places with the following geographic characteristics stand the best chance for growth, whether growth is desired or not: a connection with one or more interstate freeways, proximity to natural "amenity areas" such as national parks and monuments, proximity to ski resorts, the inclusion of a sizable college campus, and relatively close proximity to a nearby metropolitan area. This last one is extremely important. Although not all communities will benefit equally from their close proximity to a large city, this urban-rural link is clearly vital for success. After all, it is America's urban and suburban middle- and upper-middle class populations that are rediscovering small towns, and they logically tend to rediscover those located closest to their suburban homes. Small towns have essentially become the country cottage or back-yard playground for suburban America. Consequently, it should come as no surprise that the fastest-growing small towns are those located within a couple hours' drive from metropolitan areas such as Atlanta, Chicago, Phoenix, St. Louis, Denver, Boston, Seattle, New York, Los Angeles, and many others.

Of course, success is in the eye of the beholder. For smaller communities enjoying the economic benefits of recent population growth and increasing numbers of visitors, growth necessarily brings with it a host of challenges and new community issues. These issues range from complex "native versus newcomer" controversies and conflicting urban and rural ideologies to more practical issues of increased traffic congestion, skyrocketing property values, urban sprawl, air and water pollution, and loss of small-town character. These are hardly unique issues to any given town. Essentially, if a small town is to grow, it must invite "the city" to move in. And sometimes the city moves in much more rapidly than a community anticipates or desires (Figure 3).

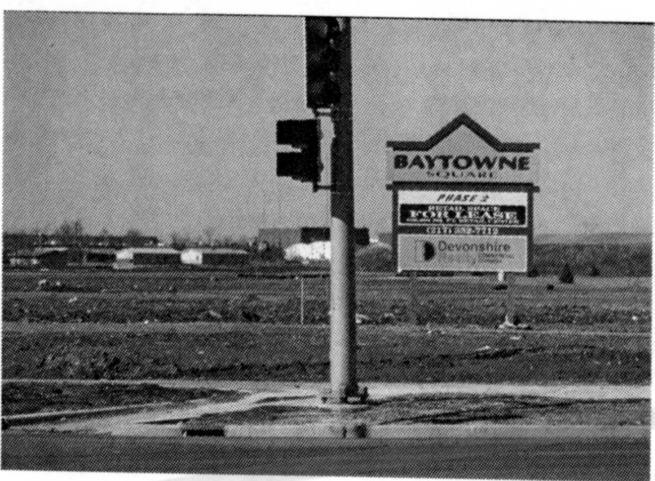

Figure 3. Prospect Avenue, Champaign, IL. Farmland is rapidly giving way to suburban development on the northern periphery of Champaign. Such transition zones are often indicated by new sidewalks, traffic lights, survey markers, signs advertising future developments, and plenty of trash littering the former farmland. (Photo: Author's collection)

Flagstaff presents an excellent opportunity to investigate one small town's screaming ride into America's new, postindustrial economy. Flagstaff is virtually a textbook case in terms of meeting the geographical criteria required for growth mentioned above. Unlike many small towns, Flagstaff is located along not one, but two major interstate freeways that provide easy access to this 7,000-foot-high community. Just over 2 hours away by car along I-17 is the booming Phoenix metropolitan area. The largest employer in Flagstaff is Northern Arizona University, hosting some 15,000 students. Just north of town is the popular Snow Bowl ski area and an impressive 12,633-foot volcanic mountain that comes with it, known as the San Francisco Peaks (Figure 4).

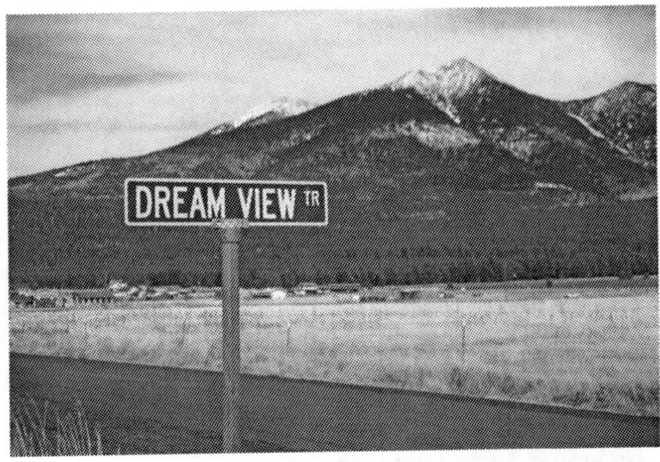

Figure 4. Fort Valley and the San Francisco Peaks, north of Flagstaff, AZ. Smaller towns and cities including Flagstaff are increasingly promoting various natural and quality-of-life amenities to prospective developers and residents. (Photo: Author's collection)

Further, Flagstaff is literally surrounded by evergreen trees—much of it available to public recreation and arguably the largest continuous ponderosa pine forest in the world. Immediately surrounding Flagstaff are a wide assortment of national and state parks and national monuments, not the least being Grand Canyon and Petrified Forest National Parks. Within a 20-minute drive are Walnut Canyon National Monument, Sunset Crater and Wupatki National Monuments, and the nationally famous Oak Creek Canyon to the south.

This book, then, investigates a place called Flagstaff, interpreted as an all-American town. Various statistics on growth and change, although useful, provide little information to comprehend the social dynamics of a particular place. Instead, one must be willing to dive into the community itself—by talking to some of its people, taking part in various events, reading its newspapers, and trying to understand the planning process that dominates many important local issues. In turn, we should seek to understand the interrelationships between a community and its own human landscape.

PLAN OF THE BOOK

The book is organized into three main parts. The first consists of one chapter that introduces readers to the community of Flagstaff and also to important geographic concepts encountered throughout the text. I discuss the discipline of geography and what it is that geographers do, because many Americans continue to be baffled about this diverse field of science. I also introduce the concept of human landscape and landscape studies, an ongoing theme of the book and its inclusive walking tour. Simply, the human landscape refers to everything that humans build and create on the surface of the earth (above and below the earth as well), including all the common, ordinary things that we take for granted every day: car washes, fences, lampposts, apartments, streets, ornamental landscaping, railroad depots, department stores, and so on. Geographers spend much effort studying American landscapes and how and why they change (or stagnate) over time. Part 1 will therefore provide a "crash course" in the geography of human landscapes.

Part 2 of the book relates specifically to the historical and current development of Flagstaff, focusing on the role of the railroad and its various impacts on the community and vice versa. Located on one of the busiest main-line railroads in the nation, Flagstaff finds itself experiencing challenges in part brought on by its own growth and the continuing growth of the freight railroad industry. In short, the railroad in Flagstaff remains a paradox, both cherished and despised by the community. Perhaps most important, the two chapters focusing on Flagstaff and the railroad provide an excellent geographic case study to illustrate how geography affects all of our lives, all of the time.

The final and most lengthy part of the book consists of a detailed walking tour through part of Flagstaff's own built environment. A total of 22 stops are included, along with substantial discussions about the development and geographical significance of each. I could have easily added many more relevant and educational stops to a book like this, though the project would have turned into several volumes easily. Still, every local place, no matter how ordinary it seems, has an interesting story to tell, and geography almost always becomes part of the story in some way. Specifically, the text not only teaches something about each of the 22 stops along the tour, but also relates it somehow to the larger American scene; the human landscapes encountered at each stop can teach us something about the geography of America as a whole. For this reason, Flagstaff serves quite nicely as a sort of outdoor laboratory through which people can learn much about North American geography as well as that of Flagstaff. This is why I call it *Flagstaff's America Tour*. Throughout the text I refer to it simply as "the Tour," for simplicity. Although it must be an awesome experience to literally put on one's shoes and walk across the continent, something not just a few individuals have accomplished, we can do the next best thing—that is, to focus on a place like Flagstaff and learn about America from our own local scene. I think you will find the experience enlightening and fascinating—as well as much easier on your feet.

You will experience four distinct landscape scenes along the Tour: a revitalized downtown business district, a culturally diverse working-class neighborhood, a university campus, and a bustling commercial strip. The Tour is designed for walking, not biking or driving. Actually, one will find it extremely difficult to drive this route, for several reasons: (1) Many stops are located in close proximity to one another, and the needs of your automobile or bike (e.g. parking) will simply be a distraction; (2) the route is actually aligned in places against traffic, along one-way streets (with sidewalks), and through pedestrian areas of the Northern Arizona University campus without easy access by car; and (3) walking is the best way to experience these places while paying attention to them carefully. We often miss much of the American scene by zooming by in the car, and this walking tour will allow you to take your time and notice all the fascinating details of places so that you might better understand what they all mean. The Tour is reasonably wheelchair accessible as well, given that the route was chosen in part to be as pedestrian and wheelchair-friendly as possible. The only major highways that must be crossed are Route 66 and Butler Avenue, both at relatively pedestrian-friendly intersections where pedestrian-type traffic crosses regularly.

I should also emphasize that Flagstaff's America Tour is not designed like other walking tours, which are read during the walk. Of course, you may do precisely that if you are so inclined. However, there is much detail in the text pertaining to each of the 22 stops, and it may be an exercise in futility to attempt a thorough comprehension of each place with all of the outdoor distractions you will encounter. I therefore suggest that you read the text prior to setting out on foot, perhaps highlighting specific aspects to keep in mind while experiencing each stop specifically. If you are visiting Flagstaff, you may wish to select particular stops to visit at some point on your trip (see map in Figure 21). However you decide to tackle it, I hope that you will enjoy Flagstaff's America Tour to its fullest extent, and I strongly believe that after experiencing the Tour—either from your living room or from the streets of Flagstaff—you will never *see* America's or Flagstaff's ordinary human landscapes in the same way again.

Part I

The Geographer's World and the American Scene

CHAPTER I

THE DISCIPLINE OF GEOGRAPHY

Interpreting American landscapes through a geographer's eyes requires an understanding of what geographers do. This point tends to baffle the typical American citizen for very good reason. Few are taught to think of geography as the social and physical science that it is, and fewer still seem to value its importance. Perhaps this book will play a small role in reversing these common notions. Despite the slow return of geographical education to our nation's classrooms, most Americans tend to view geography as something between the act of reading maps and watching a TV game show. Perhaps the most common perception of geography is indicated by the questions presented on the popular show, "Who Wants to Be a Millionaire?" Geography questions are often asked on the show, such as these: "Put in order these capital cities from east to west," or "Name the states that border Connecticut," or "What is the longest navigable river in the United States?" Though all in good fun, this and other programs like it reinforce our nation's common view of geography—the naming and memorization of places and locations. Who in America did not have to memorize all 50 state capitals sometime in grade school or college, even though these places aren't necessarily the most important economic or cultural centers in the country? I am the first to admit that except for some initial thrill of memorizing geographical facts, this aspect of geography gets old very quickly, and it is no wonder that many Americans are less than enthused about learning geography!

Americans are often astounded to learn that geography is a social science, similar to the more commonly recognized fields of psychology, sociology, economics, and political science. It is also a physical science that strives to understand how our physical landscapes are formed and altered over time, how humans impact the physical environment, and how the environment impacts us. Students can even major in geography and continue on for a masters or doctorate. A bachelor's degree, for instance, will open up a wide variety of opportunities for students, especially in the technical areas of cartography (the techniques of map-making), remote sensing (interpreting satellite and aerial photo data), GIS (geographic information sciences), and urban or environmental planning.

I find it useful to introduce the field of geography to newcomers by explaining the three basic questions that geographers ask when investigating places or regions: What is where? Why is it there? So what? The first question is merely *descriptive* in its application. Where are the features located, and what is their geographical pattern? For most Americans, this is as far as geography goes. For instance, we can map the location of volcanoes in northern Arizona or churches in Flagstaff or land controlled by the federal government in the Southwest. Or, we can locate and map our 50 capital cities. When geographers ask "What is where," we wish to *describe* a place or region in every way we can: what it looks like, how it functions, and what are its component parts. All of this can be mapped, of course, to determine the geographical distribution of things, places, and people on the earth's surface. Because geography is the only academic field whose primary concern is *spatial distribution*, the most useful analytical tool, even today, is the map. For geographical analysis, then, this first question is imperative, but it is only the first step in understanding what it is that geographers do.

The second question is inherently more interesting, and it constitutes a much more exciting aspect of geographical inquiry. When the distribution or feature in question has been mapped and described, we seek to *explain* it—to answer the question, "Why is it there?" Depending on the topic under investigation, the search for explanations can become quite complicated and controversial. For instance, geographers are still debating various theories that attempt to explain the great "white flight" to the suburbs in the 1950s and 60s. Cultural geographers prefer explanations that focus on dominant American cultural values, such as our anti-urban sentiments that include our desire to escape the dirty, congested, polluted city. Cultural geographers have collected decades worth of evidence in support of their theories. Economic geographers, however, might reply, "Hold on, it's not just cultural tastes and values that explain America's move to the suburbs." Instead, they would claim, various economic and political forces were at work, with the help of advanced transportation technology. Without the automobile and urban freeway system, the distances would be too great for commuters to live 20 miles outside and around the city's core from day to day. Explanations for suburban development are also found in the drive for profits in the construction, real estate, and auto industries. Speculators purchased large tracts of farmland on the periphery of these cities so that it could be subdivided and resold. These same developers thus *created* a demand through promotions and advertising, encouraging middle-class Americans to move to the new suburbs. Low-interest loans provided by the federal government helped to make it all affordable. Aside from cultural and technological factors, then, a variety of economic and political forces were at work as well. Indeed, the explanation for suburbs just becomes more complex from there.

As geographers continue to develop answers and theories related to the second question, the third question adds yet another layer of inquiry and importance to the research being conducted. In short, the "so what" question is meant to ask, "Why is this important" and "What are the implications" of what was found in questions 1 and 2. It is this third question that tends to link the field of geography to our everyday world. Implications of maintaining our suburban lifestyle, for instance, include a wide variety of social, economic, and environmental issues that affect our society today. These include the serious and highly contested concerns of urban sprawl and the costs of gobbling up prize farmland at a rapid rate, our dependency on the automobile for getting anywhere, our relative isolation from neighbors and friends, and our chemical-dependent lawns and gardens that can lead to contamination of ground water supplies and to air pollution through the constant use of gas-guzzling lawn mowers.

The implications of America's life in the suburbs are quite complicated, and scientists have only recently begun to understand them. Further, like implications of most human actions, they tend to be highly debatable, with no easy solutions or answers. We are all impacted by spatial patterns in many ways regardless of where we live, work, and play. It is these very implications of "what is where" that ultimately form an intimate connection between human landscapes and their communities. Such implications reveal how geography influences our society, our landscapes, and the choices that we constantly make within those landscapes. Many geographers focus much of their time and energy studying this "so what" question with regard to particular spatial problems and inquiries. You will soon find that this book and its inclusive walking tour of Flagstaff focus fairly equally on all three geographic questions.

THE CONCEPT OF PLACE

Although seemingly mundane, the term *place* is actually a central concept in the academic field of geography. Place is, for many people, synonymous with location, area, or locale. Its precise meaning, however, is not so clear, even among geographers. In fact, some geographers have dedicated much of their writing to providing a better theoretical understanding of place. Nonetheless, it remains one of those "contested concepts" that geographers continue to debate. Although the common belief that "all [towns, commercial strips, skylines] look the same," holds some limited truth—given their initial settlement by people with similar cultural backgrounds, available technology, and political economic systems—every place always exhibits geographical qualities unique to itself. Thus, all places maintain a variety of standardized patterns more or less blended with specific local characteristics and nuances; it is the local nuances that provide a special character to each place. Some would refer to these nuances as "a sense of place." For this reason, geographer John Agnew's conception of place is quite useful. His particular version of place is well respected, and thus it constitutes an underlying theme of this book.

Place, according to Agnew (1993), consists of three distinct components that continuously influence one another: *location*, *locale*, and *sense of place*. A place cannot be thoroughly understood without considering all three elements and the interactions that occur among them. "Locale is the core geo-sociological element in place," Agnew has explained, "but it is structured by the pressures of location and gives rise to its own sense of place that may in certain circumstances extend beyond the locality" (Agnew 1993, 263). In this context, then, *locale* refers to the local setting in which social activities and behaviors take place, among and throughout the local community. Social activities within the locale generally influence the creation of local landscape elements through a wide variety of social processes. These may include the law-making influence of a local governing body such as a city council, the formation of a local interest group to promote or oppose a particular development project, or the countless individual decisions made by business people and other local residents regarding how their particular commercial or residential properties are altered. Thus, the locale constitutes all organized and spontaneous interactions that occur among humans within a particular place, which transform human landscapes, ultimately manipulating that place.

Although the locale refers to all social activity generated from *within* a particular place, *location* involves the various effects *upon* locales of social and economic processes that operate at larger geographic scales. In short, location refers to the various external influences on the locale. You may be familiar with the simple though powerful mantra pertaining to real estate: "location, location, location." In part, the economic and social values of individual properties depend on what is located around them—the locational component of place. The same two-story Dutch Colonial house situated within a quaint urban historic district will not maintain the same value—economic or otherwise—as it would if it were located within a heavy industrial and manufacturing area. In Flagstaff, for instance, real estate agents are quick to advertise new houses based on their location with respect to other surrounding features presumed as desirable, including views of a golf course or scenic vista, distance from nearby schools or downtown, and—most important—the number and density of coveted ponderosa pine trees growing on or around the given property. Thus, each particular property is always influenced heavily by various external geographic factors.

The same is true for entire towns or cities regularly influenced by trends, processes, and places located *outside* their immediate jurisdictions. For instance, Flagstaff's local economy depends heavily on the tourism industry, a situation that can be controlled and promoted locally only to a limited degree. Even without Flagstaff's relentless promotional campaigns to attract more visitors, some tourists would still find their way to Flagstaff. Although local promotional efforts that attempt to sell Flagstaff to prospective visitors are arguably quite effective, the fact that Flagstaff has become a tourist town is contingent primarily upon geographic situations from outside the locale. Located some 80 miles south of Grand Canyon National Park, Flagstaff has served through most of its history as a convenient stopping-over point, or gateway town for Grand Canyon visitors. Even more important is

Flagstaff's geographic relationship to the growing Phoenix metropolitan area, from which approximately 65 percent of Flagstaff's visitors come. Another related external influence involves the continued attraction of national chain stores and retailers to Flagstaff's commercial strips and freeway interchanges. Familiar national fast food chains, hotels, and "big box" stores including Wal-Mart and Target have decided to locate in Flagstaff to take advantage of the increasing tourist traffic as well as Flagstaff's growing regional population.

An abnormally heavy amount of railroad train traffic through town exemplifies well the influence of location on a particular place. Witnessed and heard by Flagstaff residents some 90 times a day, the increasing number of freight trains through town is largely explained by the town's location along one of America's busiest main-line railroad routes. The product of previous corporate mergers, the mammoth BNSF Railway (see Chapter 4) has learned to take advantage of the expanding global economy by effectively transporting freight cargo between Chicago and Los Angeles—via Flagstaff. Thus, Flagstaff's railroad is just one component of a larger global network of transportation routes that connects America with the economies of Japan, China, the entire Pacific Rim region, and Europe. A global economic process is therefore influencing Flagstaff's locale in various ways, due to the town's location along one of the world's busiest railroad corridors. This locational situation has directly influenced community-related issues within Flagstaff's locale, the specifics of which are explored later. The important point here is that not all of Flagstaff's human landscapes and geographic characteristics are a product of local processes controlled entirely from within the community. Instead, a place like Flagstaff is constantly influenced by processes and circumstances external to the locale.

The third component of a place is referred to as *sense of place*. This concept, too, can give geographers headaches due to its ambiguous meaning, but it is vital for understanding why humans become attached to the places in which they live, work, and play. On a basic level, we must recognize that all human interactions have to *take place* somewhere, so our lives are intimately tied to particular geographic regions and places. A sense of place, therefore, refers to the ways in which we become attached to places, usually in a positive sense, derived from our own personal emotions and sentiments. That is why sense of place is exceedingly difficult to measure, though some social scientists have attempted to do just that, with limited success. After all, how can the ways in which we feel at home in a given place be quantified? Sense of place here can best be understood as a sense of being at home in a town, city, or region as we become accustomed to a particular place and become more familiar and comfortable with it over time (Jackson 1994). It is now recognized through research that humans tend to gain a strong sense of place, or attachment to place, through social activities with family and friends in a particular locale. Such activities include regular family visits, eating out with friends, shopping downtown, or participating in local community organizations such as clubs, churches, schools, and politics. Generally, the more we become involved socially within the locale, the stronger our sense of place becomes.

An individual's sense of place is also commonly enhanced by a long-time familiarity with a place's distinctive human landscapes, and by the natural environment in which a place is situated. In the latter case, many residents claim a strong sense of place for Flagstaff in part due to the breathtaking scenery around town provided especially by the San Francisco Peaks to the north and the veritable carpet of ponderosa pine forest blanketing the region. That Northern Arizona University is often dubbed the "Mountain Campus," and that local historian Platt Cline titled his monumental book *Mountain Town* (Cline 1994), is indicative of how Flagstaff's surrounding environment elicits its own special sense of place for residents and visitors alike.

An interesting exercise that you can try yourself or with others is one that I commonly use in my college classes to help people understand what it means to have a strong sense of place. Simply ask yourself or people you know if they "feel at home" in a particular place, whether it is their current hometown, neighborhood, city, or their childhood home. The answer will invariably be "yes." The important follow-up question is "*Why* do you feel at home there?" After a quizzical look, a pause, and some heavy thinking—these are not issues that people tend to think about every day—the respondent will usually mention aspects of family memories and activities, memberships in community organizations, and fun times had with friends in various local settings. Given that one's sense of place is by its very nature subjective and personal, answers to this question will of course vary from one individual to the next. Still, these particular answers can generally be considered as standards. No matter the individual answers, however, it is this notion of sense of place that ties all of us intimately to geography. In part, that is why it is so important for us to gain a better appreciation and understanding of the physical and human environments in which our lives are so intertwined. As a whole, not only are our lives engrained within a *locale* defined by social activities, community-related issues, and local decision making, but we are also affected by the outside world, the influence of *location*. In turn, we come to feel specific sentiments and emotions about our locale and location that can be interpreted as a strong *sense of place*. In short, place matters. Just as we affect place, place affects us throughout our lives in very powerful ways that geographers and others are still working to better understand. As one geographer recently put it, "Where you live is what you are" (Cohen 1998).

Throughout this book we will experience in some detail a place called Flagstaff, Arizona. Like many other places, Flagstaff has developed its own distinct geographical qualities and local histories that contribute to its strong sense of place. At the same time, residents increasingly believe that Flagstaff's distinctiveness is being threatened and perhaps lost to complex external pressures of location, especially through the homogenizing influences of globalization. In Flagstaff as in all places, aspects of locale, location, and sense of place are deeply intertwined and are ceaselessly interacting with and influencing one another in profound ways. Often, such aspects are manifested within the human landscape for all to see and experience.

Understanding Human Landscapes

This book concerns the geography of ordinary, American human landscapes and the communities that ceaselessly create and alter them. In Flagstaff's America Tour we explore four distinct though interdependent landscape scenes found in the growing community of Flagstaff—namely, a downtown business district, a pre-World War II working-class neighborhood, a growing university campus, and an evolving automobile commercial strip. From the geographer's perspective, *landscape* refers to neither English paintings of the countryside nor the "scenic" landscapes that we visit in national and state parks. When advertising a suburban lot as *landscaped*, explained Peirce Lewis, "it is generally understood that somebody has fussed with the shrubbery on a small bit of ground, perhaps planted a few trees, and has manicured the bushes—more or less artfully" (Lewis 1979, 11). For geographers, however, human landscapes consist of the total accumulation of material objects and things that humans have built and arranged for themselves to make their world habitable and agreeable. Basically, everything we build on the surface of the earth—and more recently, above and below the surface as well—is part of our human landscape.

All of us live among and interact with "ordinary" landscapes all of the time. I suspect that this is one reason why most people tend to take them for granted. Features in the human landscape include obvious things to which we rarely give a second look: sidewalks, tree-lined streets, trailer parks, freeways, skyscrapers, train stations, lampposts, grass lawns, dumpsters, road signs, barns, alleys, churches, and so forth. All of these things hold meaning and significance because they have stories to tell about our own culture and society. Specifically, I approach the interpretation of Flagstaff's own ordinary landscapes from a geographer's perspective. As a geographer, I view our landscapes as a product of numerous forces both local and global in origin—forces attributable to a variety of economic, political, cultural, social, and historical processes that are constantly at work in our society. It is the combination of these complex forces that communities are constantly trying to come to terms with. Some of these forces can be controlled and manipulated by local communities themselves, whereas others cannot.

Why should we even attempt to study and pay attention to such common, ordinary places? Simply, it will help us forge a stronger connection to the places we interact with all of the time. Some argue that we are losing that connection with the land, with society, and with the very geography that supports us. Many people, and even scholars, have rejected our everyday world as not being worthy of our attention. Instead, we tend to focus on *superlatives* in our dominant American culture—that is, the features of our lives and places that we consider unparalleled, exceptional, and outstanding. This approach to understanding our world unfortunately leaves a lot of important things ignored. We are taught—often unknowingly and benignly—by our media, family, and schools to pay the most attention to anything that can be described as best, most, highest, tallest, biggest, newest, first, last, poorest, widest, safest, and tastiest. The list of superlatives continues indefinitely. We readily learn about the tallest skyscraper, the most advanced technology, the oldest house, the safest car, the first state to enter the Union, the deepest canyon, and the most dangerous intersection.

America's love of superlatives reveals itself constantly in our ordinary human landscapes. For example, Grady Clay (1996) recognized the *capital* as a specific landscape element, a product of our culture. It seems that every city and town either strives to be identified as the "capital of" something important, or conversely, earns such an identity without much effort or planning. Although we usually associate the "capital" with the location of the state capitol building, or the United States Capitol in Washington, D.C., many more capitals have arisen upon our American landscape. Beyond our political hubs, places both large and small have achieved capital status through *dubbing*, a practice once associated with the conferring of knighthood or other honors during the Middle Ages. "In the absence of royalty," observed Grady Clay, "dubbing today is everyman's gimmick for attaching status, celebrity, or fame to a place or product, simply by assertion, usually in print" (Clay 1996, 11). It seems that practically every city desires to be a superlative in order to secure its own unique identity. Thus, Tarpon Springs, Florida has been dubbed the "Crawfish Capital of the World" and Hershey, Pennsylvania has become the Chocolate Capital, and Corona, California was once the Lemon Capital. More recently, Roswell, New Mexico has become the UFO Capital of the World, to the chagrin of its more conservative residents (Figure 5). This list of dubbed capitals could fill several pages, and their capital status is often displayed proudly on city welcome signs, billboards, water towers, and Web sites.

Figure 5. International UFO Museum and Research Center, Roswell, NM. Housed in Roswell's old Plains Theater since 1996, this museum has stimulated theme development within the downtown area. (Photo: Author's collection)

One important implication of our nation's focus on the biggest, tallest, and first is that Americans as a whole pay little attention to our common, ordinary landscapes. I personally believe that if people took more interest in their surrounding environment and learned something about how our human landscapes have developed over time, the word "boredom" could be nearly eradicated from the English language. There is always something interesting to see outside if we have some idea of what to look for. One of the primary tenets of contemporary landscape studies is that "there is no such thing as a dull landscape" (Groth 1997, 3). Ordinary landscapes serve as important archives—America's "unwitting autobiography" as Peirce Lewis put it (Lewis 1979, 12)—of social experience, cultural meaning, economic change, and political processes. To learn more about our everyday environment, then, is to learn much about ourselves—our values, interests, cultures, and ideologies as American citizens. More than that, I believe that if we learn some basic geographical concepts, we can all effectively "read" the American landscape on our own. With a little training, you will undoubtedly find our world a much more interesting and fascinating place in which to live.

As you continue through this introductory journey of some typical American landscapes, you should keep in mind that everything in the human landscape is more or less significant and meaningful in some way. Everything out there is important, regardless of whether a landscape is pretty or ugly, trendy or obsolete, tasteful or distasteful. As humans, we make value judgments about landscapes all of the time, and there's nothing wrong with that—until we make a true effort to *understand* these places for what they are, and why they're there. Thus, I suggest that you set aside your value judgments for the time being. Everything in the landscape—from skyscrapers to picket fences—is fair game for geographical inquiry, and all of it has been created by our own society, whether we like it or not. Therefore, it is necessary first and foremost to explain *how* these landscapes function, *why* they appear as they do, and *why* they are located where they are, before we allow ourselves to decide if a particular landscape is "good, bad, or ugly." This is your challenge for the remainder of this book, and for any landscape analysis you may undertake beyond it.

The next chapter serves as a guide to the various social, economic, political, cultural, and historical factors responsible for shaping the landscapes in which we live—that is, the primary explanations that help us to answer geographical question 2: "Why is it there?" Although one of these factors may dominate in any particular case, the others are always influential in some way. Further, I separate these factors here for the purpose of discussion and understanding, but these factors do not operate independently of one another. To the contrary, places of any scale are dynamic and complex, so it would be naive to assume that any human landscape could be explained merely through a simple economic or cultural influence, for instance. It is wise, therefore, to treat all of the factors in Chapter 2 as continually intertwined and interdependent.

Finally, implied throughout is the always-important influence of the physical environment, despite the continuing drive to "conquer geography" with human ingenuity and technology (Lewis 1979, 25). Virtually all modifications to the landscape must necessarily alter the natural environment in some way, and nature in turn is always impacting our built environment. To best understand a place, one is advised to pay close attention not only to the human landscape itself, but also to the ways in which physical and human environments incessantly influence one another. Therefore, aspects of climate, topography, soils, rock strata, hydrology, and plant and animal life must all be considered when investigating how a particular place looks and functions.

The interpretation of human landscapes constitutes a central part of any geographer's education and can provide an endless source of fascination for anyone. Prior to our walking tour through Flagstaff, then, Chapter 2 will provide an introduction to landscape studies, allowing for a deeper appreciation of Flagstaff's own human landscapes and those encountered practically anywhere else. During the Tour I will incorporate many of these geographical concepts to better understand places along the route.

CHAPTER 2

THE GEOGRAPHY OF HUMAN LANDSCAPES

LANDSCAPE AS HISTORICALLY CONTINGENT

First, we should reject outright the idea that certain things are "historic," while other things are not. America's tendency to designate certain places and things as historic implicitly tells us that everything else is *not* historic. We place fences around historic houses, call attention to historic monuments, and designate older sections of town as historic districts. Museums and guided tours serve the same purpose. We are conditioned to believe that the landscapes outside the confines of the museum walls or the tour route are not worth paying attention to because they are not recognized as being important. To the contrary, geographers recognize that the production of all human landscapes is *historically contingent.* In other words, the landscape features that we see and interact with in today's world are all contingent upon the societies, processes, decisions, and philosophies of the past, whether from 2 or 200 years ago.

According to Peirce Lewis, "the landscape is not something to be admired or denounced. Instead, it is like one vast archaeological dig—a layered accumulation of artifacts created by that disorderly accumulation of people we call our ancestors" (Lewis 1987, 23). This is not to say that museums and historic districts are bad things—quite the contrary. These places play a vital role in our understanding and appreciation of culture, society, heritage, art, and science. They also serve as clues to our own cultural values and interests, given that we as a society must always make choices about what to save, and how to save it. Instead, the point is that geographers take history seriously—all of it. To explore human landscapes from a geographer's point of view, therefore, we need to resist the temptation to believe that certain places are somehow less historic than others. Peirce Lewis has clarified this point with his example of a historic tour through Pennsylvania:

> In my home state of Pennsylvania, history is much touted as a tourist attraction, and there are self-guided tours across the state from one designated spot to another. These historic tours are predictable. They always start in Philadelphia, and Stop One is Elfreth's Alley. Stop Two is Betsy Ross's house. Stop Three is Longwood Garden in the Philadelphia suburbs, and so on until you drop into Lake Erie at Presque Isle, which is Stop 28. Now somewhere between Historic Stop Three and Historic Stop Four is, well, South Philadelphia, a large area of middle-aged rowhouses, mainly inhabited by blue-collar blacks and third-generation Italians. South Philly, of course, is not on any of those tours, and it is not likely to be. Most people I know on the Historical and Museum Commission in Harrisburg would think you were crazy if you suggested such a thing. Yet the fact is that South Philly is a more truthful historical museum than Betsy Ross's house will ever be. (Lewis 1987, 26)

It follows that to best understand our human landscapes, we must strive to uncover their histories of development. As an example, most towns and cities settled prior to 1920 include a *central business district* (CBD) designed specifically for commerce, where the commercial buildings are compact and often lined up flush with the street. As noted earlier, most Americans refer to this type of geographic space as *main street.* Often, the CBD is focused directly on the railroad, the vital lifeline for many cities and towns a century ago. Today the same railroads are cursed for causing too much traffic congestion. Additionally, countless downtown buildings have been demolished since the 1940s to make way for parking lots and development projects through an ill-fated process known comically as "urban renewal." The truth is that these business districts were not designed for the automobile in the first place, and few communities have not had to somehow come to terms with that reality. The downtown of the nineteenth century was designed to minimize the impact of geographic distance, to cluster together as many functions as possible, and to facilitate the most common means of local transportation—foot traffic (Figure 6). That many towns and cities still have yet to solve the "parking and congestion" dilemma is directly contingent upon the technologies and philosophies of the past. The downtown landscape as it appears and functions is thus a *historically contingent* place. Given the importance of history in the landscape, therefore, much of this book is devoted to looking at historic processes, events, and people to better comprehend the landscapes we live among today.

Figure 6. Main Street, Galena, IL. Now a bustling tourism business district, Galena's Main Street "wall" of nineteenth-century commercial buildings attracts throngs of visitors every weekend, mostly from the Chicago area. The district's curving and narrow streets are a product of its location on a small shelf of land adjacent to the Galena River. (Photo: Author's collection)

The Seen and Unseen of Landscapes

In one sense, landscapes can be interpreted as three-dimensional, visual "texts" that we can "read" like a book if we know what to look for and if we know some basic history and geography. When you have mastered some basic concepts (highlighted in italics throughout this book), you will most likely never "see" our ordinary landscapes in the same way again. Soon you will be impressing your friends and family at the dinner table with conversations about Victorian architecture, the evolution of the motel industry, and the Township and Range land survey system.

It is important to recognize, however, that there is much more to our human landscapes than that which is visible (the *seen*). If we are seeking a deeper understanding about a particular landscape in a particular place (say, a suburban neighborhood), we will need to investigate behind the scenes, so to speak, into the realm of the *unseen* (Upton

1997). Visual information (in the landscape itself) provides seemingly countless clues about human and physical geography, and thus the landscape can be read somewhat like a textbook. However, to determine more precisely the complex processes contributing to the creation of a place, further background research is often necessary.

Although the visible landscape itself holds a wealth of information, it rarely (if ever) provides us with the whole story. If we are inclined to dig a bit deeper, we will discover that there is much more than meets the eye, because landscapes are produced by humans who in turn operate within an almost endless variety of social situations. Human landscapes are *social productions.* They are produced by an amazing variety of social processes through which humans are constantly interacting with one another. For instance, various interest groups compete for various land uses or development projects, and volunteer organizations seek to help others in need. Petitions are signed, economic and political deals are made, and protests are conducted in the name of protecting particular values and interests. People choose to shop in some places and not others, or to behave in certain ways in certain places. Goofy clothing and clown hats might be more socially acceptable, for example, at the county fair than at church on Sunday morning. These social interactions and human decisions are collectively part of the *unseen*, and it is important to consider the unseen aspects of landscape to better understand them.

How does one investigate the *unseen*? There are numerous methods that require varying levels of effort. Discussions with people directly involved in some way with particular landscapes are often wonderful sources of information. Business owners downtown can tell you stories about how the business district has changed over time, because they may have been directly involved with the process of change. They can volunteer their own perspectives on the positive and negative implications of that change, and how it has affected them directly. Another useful source of information consists of local newspapers. From a series of daily or weekly issues, one can often determine the dominant community topics and places important at a particular time. You can learn something about the community and its social dynamics through letters to the editor and headline stories about topics of local interest.

Other sources of information can be found at local or university libraries and museums, where historical archives are typically located. Historical maps of land ownership patterns or of city and county streets are also useful to determine how and where cities have grown or stagnated. Promotional materials from the local chamber of commerce or convention and visitors bureau provide excellent sources of information that highlight the unique and special attributes of a specific place. Historic photographs can be used to determine changes and alterations to landscape scenes over time. Searching out local historians can be useful for gaining an overall perspective of a place's geographical development and characteristics. More recently, Web sites featuring various cities and their dizzying number of organizations provide yet another perspective on these places. These are only a few of the common sources of information that can be used to investigate the unseen aspects of our human landscapes, to provide some qualitative perspectives about particular places of interest. In fact, I have used many of these methods to investigate the unseen aspects of Flagstaff's own landscapes for this book.

Perhaps a rather detailed example of the seen and unseen will be instructive. The example I offer here consists of skyscrapers, or office towers, making up the skylines of our world's major cities. When using our skills as geographers, we can first focus on the technologies required to create such impressive structures. These super-human towers would simply not exist without a necessary collaboration of technologies that support their creation—technologies that involve the use of central air, interior lighting, structural steel, fire-retardant building materials, and of course the elevator. For these reasons the skyscraper as a landscape element is historically contingent—upon past technological advances and the mass marketing and consumption of those advances. Prior to the elevator, buildings rarely exceeded six floors.

Culturally speaking, we can read the landscapes of skyscrapers and interpret their symbolism and meanings. First, the skyscraper can be viewed as quintessentially American. Although European and other architectural traditions have influenced American architects throughout the twentieth century, it was in the United States that the skyscraper became a powerful symbol of corporate expansion, industrial and commercial success, and American superiority. As Paul Goldberger (1981) commented, "The skyscraper is at once the triumphant symbol of and the unwelcome intruder in the American city. We seem, after nearly a century, still not fully at peace with tall buildings: they shatter scale and steal light, and it is no surprise to hear them denounced as monstrous constructions; yet we also hold them dear." This debate surrounding the implications of skyscrapers became all the more intense with the recent destruction of the World Trade Center in New York. As of this writing, Americans and others around the world are discussing the pros and cons of rebuilding the towers in some form.

We could speak further about the evolution of architectural styles adopted for these "monstrous constructions," as well as the imagery that their corporate owners wished to promote. It is no surprise that corporations use their buildings as expressions of their corporate success and competitive edge—hence the drive to create the tallest and most impressively designed structures.

There is much about the skyscraper that we don't see, however. It is difficult to tell exactly what is happening *inside* a building by simply looking at it. Yes, it is probably used as office space for various companies, rented out at various rates by a landlord. Still, which companies are using the space, and for what activities? We wouldn't know anything about what is actually going on inside these glistening towers by simply looking at their exteriors. Instead, it would be wise to inspect the list of tenants who occupy its floors to provide a much different, more informed interpretation.

For instance, Deryck Holdsworth (1997) discusseed the Singer Building in New York City (of the Singer Sewing Machine Company), once famous for its remarkable 612-foot tower. When completed in 1908, this was the tallest building in the world. What is *unseen* is that the tower itself was only the latest of a building project that had begun some 10 years earlier with a variety of 10 and 14-story buildings. These smaller buildings received much less attention after the tower was built, but it was in these lesser structures that the Singer Company actually conducted its operations. "While the Singer, Metropolitan Life, and Woolworth towers certainly attract the eye, dozens of other new skyscrapers being built nearby offered many times more office space. If the landmarks on the skyline are the bold headlines," explained Holdsworth, "this broader volume of real estate—researched through commercial directories and corporate histories—provides the fine print" (1997, 49). The visual landscape, as seen, therefore comprises only part of the geographical story. It is for this reason that we focus throughout this book on both the seen and unseen aspects of Flagstaff's own human landscapes.

LANDSCAPE AS A CLUE TO CULTURE

The concept of *culture* is not simple. For our purpose we can view culture as the totality of customary beliefs, tastes, values, social forms, language, and material traits that reflect the traditions of specific ethnic, religious, or social groups of people. This definition is similar to those found in typical social studies textbooks that often sit idle in front of bored high school students. If we realize, however, that all of our human landscapes are the product of a specific and intricate cultural process, the study of culture can instantly become an endless source of fascination. The wide variety that we observe in the landscape results from different human actions—actions of both individuals and groups—across the earth's surface. Particular cultural and social traits combine to produce distinctive cultural landscapes. Recall that everything people accomplish has to take place somewhere, so we must recognize that geography is linked very closely to culture—because it has to be. People do not, and cannot, behave and interact on the head of a pin. Further, humans are always interacting in some way with nature, and different cultural groups tend to interact in different ways. Therefore, our own human landscapes can provide strong evidence about the cultural traits and values of the people who produced them. In this section I introduce some of the more important concepts of cultural geography useful for identifying the mark of culture in the landscape.

One case in point is the typical suburban single-family house. Often consisting of a living room, dining room, kitchen, two baths, three bedrooms, laundry, two-car garage, front lawn and back yard, the house silently reveals a surprising amount of information about American cultural values (Figure 7). It assumes a nuclear family structure, consisting of a mother, father, and children, still a powerful social ideal in American society, despite the fact that this way of life constituted less than 30 percent of American families in 2000 (Pulsipher 2000). The house also assumes certain ideas about public and private spaces. The front yard is a sort of public place, at least for viewing, so it is immaculately maintained by today's latest technologies, especially the ubiquitous lawn mower and leaf blower. More than anything else, the front yard is a space used to show off to the neighbors and the world, to indicate how well the family is doing. This is a space that indicates one's socio-economic status. The back yard, however, is traditionally a private space, often an extra room or a spillover from the house itself. Thus, it is most often fenced in with 7-foot walls, indicating that public viewing is not allowed. Further, the house symbolizes American ideas about private property and polite neighborliness and mobility. "Because we move so often in our quest for a better job and standard of living, yet insist on privately owned homes," explained Lydia Pulsipher (2000, 16), "a vast system of interchangeable dwellings has evolved across America, supported by an institution: the American domestic real estate market." Thus, it is possible to find similar houses with recognizable room layouts, sizes, and styles practically anywhere across the country.

Figure 7. Suburban neighborhood in Champaign, IL. Notice the immaculately trimmed lawn and shrubbery, and the grand entryway. This is the public view; the backyard is not as likely to be this neat and tidy. (Photo: Author's collection)

Cultural geographers generally agree that specific culture traits have to originate somewhere—that is, in a particular place or region. A *culture hearth* is the place where the core characteristics of a culture evolve. To develop a culture hearth, a group of people must be willing to try new things and to allocate various resources to develop innovative ideas. Some kind of economic structure is also necessary to facilitate the creation and adoption of those innovations (Rubenstein 1989). As geographers, we can trace many of the world's dominant religions, languages, technological advances, agricultural practices, and political systems to a limited set of cultural hearths around the planet. Globally speaking, culture hearths in Europe and the Middle East have contributed to our own dominant cultural traits here in North America. Closer to home, geographers have identified several important culture hearths in the United States that have impacted American culture as a whole since colonial times. These culture hearths are found in southern New England (primarily Massachusetts and Connecticut, focused on Boston), southeastern Pennsylvania (focused on Philadelphia), and tidewater Virginia (the Chesapeake Bay area). Other geographers have suggested that the metropolitan area of southern California, focused on

Los Angeles, provided an emerging culture hearth in the twentieth century. Overall, these particular American hearths represent the primary sources of America's cultural traditions, human geographies, dominant language and customs, and religions.

How do culture hearths, located in relatively small regions, spread their cultural characteristics to other places? The answer, in part, is the process of *cultural diffusion*. After a cultural idea appears in the landscape, it spreads outward from its cultural hearth. Thus, the process of diffusion can be defined as the spatial spreading or dissemination of a culture element or some other phenomenon from one place to another.

Returning to our earlier example, the suburban "dream home" can be interpreted as a product of diffusion, in this case from New England. By the 1820s, New Englanders were building their homes set back from the street on their own separate lots, often constructed with wood instead of brick. This was quite a divergence from the old English building tradition of constructing adjoining brick row houses close to the street. It is interesting that Pennsylvanians continued building English-style row houses in their cities and towns right up through the 1860s. Thus, it was New England that supplied the westward-moving nation with a socially acceptable form of residential dwelling. From the New England culture hearth the idea of separate houses on separate lots with front and back yards diffused westward.

How does the process of cultural diffusion happen? First, the landscape is often changed through *imitation*. That is, people in one place learn about a new style, innovation, or way of life, and they seek to adopt it for themselves. The recent proliferation of icicle-shaped Christmas lights dangling from the eaves of American homes is a case in point. I presume that imitation has played a large role in the successful diffusion of icicle lights across the country, even into warmer climate regions that rarely see real icicles. All it takes is one household to install these trendy lights before neighbors see them, like them, and travel to Wal-Mart to purchase them for their own homes. Eventually, there may even be a backlash, or resistance, to a particular innovation, whereby some people rebel due to their individualistic tendencies. I have spoken with several people who rejected these icicle lights simply because "everyone else is doing it." Thus, the choice to adopt a new innovation can spark sentiments of individuality or, conversely, can become a social symbol of conformity.

Another common process that encourages the spread of cultural elements is *migration,* the physical movement of people across the land. When people move, they bring their cultural "baggage" with them. North America owes most of its dominant cultural patterns to three particular European sources: England, France, and Spain. Our own American culture is primarily contingent upon the historical settlement of these three groups in North America, a process that began more than 400 years ago. Of course, all three of these dominant European-based cultures collided with a wide diversity of Native American cultures already in existence throughout North and South America. Our regional landscapes in the United States are therefore contingent upon the relative influence exerted over time by English, French, Spanish, Native-American, and African-American societies.

Flagstaff was settled in the heart of the Southwest, a culturally diverse region typically thought of as including western Texas, New Mexico, Arizona, and southern portions of Utah and Colorado. The term *Southwest* is actually an Anglo-American concept used to define a territory located south and west of America's traditional culture hearths in the Northeast (Meinig 2001). To the Hispano-American, however, this region may be perceived as the North, oriented more to the cultural hearth of central Mexico. In addition to the Native Americans already living here, the Spanish first migrated into the region from Central America after 1500, only to be followed some two centuries later by Anglo Americans of British descent from the eastern United States. Today the American West is forging a closer association with the *Pacific Rim*, that region consisting of nations encircling the Pacific Ocean. As such, the West has been experiencing its most recent wave of immigration—this time from the Pacific Rim countries of China,

Japan, and South Korea, and from South Asian countries such as India and Pakistan. On top of that, the close proximity of the Southwest to Mexico has led to increased immigration of Hispanic people from the south.

This dynamic and historical process of successive occupation by different cultural groups over time is referred to as *sequent occupance.* Each group, in turn, comes to occupy a place, thereby modifying the landscape in unique and characteristic ways. If a place or region is occupied by a group of people that possesses attitudes, objectives, and economic practices different from the previous occupants, then you can bet that the landscape will be modified to reflect these newer cultural values.

Most recently, non-Anglo ethnic groups have been immigrating in greater numbers and have consequently added their own cultural diversity to the American scene, largely through the process of cultural diffusion. Between 1961 and 1970, Europeans still constituted a sizeable immigrant group, which accounted for a third of all immigrants into the United States (Getis, Getis, and Quastler 2001). During those years, the top three sources of European immigrants were the United Kingdom, Italy, and Germany (in that order). Only Mexico, Canada, and Cuba supplied more immigrants to the United States than did Europe during the 1960s.

By the 1980s, however, the situation was very different. Less than 10 percent of all immigrants came from Europe. Instead, most were now coming from Mexico, the Philippines, Vietnam, China, Korea, and India (in that order). The United States is thus witnessing an emerging new pattern of non-European ethnic diversity. In the year 2000, non-Hispanic whites accounted for 71 percent of the U.S. population, followed by African-Americans (13%), Hispanics (11%), Asians (4%), and American Indians (just under 1%). The increasing ethnic diversity of the United States is further indicated by the fact that between 1990 and 2000, the non-Hispanic white population declined in its share of the total from 75 to 71 percent, whereas all other minority groups increased (Getis, Getis, and Quastler 2001).

Despite this continuing trend of immigration and increasing diversity, the entire United States remains dominated by an Anglo-American culture, one that has proliferated due to the "automatic acceptance of the resulting [cultural] package by millions of later arrivals and their progeny" (Zelinsky 1997, 157). According to geographer Wilbur Zelinsky, who has made a career out of studying America's ethnic diversity, "what we find in geographic fact, in some three million square miles of territory sandwiched between Quebec and the borderlands of middle America, is a single dominant culture—one pervasive ethnic group—an entity we can properly label Anglo-American" (Zelinsky 1997, 157).

By the middle 1800s, Anglo-American society in the United States had developed a powerful set of cultural values and ideals that still dominate American culture today. These values include (but are not limited to) an insatiable appetite for anything that is new; a strong desire to be near, and surrounded by, nature; the need to "conquer geography" (Lewis 1979) with grand technological feats such as building bridges, dams, and building airplanes; a rugged individualism with an aggressive pursuit of goals; an unprecedented freedom of mobility; a constant desire to obtain social acceptance while seeking a distinct level of socio-economic status; a unified belief in an (ideal) society of equality, as specified by the U.S. Constitution; and a strong sense of community. Many other Anglo-American cultural traits reveal themselves clearly within our human landscapes, but the ones listed above are perhaps the most dominant and pervasive.

Some of these traits are rather contradictory, providing some significant paradoxes in American culture. For instance, America's desire to be near nature sometimes contradicts our desire to conquer and tame that very same nature. Further, our rugged individualism is countered by our equally powerful need to belong to a larger community of people who are like us in numerous ways. All together, however, these collective American cultural values constitute, to use Zelinsky's (1997, 158) words, a "largely subconscious code governing the proper ways in which to arrange human affairs over American space: how to cope with natural habitats; how to design towns, cities, houses, roads, other structures, or cemeteries; how to occupy rural territory; and, in general, how to relate to our surroundings."

Despite all the fascinating regional and ethnic variations that continue to produce a wide array of human landscapes, this cultural diversity has yet to impart a serious challenge to the dominant Anglo-American ideals described above. Most often, what one finds in places occupied by non-Anglo cultural groups are *ethnic markers*, or indicators in the landscape of an identifiable cultural presence. Such markers may include distinct store-front signs, religious objects in yards or porches, fanciful color schemes on buildings, wall murals depicting some aspect of ethnic heritage, architectural details that reflect the stylistic traditions of elsewhere, and entire structures that represent non-Anglo cultural or religious traits (such as synagogues or mosques). Specific markers of African-American culture, for instance, may be found in the form of some southern African-American church buildings, grave sites, certain gardening practices, and their traditional bare-swept front lawns (Zelinsky 1997, 159). In America's various urban "Chinatown" neighborhoods, it is the building facades that comprise perhaps the most striking landscape trait of these places (Lai 1997, 81). Chinatown structures usually contain certain distinctive features found in few other places, such as recessed or projecting balconies, upturned eaves and roof corners, sloping tiled roofs, flagpoles, and parapets bearing Chinese inscriptions (Lai 1997, 81). Thus, various design traditions for outdoor spaces can be associated with specific ethnic groups. If one knows what to look for in the details of yards or gardens, for instance, it is possible to identify the presence of Latino, African-American, Portuguese-American, Chinese-American, or Italian-American communities (Hayden 1997, 127).

Ethnicity, as well as race, class, and gender, continue to be a shaping force in American urban and rural places. American Studies professor Dolores Hayden has observed that "in Eastern European Jewish neighborhoods, distinctive ethnic building types include synagogues; in Chinese-American neighborhoods, laundries, herb shops, and association boarding houses; in Japanese-American neighborhoods, temples, nurseries, and flower markets" (Hayden 1997, 127). Ethnic markers such as these provide for the rich diversity that describes America's cultural landscapes. By recognizing this diversity, one can more successfully look beyond the dominant culture, "to learn how all those many…peoples have fared as they tried to cope with that huge, absorbent phenomenon we call the American cultural system" (Zelinsky 1997, 161).

Most important in explaining the prominence of Anglo-American culture in the United States was the incessant population growth in the eastern colonies, and their ultimate success at forming a nation state known as the United States of America. By the year 1780, the time of our nation's official birth, more than 2.7 million people were living along the eastern seaboard, from Georgia to Maine (Lemon 1990). That number increased to 4 million only 10 years later in 1790, the year of the first U.S. Census count. These growing populations ultimately exerted a powerful influence on the future American economy, culture system, settlement patterns, and political agendas of the United States. In fact, it was in the Northeast that not only the American Revolution was fought and won, but also the country's political and economic power has been concentrated since the beginning. The nation's most important financial decisions and business deals were made there, especially through the nineteenth century, and a huge proportion of America's wealth was controlled by Northeastern financiers and corporations. Further, many of the nation's prestigious educational institutions were, and still are, located there (Lewis 1990). It is not surprising, then, that the Northeast—consisting of two of the nation's three dominant culture hearths (Pennsylvania and New England)—played a significant role in the development, settlement, and cultural production of the United States.

It is safe to say that Anglo-American culture is responsible for the most profound and immediate impacts on the American Southwest. Although important and numerous patterns of Hispanic and Native-American culture are still quite evident, it is the Anglo culture that has become dominant, and only within the past 150 years (Francaviglia 1998). Through a veritable obsession with large-scale geometric order and planning, combined with rapidly advancing technologies, the Anglo-Americans shaped, transformed, and reshaped the Southwest landscape in ways never seen before. Significantly, the Anglos brought with them the Township and Range land survey system—a massive land distribution scheme of continental scope that arranged much of the West into the familiar square-mile sections (more about this later). Only decades after their first arrival, they also brought the technology of the railroad. No less than five transcontinental railroads ultimately integrated the West with the eastern United States. Shipped on those trains was a continuous supply of new settlers from the East, along with manufactured goods and food supplies from eastern and midwestern factories and farms.

Flagstaff was founded during the height of this growth, located in the heart of the emerging Southwest. New economic activities came with the Anglos as well, including the extractive industries of mining and logging, and agricultural practices often involving cattle and sheep ranching. Later still, the Anglo-Americans built new roads, freeways, and bridges, and brought large-scale, high-tech manufacturing, providing a new job base for Southwest cities. This development has continued to attract waves of new settlers to the Southwest since the 1950s for the purpose of professional careers, retirement, recreation, and sun. Known to geographers as America's continuing shift to the *Sun Belt* from the *Snow Belt* (or *Rust Belt*, due to the decline in manufacturing in the northeastern United States), this continuing migration of corporations, investment, and people signifies the most recent wave of Anglo-American influence in the Southwest.

Of course, the Southwest is not alone with regard to its rich cultural history and diversity. Because a wide variety of cultures have influenced different places and regions around the world, you will probably never encounter a landscape that represents only one "pure" culture. Although we can discuss the history and significance of specific cultural groups as I have done here, much of what we see is usually a product of *acculturation*. When two or more cultures interact over time, the more dynamic and powerful culture will likely dominate the weaker one, either through peaceful or other means. Regardless of which culture is the most dominant, however, both cultures coming into contact with one another will invariably borrow from each other.

For instance, much of the initial Spanish settlement was focused on earlier Indian pueblos, especially in New Mexico and Arizona. Though the Spanish often failed to assimilate these pueblo people into their own culture, they kept trying to do so, especially through the missionary efforts of the Roman Catholic Church. Thus, Indian pueblos in New Mexico and Arizona often contain a Spanish mission church at the heart of the village. Francaviglia has further described the process of acculturation that occurred within these pueblos:

> The Spanish brought many building traditions to the region, including the extensive use of adobe brick, doors for access to individual rooms, and a wealth of colonial architectural details; but they also borrowed from the native peoples. Touristic literature to the contrary, it is virtually impossible to find Native Americans living in "pure" Indian settings today, even in the pueblos. (Francaviglia 1998, 13)

The acculturation of Spanish and Anglo traditions is even more apparent in the southwestern landscape, sometimes including the influences of Native Americans as well. Spanish adobe churches in northern New Mexico's Hispano villages, for instance, often serve as the focal point of their communities. The churches themselves may include a blend of Spanish and Anglo influences, indicated by their inclusion of the characteristic Spanish mission towers and adobe construction, complete with the characteristic Anglo gable-front roof. Similarly, the meeting of Hispanic and Anglo cultures is illustrated in Tucson, Arizona's historic district where one can still find Spanish colonial adobe buildings with Anglo-derived pitched roofs, dormers, and storefront windows inserted into the original adobe structures (Hornbeck 1990b).

Aside from these examples, architecture can serve as one of the most recognizable clues to culture. It is useful to think of architecture as something similar to clothing fads, in that the dominant society comes to accept new clothing styles over time as the popularity of others fades away. Sometimes, older clothing styles can even make a comeback and reappear; the same holds true for architecture. The architectural styles displayed on our various buildings and structures represent a similar process of shifting cultural tastes through time. Since colonial days, Americans have continuously fallen in and out of love with a wide variety of architectural styles and ideas. Much of the ornamentation adorning America's buildings is of little practical or functional value at all. Instead, our buildings often take on different shapes and appearances due to changing cultural values. It should come as no surprise that our ensuing walking tour through Flagstaff will feature a good deal of instruction relating to American architectural styles. They serve as important clues to the various cultural values that have shaped Flagstaff's own human landscapes.

The Political Economy of Landscape

For all the influence that culture has on shaping our everyday landscapes, it is only part of the story. All cultural groups operate within an economic system of some kind that is always influenced by political decision making. Although it is tempting to separate notions of economy from politics, the two are always fused together and closely interdependent. For this reason, scholars often refer to *political economy* when describing the ways people earn a living, produce and consume goods and services, and organize their spaces of consumption and production across the landscape. Just as the patterns of our human landscapes reflect various cultural traits, these places further reveal the complex dynamics of their respective economic system. Sometimes a challenge is presented in determining whether a landscape feature—a suburban tract home, for instance—is primarily the result of cultural, economic, or political influences. Instead of choosing one or the other, however, as many scholars have naively done in the past, it is important to recognize the contributions of all of these processes simultaneously. One explanation often overlooked by cultural geographers relates to various economic processes, rooted as they are in America's capitalist economic system.

Perhaps it is easiest to comprehend the link between political economy and landscape by reviewing the four dominant political economic systems that are found on the planet today. Briefly, these systems are *pure capitalism*; the *command economy* of Marxism; a *mixed political economy*, including fascism and socialism; and the *traditional economy* of peasant farmers and indigenous populations (Stutz and de Souza 1998).

Pure capitalism is the political economic system with which Americans are most familiar, and it is this system that contributes greatly to the shaping of our American landscapes. Also referred to as the *market economy*, or *laissez-faire capitalism*, pure capitalism is based on the notion of free-market competition and private enterprise that is minimally regulated by government structures or policies. In pure capitalism, all individuals and firms seek to maximize their own self-interest. Two groups of decision makers dominate this political economic system: households and businesses. The well-known laws of supply and demand help to regulate what is produced and consumed in the marketplace.

Consequently, in America we do not necessarily need to wait for governments or corporations or other large and powerful organizations to make decisions about creating or altering our landscapes, because we live in a society that champions political democracy with its associated individual freedoms and *laissez-faire capitalism.* When it comes to issues of property ownership and the operation of businesses for profit, we are one of the most anti-government societies to be found anywhere on earth. Laissez-faire capitalism is basically the idea that government should stay out of our business—literally. The overwhelming philosophy in America is that private businesses should be able to operate without burdensome restrictions from the government. Richard Schein (1997, 663) explained that "one of the principal tenets in the historical formation of the American cultural system is the establishment and protection of property rights and freehold land tenure. Americans firmly believe in their lawful ability to do what they like with their individual pieces of the planet." What this means is that "most landscapes in the U.S. are the result of countless individual, independent, self-interested decisions that create, alter, and maintain landscapes, their meaning, and their symbolism" (Schein 1997, 663).

Despite America's relatively anti-government mentality, there is no such thing as a completely pure capitalist economy where the government has no influence whatsoever. In fact, the role of government in our economy is profound, from federal to state and local levels of control. From local sign ordinances, zoning laws, and building codes to state and federal legislation and funding choices that encourage or discourage certain economic behaviors, America's governmental structures make it clear that our country's version of capitalism is anything but pure. Still, the role of government in a nation's economic system is relative. The United States comes closer to this ideal than any other nation or region in the world. That means that individual decisions and actions matter more here than perhaps in any other country, so our landscapes are apt to be shaped in part by individual economic decisions (Figure 8).

Figure 8. Main Street of Oatman, AZ. Family-owned businesses like this T-shirt shop demonstrate free-market capitalism at work in the landscape. Once a booming gold mining town, Oatman has become a tourist attraction due to its proximity to Laughlin, NV, and its location along old U.S. Route 66. As the number of visitors increased, so too did the number of entrepreneurs who have converted older mining-era buildings into souvenir shops. (Photo: Author's collection)

Take the case of Moscow, Russia, for instance. Dominated until recently by strict Soviet planning and a *command* political economic system, Moscow's cityscape does not exhibit a striking skyline of tall office towers as one might expect to see. During the Soviet era between 1917 and 1991, the holding of private property and the growth of large, private corporations simply were not allowed. With no large corporations or private land speculation, there are no office parks, and therefore no skyscrapers. Throughout Russia, locations of production, agriculture, housing, and transportation were determined more by governmental decision making and planning than by private, individual interests. The idea of "keeping the government off my land and out of my business" would have constituted a sick joke until 1991. Now, the old Soviet system is becoming privatized, though at a much slower rate than many in the Western world would like to see. Even suburban housing developments are materializing around Moscow, and communal farms and buildings are being sold as private property.

Surely, Russia's transition from a command to a capitalist economic system will hold profound and still-untold implications for Russia's society and landscapes. In America, however, capitalism has been a way of life—and thus a major contributor to our own landscapes—since colonial times. We must recognize this fact if America's human landscapes are to be understood with any degree of completeness and accuracy.

One implication of a free-market system relates to the economic treatment of private property. Land can be viewed as a commodity to be bought, sold, rented, leased, and altered (Logan and Molotch 1987). It follows that any piece of land always maintains both use values and exchange values. In short, the *use values* of land include the social, behavioral, or sentimental values of property, whereas *exchange values* are those related to the treatment of property as a commodity, giving rise to a constant exchange of property enabled by our free-market system. These exchange values appear most visibly as "rent," or the outright purchases or payments made to landlords, realtors, and mortgage lenders. The most common conflict of interest occurs between residents and entrepreneurs. As residents, people attempt to make a life for themselves through the various use values of their property, whereas *entrepreneurs* are business people who treat land as a commodity to be bought and sold with the goal of maximizing their monetary return (Logan and Molotch 1987).

This tension between residents interested in use values and entrepreneurs focused on exchange values is found in small town and large city alike, and often results in various intercommunity conflicts. The formation of various interest groups is often the result, each pushing for their own agenda with respect to how certain properties are put to use. More often than not, the entrepreneurs win these contests, represented on the landscape by their various development projects such as new highways, housing developments, or business parks, to name a few.

Still, cases abound in which various interest groups concerned with non-economic aspects of land use have prevailed in such contests. Free and democratic elections, for instance, can provide an advantage for those fighting against a certain development project. Through local referendums or state and national elections, the people themselves are sometimes provided with the decision-making power to determine what type of economic growth happens at what location, and how that growth is ultimately materialized in the human landscape.

In Flagstaff, a local referendum (election) in May of 2000, for instance, allowed city residents to basically choose—within the limits specified by city planners—the types of transportation developments they preferred. The results of this election have already led to improved mass transit in the form of expanded bus service, new bicycle lanes throughout much of the city, and planning for a new overpass at Fourth Street. All of these projects will hold variable implications for the future growth of Flagstaff and for continued changes in the city landscape. It was clear that those promoting more environmentally sensitive, or "smart," growth for Flagstaff gained more power through this election to influence change than they might have had otherwise.

It is the entrepreneurs, however, who enjoy the bulk of power and influence when it comes to community struggles over land use and development. The explanation for this, in part, is rooted within our own political economic system of capitalism. Those individuals and organizations seeking exchange values often share interests with others who maintain common economic goals (Logan and Molotch 1987). Whether at a neighborhood or national scale of interest, entrepreneurs often form alliances with other business people, government bodies, and various organizations that will benefit mutually from economic growth. Harvey Molotch has referred to "an apparatus of interlocking progrowth associations and governmental units" as a *growth machine* (Logan and Molotch 1987). More generally referred to as *growth coalitions* in the discipline of urban geography, the growth machine tends to oppose any intervention that might lead to the regulation of development in the name of use values. As Logan and Molotch (1987, 32) have explained, those associated with a growth machine in a particular locale, such as a metropolitan area, "unite behind a doctrine of value-free development—the notion that free markets alone should determine land use." From this perspective, aggregate growth is considered to be a public good, and virtually any increase in economic activity is believed to help the entire community. Consequently, growth, according to this argument, "brings jobs, expands the tax base, and pays for urban services. City governments are thus wise to do what they can to attract investors" (Logan and Molotch 1987, 33).

This is precisely what city governments do, by participating in various growth coalitions consisting of the mayor and city council, local business associations, the chamber of commerce, the convention and visitors bureau, and even—in smaller towns—the local Main Street program. Depending on the particular growth issue at stake at a given place and time, the growth machine may gain the additional support of local universities and colleges, professional sports organizations, state politicians, local media, utilities, and organized labor. All of these entities tend to benefit economically from progrowth policies in a particular locale.

The informal members of a particular growth machine will vary from one place to another, but the primary association will necessarily include a public-private partnership, whereby private business interests are working together with local governing bodies. In this way, the actions and decisions of the growth machine will mutually benefit all those involved in seeking the economic benefits of exchange values. This process represents the heart of the political economy of capitalism, in that both government and private property owners become aligned to promote some form of economic growth. For this reason, growth is more or less inevitable, as long as entrepreneurs are interested in investing in a particular place. On the flip side, those interest groups promoting various use values involving certain social, historical, or environmental attributes of a property are more likely to successfully alter the way in which growth happens rather than prevent it outright. Even in smaller communities, local growth machines can wield the necessary power and influence to transform the human landscape to their liking.

Consequently, geographers must consider political economic explanations as well as cultural contexts to understand why our landscapes look and function as they do. The combined role of politics and economics is always paramount. Like it or not, this is the way in which American society operates within the larger system of free-market capitalism. The motto for such a system, then, might be "growth happens." The question is whether or not society as a whole can manage economic growth by successfully promoting use values that reflect aspects of community, history, environment, and quality of life.

Globalization in the Landscape

Related somewhat to political economy because of its roots in capitalism, *globalization* can be defined as the increasing interconnectedness of people and places throughout the world through converging processes of economic, cultural, and political change (Rowntree, Lewis, Price, and Wyckoff 2000). As one of the most powerful forces affecting change around the world today, globalization has played an increasing role in shaping our human landscapes. Cities, regions, and countries once distant from each other are now finding themselves increasingly linked through new communication technologies, transportation improvements, and electronic trade. The *friction of distance*, or the resistance to the flow of ideas, people, and commodities across space, has become the target of new global communication systems, satellite and Internet technologies, and transportation advances that have practically annihilated space and time. For those individuals and businesses fortunate enough to have access to such technologies, communication is virtually placeless; people can communicate with others around the world regardless of their location. This situation is unprecedented in the history of the human world.

Other factors contributing to globalization include the following: the rise *of multinational corporations* that maintain plants and offices around the world (such as Sony, Ford, McDonalds); international financial institutions (such as the New York Stock Exchange) that can collectively conduct global trade 24 hours a day; international agreements that promote free trade, thus reducing the economic significance of national borders; the standardization of global transportation systems for the movement of people and goods by land, air, and sea; and increasing international tourism, whereby more humans travel to other countries and places for leisure and entertainment than ever before. Global tourism, not just incidentally, is now the world's largest industry, having surpassed oil and gas in 1992 (Brass 1994, x-1). Although different forms of globalization have been taking place roughly since the 1500s, all of these factors have emerged with a vengeance since roughly the 1960s. Thus, we consider our current period of history to be in the midst of the most recent—and probably most intense—*round* of globalization.

The process of globalization primarily involves economic activities associated with the global expansion of capitalism. Its consequences are far-reaching. Cultural patterns and traits, social processes, and political arrangements at all geographic scales are profoundly influenced by globalization—and no place on the planet is completely immune from these changes. We are truly becoming a global culture and society in many respects, though not everyone and every place is affected in the same ways. Globalization is a very uneven process, positively affecting some societies and places while negatively affecting others. This is why the merits of globalization are debated heavily around the world. These debates are visible in many forms and venues, such as recent protests at meetings of the World Trade Organization.

Most important, many argue that because the market (capitalism) is the driving force in globalization, inequality will be made worse as winners and losers are created. "If globalization makes the world more homogenous," explained sociologists Frank Lechner and John Boli (2000, 3), "many cultures are in trouble. Loss of local autonomy may mean that more people will be vulnerable to economic swings, environmental degradation, and epidemics. For these and other reasons, globalization has become an extremely contentious process." Indeed, the term *globalization* is, for many non-western societies around the world, synonymous with *westernization*, or the expansion of western cultural values and economic processes into non-western regions.

The whole process of globalization is centered on the idea of the *global product*. Basically, as more people gain access to information from around the world, they tend to develop global "needs," and in turn demand global commodities. In the sense of consumerism, they effectively become global citizens. For all intents and purposes, Americans are the quintessential global citizens, as we regularly purchase and consume products from around the world—from international automobiles and clothing to international food and music. Global citizens consume global products—that is, the seemingly countless products that corporations manufacture and make available for sale around the world. Just a few examples include McDonalds Big Mac sandwiches, Suburu automobiles, TVs and television shows, music CDs, computer software, Nokia cell phones, Lipton tea, Coca-Cola, Nike sneakers, and Pokemon cards. The list goes on indefinitely, and it continues to grow ever larger as consumer products are increasingly tied to the global economy through the multinational corporations that produce them. Corporations must successfully generate stronger consumer demands for their own global products, which means marketing and advertising—and lots of it! Thus, we not only see and use these products, but we are bombarded almost everywhere with the images (and sounds) of global advertising: strategic and recognizable logos and themes, corporate slogans and jingles, towering billboards, and many others. These images constitute our new landscapes of global capitalism (Figure 9).

Figure 9. World's largest Coke bottle, Las Vegas, NV. Signs of global consumerism are rampant throughout today's American landscapes, revealing the diffusion of global products and their corporate identities around the nation. (Photo: Author's collection)

Not surprisingly, globalization is most often viewed as a *homogenizing* process, in that global culture and economy are becoming more uniform and standardized. Many claim, therefore, that we are headed for the creation of an eventual world culture at the expense of the diversity and uniqueness of places and people. In the United States, this homogenization is easy to identify in the landscape, in the form of standardized fast food chains, motels and gas stations, big-box discount stores (e.g. Wal-Mart, Target), and replicated architecture from coast to coast. The uniqueness and diversity of places and regions seems to be de-emphasized while the omnipresent Burger King invites us to experience the "Home of the Whopper" from Maine to California.

Few geographers, however, view complete global homogenization as even remotely possible. Associated directly with the process of globalization is the reverse process of localization. The reality around the world is that not everyone, nor every nation, looks forward to further globalization and its associated tendency to severely disrupt local economies and cultural identities. In the face of threatened homogenization, therefore, many local societies, regions, and culture groups have been attempting to recapture their own identities or create new ones. Localization, therefore, is a process that globalization breeds. Both are highly contradictory but closely interdependent. As Kevin Robins has claimed, globalization "should not be seen as an absolute tendency. The particularity of place and culture can never be done away with, can never be absolutely transcended" (Robins 1999, 23). There is much evidence of a rapid resurgence of local traditions, languages, and cultures around the world. Although local places are increasingly overshadowed by an emerging world culture of sorts, it is important not to ignore the power of *localization*—the place-based efforts to increase the vitality of local cultures and economies.

Further, we've got a long way to go before achieving a global culture. Currently, less than 10 percent of all countries around the world are considered to be homogenous with regard to ethnicity, and in only half of the world's countries is there a single ethnic group that represents more than 75 percent of the population. In the United States itself, "multiculturalism is the rule, homogeneity the exception" (Barber 2000, 24). And, according to Benjamin Barber (2000, 24), if a common language—a nation's primary attribute—is the most important criteria for forming nations, then "a count of the number of languages spoken around the world suggests the community of nations could grow to over six thousand members"—hypothetically, of course.

Localization can sometimes occur through the splintering apart of larger countries. The world now consists of many more, often smaller, nations than it did in the 1980s. The world gained 15 new countries instantly from the breakup of the Soviet Union in 1991, including Russia itself. Yugoslavia, a country originally the size of Wyoming, is now much smaller, having splintered into no less than five separate nations, leaving Serbia and Kosovo to comprise the current Yugoslavia by default. If current history is any indicator, then, local identities and characteristics still remain strong and appear to be getting stronger, even in the face of ongoing global integration.

Closer to home, the process of localization is exhibited in a wide variety of common landscapes throughout America. Localization does not require nations to splinter into smaller states through ethnic warfare or other destabilizing means. More commonly, towns and cities of all sizes are struggling harder than ever to stand out in some way, apart from the rest. They are promoting, sometimes even inventing, their own local identities. Often this is accomplished through the use of local heritage that is perceived as distinct in some ways from other places. Few places in America today fail to promote some type of *heritage landscape*, those human landscapes that celebrate some aspect of the past deemed important to a local community. We're all familiar with them, the so-called historic district, Olde Towne, pioneer museum, and heritage corridor, to name just a few.

In part, this focus on local heritage is a countering force to intensified economic globalization. As businesses and industries scan the world for preferential locations, particular places are forced to compete more than ever in the race to attract investors. Therefore, as Kevin Robins has explained, "cities and localities must actively promote and advertise their attractions...It is necessary to emphasize the national or regional distinctiveness of a location. In this process, local, regional or national cultures and heritage will be exploited to enhance the distinctive qualities of a city or locality" (Robins 1999, 25). Heritage is similarly exploited in the drive for places to attract visitors, now that towns and cities rely much more on tourism and local *amenity values* (e.g. environmental features, recreational opportunities, quality of life benefits) for their economic prosperity and less on traditional manufacturing and industry.

Consequently, places of all sizes promote and capitalize on their own unique set of amenity values that are attractive to visitors, retirees, and other potential new residents. Rare is the town or city that does not maintain an ambitious chamber of commerce or convention and visitors bureau that eagerly promotes the positive economic and social features of their communities. Flashy Web sites managed by these same organizations act as city boosters for a global audience, highlighting all that is great about living, working, and investing there. To be sure, the process of localization is in full swing across America. Our continuing obsession with heritage landscapes is a clear testament to that fact—an expanding celebration of local economies and cultures.

LANDSCAPES OF CENTRALIZED AUTHORITY

Americans are accustomed to living in one of the most unregulated free-market countries in the world. It may therefore come as a surprise when we discover how influential our federal and local governments have been in shaping the American scene. For instance, to understand the origin of our nation's interstate freeway system, land survey systems and countless other American landscapes, we must turn to their most influential "author," that of our own government. As geographer Wilbur Zelinsky claimed, it would be quite an oversight to try to explain our human landscapes without considering the powerful role of *centralized authority*, "the workings of our more-or-less sovereign nation states and their varied agents and deputies" (Zelinsky 1990, 311). To not consider the historical and contemporary influences of the U.S. government and thousands of state, county, and municipal (city) governing bodies across the country is to miss a substantial explanation for why our landscapes look as they do and how they came to be.

As you might imagine, the collective influence of these governing bodies goes well beyond our cherished freeways. The magnitude and influence of America's governments from the local to federal level is impressive. By 1984, more than 16 million persons were on government payrolls, with 2.8 million of them employed by the federal government. This made the U.S. government by far the nation's largest employer (Zelinsky 1990). In this section I offer two particular examples of how the federal government has been at work shaping the American landscape: the Township and Range land survey system and the federal interstate highway program. Later we will repeatedly come across these and other, more local examples of centralized authority revealed in Flagstaff's own human landscapes.

"It looks like a checkerboard down there" is a common reaction heard while jetting over the expansive Midwest (Figure 10). What we see from the air is one of the most striking examples of the federal presence on the land. A more accurate technical term for our national checkerboard is the federal *Township and Range Survey System* or, more simply, the *National Grid.* The story behind the checkerboard began with Thomas Jefferson, who chaired a committee in 1784 to prepare a plan for governing the nation's new western territory (Johnson 1990). The committee was concerned primarily with the challenge of systematically dividing up the incomprehensible amount of land that was coming under the control of the federal government. Jefferson's initial proposal divided the land into *hundreds*, each of which would consist of 100 one-square-mile sections of land in a ten-by-ten grid plan. The survey lines for these square-mile sections would be aligned directly north-south and east-west, crossing each other at right angles. When all was said and done Jefferson's hundreds were altered slightly, though his basic concept for dividing up the nation's real estate survived intact.

Figure 10. The "Great American Checkerboard," somewhere over central Illinois. From the air, the square-mile sections of the Township and Range survey system are obvious due to the embedding of access roads, farmsteads, and cropland. (Photo: Author's collection)

Immortalized in the federal Land Ordinance of 1785 was the plan for "ascertaining the mode of disposing lands in the western territory" (Johnson 1990, 128). The main purpose for such a grand plan was basic: to efficiently transfer title of land from the current federal owners (as public lands) to future private ownership through sales. The government had little interest in becoming a national landlord. Such an organized system of land surveying would encourage Americans to settle the West in an efficient and uncontroversial manner, on lands that had been poorly explored. With a systematic grid on paper, lands could easily be sold in the East to western settlers who had never set foot on their new properties.

Under the Land Ordinance, Jefferson's hundred became instead the "township," each a 6-mile by 6-mile square that formed 36-square-mile sections of land. As one might imagine, the initial surveying was not easy, and the process of surveying the ever-expanding nation continued throughout the nineteenth century and into the twentieth. Today, much of the nation has been surveyed under the Township and Range system, including most territory extending from eastern Ohio to the Pacific Ocean. After the land was officially surveyed and recorded, a federal land office was opened in a convenient place so that the sale of land could begin in that area.

The size of the parcels for sale became a topic of intense controversy from the start. Initially, the government only allowed a minimum purchase of one square-mile section, or 640 acres. In 1800 the minimum purchase size was reduced to a half section (320 acres), then to a quarter section (160 acres) in 1804, and finally to a quarter of a quarter section (40 acres) in 1832 (Meinig 1993). These reductions allowed more people to purchase land, and this practice ultimately led to a greater diversity of land holdings throughout the newly settled lands west of Pennsylvania. In this context, the National Grid can be interpreted as a strong symbol of Jeffersonian democracy, due to the grid plan's uniformity across space and its non-hierarchical, non-centrist organization. As landscape architect Robert Riley has written,

> [The National Grid] is an organization so powerful that even the few departures seem to reinforce it: the wrinkling of the land in Iowa like a topologist's diagram, or the interstate gracefully curving across it only to return to the half section line. The buildings as simple, abstract cubes set square to the road with the circular counterpoint of bins or an occasional irrigation circle look like pieces of a gigantic monopoly board, based on the rules of commodity and political equality. It is a visual landscape that contemporary high technology farming has molded but not disrupted. The disruptions are the landscapes brought by new residents: the curving roads and artificial lakes of the wealthier exurbanites seeking that original niche of human occupation, the wooded stream valley; or the one-side-of-a-quarter section, small-lot subdivision of strip septic tank suburbia; or the single lot with its long, low, dark-stained ranch house, set on a "welcoming" diagonal. The farmer has a clear and bold vision of the landscape; the newcomers do not. (Riley 1985, 26)

Left alone without further human influence, the Township and Range survey lines are themselves invisible. One cannot spot the surveys from the air, as they exist only on paper and can be recognized on the ground only if there are physical property markers. What makes the landscapes of the National Grid come alive are the settlement patterns that have played out within the grid's framework. Somewhat humorously, the Township and Range system proved to be an efficient means of land distribution, but no one had bothered to include any provisions for roads or townsites. Where would the roads to access these western lands be constructed? The answer was, naturally, along the section lines—the boundaries of the square-mile sections themselves. The ad hoc practice of creating roads along the section lines not only buried the original survey markers but also became engrained as an American habit (Johnson 1990). With few exceptions, diagonal roads were rejected so that even today a trip from one rural townsite to another might require driving in stair-step fashion, across and over, instead of along a shorter, direct-line route. Not until the construction of our U.S. highways would a particular roadway plan diverge off of the four *cardinal directions*—due north, south, east, and west. In the Midwest and West, few of these section roads were even paved until the 1980s, and many remain unpaved today. In 1900, "the nation with the greatest railway system in the world had the worst roads" (Johnson 1990, 139).

Of course, the national habit of constructing roads along the section lines has had far-reaching geographical implications. As the roads are oriented north-south and east-west and intersect every square mile at 90 degree angles, so too are the houses and farmsteads oriented to the National Grid. Given that most homes feature box-like shapes and square or rectangular rooms, the rooms themselves are oriented to the grid, as is the furniture within them. Given that even cemeteries tend to be oriented to the four cardinal directions with their grave markers lined up like military regiments, it is quite common for people to live their entire lives oriented to the National Grid. They eat, sleep, play games, plow fields, ride bikes, learn in the classroom, watch TV, and even die on the National Grid. The federal system that originated more than 200 years ago has thus greatly influenced the social and spatial patterns of life throughout much of America.

The National Grid has influenced the growth of cities as well, especially those that are now characterized by miles and miles of sprawling suburbs, like Phoenix. What were once dirt section roads connecting farmsteads with nearby towns have been transformed into multi-lane commercial strips with major intersections that often conform precisely to the square-mile survey pattern (Figure 11). Replacing farms on the edges of these cities are the ubiquitous housing subdivisions placed along creatively designed curvilinear residential streets, though all of them are still constrained by the familiar square-mile sections. In this way the growth of our cities and suburbs has been *disciplined*, so to speak, by the centralized authority initiated more than two centuries ago by our own federal government. To look at the sprawling Phoenix landscape from the air, therefore, is to see this federal discipline play out for miles and miles of urban desert. Not unlike the grade school teacher who instructs us to "stay inside the lines" while drawing, the developer is similarly constrained by the existence of the square-mile grid sections and their respective streets. On approach to Sky Harbor International Airport, it appears that Phoenix developers were instructed by the powers that be to "stay inside the square." Thus the grid has not gone away, but instead has been reinforced, with former section lines now serving as our major auto corridors through town.

Figure 11. The Phoenix metropolitan area, on approach to Sky Harbor International Airport. Here, a patchwork of alternating farm fields and new housing developments coexist uneasily, all confined by the Township and Range survey system. (Photo: Author's collection)

Continuing with landscapes of the automobile in mind, we turn to a more recent though equally as influential landscape resulting from centralized authority—that of our interstate freeway system. The most noticeable impact consists of the roadways themselves, which now include some 43,000 miles of limited-access freeways. These transcontinental roads contain enough pavement to cover the entire state of West Virginia, and they form a virtual national grid in themselves, crisscrossing the nation in generally east-west and north-south orientations. The plan is systematic and rigorously planned, not unlike the

Township and Range survey system. Interstates aligned north-south are designated with odd numbers and east-west freeways carry even numbers. Low-numbered interstates are found in the West and South, with progressively higher numbers toward the East and North. Three-digit numbers are reserved for "connector" freeways that link transcontinental routes with urban areas, or for bypasses and beltways. As a whole, the enormity of our freeway system today is a superlative in itself, being as it is the world's greatest public works project ever undertaken (Zelinsky 1990).

Considering the immediate landscape implications of such an undertaking, geographer Wilbur Zelinsky wrote that

> the existence of such long stretches of uniformly engineered pavement, the thousands of standardized bridges, overpasses, and lighting installations, broad swaths of rather monotonous roadside landscaping, the totally unsurprising service plazas, and all those signs of unvarying size, shape, color, and typography has become one of the central facts of American life, and a more than trivial portion of our collective sensory input. We are not prepared as yet to assess the impact of this grandiose web of concrete on our economy, society, ecology, and life-patterns—no geographer or other social scientist has been brave enough to try—but unquestionably it is staggering. (Zelinsky 1990, 326)

The watershed event initiating the era of freeway building in America was the Federal-Aid Highway Act of 1956 and the initiation of a transcontinental interstate freeway system. Many Americans are little aware of the motives behind the Act and the historical roots of the program. I offer some highlights here, given that we will be visiting some landscapes in Flagstaff that have been strongly influenced simply by the location of two such freeways, Interstates 40 and 17.

Before there were freeways, there were parkways, and the federal government had little to do with them. The term *parkway* was coined by Calvert Vaux, who worked with the famous landscape architect, Frederick Law Olmstead in the creation of New York's Central Park.

The term first appeared in their proposal in 1868 that led to the construction of the Ocean and Eastern parkways in Brooklyn. These were the first "parkways" in the world (Patton 1986). The typical parkway of Olmstead and Vaux was characterized by the separation of pedestrian and vehicular traffic, the use of a central median to divide traffic in each direction, and linear strips of park-like green space on both sides of the corridor and perhaps in the median as well. The models for their innovative parkways came from a variety of sources, including the grand boulevards of Paris and various divided streets already found in colonial towns, such as Commonwealth Avenue in Boston. For Olmstead, the parkway was also viewed as an excuse to design more park space along its route. The auto-induced parkway was "a natural successor to Olmstead's romantic view of the park as a series of sequential vistas, with its basis in the parks of English country estates—and in the groomed landscape of New England where he grew up" (Patton 1986, 68).

What might surprise us more is the motivation for designing parkways in the first place—namely, the increasing commercial clutter, traffic congestion, and danger that characterized many early roads of the 1920s and 30s. Traffic tie-ups and hour-long commutes are certainly nothing new. The danger to motorists and pedestrians was an overriding concern of this time; fatalities and injuries from auto accidents were increasing much faster than the use of automobiles themselves. The decade of the 1920s was the deadliest ever, measured by fatalities per mile driven. In 1928 some 28,000 Americans died on our nation's roadways (Patton 1986). A long list of roadside distractions was partly to blame, especially increasing numbers of billboards, business signs competing for the motorists' attention, and buildings clustered close to the roadway. For those who were using the new roads to speedily access early residential suburbs, the roadside clutter was simply getting in the way. Overall, the northeastern region of the United States became home to numerous parkways that provided a welcome relief and a moderate solution to the hassles and dangers of previous roads.

It is not surprising that the federal government watched with great interest as these parkways evolved. The parkway idea was consequently adopted by the government to create jobs during the Depression and to construct scenic auto roads into our national parks and forests. Further, the parkway would become the forerunner to the interstate freeway system that we are all familiar with today. However, although the parkway was designed primarily for beauty and recreation, the emphasis quickly turned to speed and efficiency. E. M. Bassett, the lawyer credited with coining the term *freeway* to describe a multi-lane, limited-access highway, commented that the parkway was "a strip of land dedicated to *recreation*, over which the abutting owner has no right of light, air, or access." Conversely, the freeway was completely "dedicated to *movement*" (Patton 1986, 71). By 1942, the Roosevelt administration had spent approximately $4 billion on highways, and Roosevelt had been exploring the idea of creating a national superhighway program. The freeway, or superhighway, however, would not become reality until well after World War II.

In 1949, the Bureau of Public Roads was altered to become the new Department of Transportation. Five years later, President Dwight Eisenhower asked General Lucius Clay, a director of a large oil company at the time, to chair a committee that would assess the transportation needs of the nation (Jakle 1990). The ultimate result was immense in its implications, namely the passage of the aforementioned Federal-Aid Highway Act of 1956. The Act formalized a plan to construct some 41,000 miles of limited access freeways, 5,000 miles of which would be built within existing cities. How would such a grand scheme be funded? The solution to this problem was quite creative, and very successful. A Highway Trust Fund was established, the revenue for which would come from a series of federal taxes on motor fuel, tires, new buses, trucks, and a use tax on heavy trucks. These funds would be channeled through the Trust Fund to construct and maintain the new freeway system. Through this funding mechanism, the federal government offered to pay a full 90 percent of all construction costs, an incentive that quickly encouraged state governments to build new highways (Jakle 1990). This funding scheme was self-perpetuating: as more people drove more cars, trucks, and buses, more federal taxes would be collected for highway construction. As long as people continued to drive and use gasoline, the roads would be paid for. This system is still very much in place today.

President Eisenhower gave four basic reasons why America needed an interstate system, summarized here by John Jakle: "Existing highways were unsafe, too many roads were congested, poor roads inflated transportation costs for business, and, finally, existing highways were inadequate for the evacuation of cities threatened by nuclear attack" (Jakle 1990, 299). Although this last reason may appear somewhat absurd, it was in reality quite serious according to the government. That the Eisenhower administration added the "National Defense Highway" tag to the Interstate title was evidence of the close link between the newly enacted freeway system and the perceived threats of the emerging Cold War. The Soviets exploded their first atomic bomb in 1949, and thereafter the federal government focused on issues of national defense. After participating in a test of the military readiness system, Eisenhower declared that America should act quickly to create better highways to enhance evacuations from the cities and to facilitate the national movement of troops (Patton 1986).

As it turns out, national defense may have been a valid reason for building interstates, but it was more of a public relations effort by the Eisenhower administration to ensure that the freeways would be built. The government realized that evacuation plans were unrealistic anyway, given the probability of little or no warning prior to any incoming missile attacks. Instead, Eisenhower's primary motive for building the interstate system was apparently economic. Even today we witness the occasional military convoy rumbling over our freeways; it was particular sectors of the U.S. economy that ended up benefiting most. Eisenhower and his advisors even viewed the interstates as a method to manage the economy itself. The way to encourage economic growth, they believed, was to funnel money through the private sector, even if big business would be the primary beneficiaries. By the 1950s, the automobile accounted for, directly and indirectly, nearly a fifth of the entire U.S. economy. The building of interstates might not "add to the efficiency and productivity of that economy, but would aid its largest components directly: the auto makers, of course, and steel and rubber and plastics and construction" (Patton 1986, 87). With this in mind, John Jakle observed that "no real consideration was given to the railroads or to public transit as alternative forms of transport. No consideration was given to linking highways, new or old, with other transportation modes. No thought was given to how highways might affect the established geography of the nation" (Jakle 1990, 299).

With the automobile and its infrastructure given top priority by the federal government, the nation essentially did a flip-flop during the twentieth century. Prior to World War II the United States maintained the most extensive and elaborate railroad network in the world, but was embarrassed by its poor roads. By the 1970s the rail passenger industry had collapsed, and America now boasted of the most efficient auto road network on the planet. In turn, travel on commuter trains fell from 32 billion passenger miles in 1950 to only 8 billion by 1970. Aside from some urban rail transit comebacks, such as in Los Angeles and Washington D.C., Americans have for three decades now been restricted to a single mode of ground transportation—that of the automobile—with very few alternatives in very few places. Landscapes of the automobile have consequently dominated today's geographies of America. Thus, we will be returning to such landscapes quite extensively later in the book.

The role of centralized authority on the human landscape lies in the domain of local and state governing bodies as well as with that of the federal government. For their part, city governments usually influence local landscapes in a variety of ways, often a product of local ordinances put into place by a city council. The impact of zoning is one such example. The idea of *zoning* is generally straightforward. Zoning codes combine two basic principles: dividing entire cities into districts, or zones, and designating specific land uses and other requirements within these zones (Burgess 1996). At the National Conference on City Planning, held in 1909, the concept of zoning received national attention for the first time. There Frederick Law Olmsted Jr. and others described the overcrowded and deteriorated conditions of urban tenements and slum districts. German cities, they explained, maintained *ordinances* (local municipal laws) to deal with similar situations there, so they recommended the same for American cities. Generally, they sought laws that would effectively keep unhealthy and incompatible land uses from residential areas, and the practice of zoning ultimately became the answer. Zoning's primary purpose, therefore, was to protect residential neighborhoods, especially those located in poor and working-class areas.

One concern of legal authorities, however, was that any attempt to protect certain neighborhoods but not others might not gain court approval. A zoning ordinance that was part of a comprehensive plan for the entire city, however, would be more acceptable and feasible. As an element of planning, then, zoning could be used to direct residential, commercial, and industrial activities to particular areas zoned specifically for those purposes. During the 1920s, states across the country adopted *enabling legislation*, that is, state laws allowing or enabling cities and towns to enact local ordinances and regulations. The practice of zoning came to have two primary purposes: to protect residential neighborhoods from unwanted land uses (such as factories) and to direct growth and development into specific geographical spaces. By 1930, local zoning ordinances had been adopted by more than 500 cities, and more than 80 percent of the U.S. urban population lived in cities that were zoned (Burgess 1996). Therefore, by World War II, urban America had brought the concept and application of zoning into the national mainstream.

What zoning allows for is a *disciplined landscape*, as Richard Schein (1997) called it, in that residents cannot alter their properties in limitless ways despite our existence in the most unregulated capitalist society on the planet. As we will see with Flagstaff, zoned landscapes can reveal different degrees of discipline, imposed by various regulating bodies and laws. Zoning creates one level of discipline at the city or county level, while neighborhood associations and historic preservation ordinances may provide additional disciplinary measures that further direct how private landscapes may or may not be manipulated. In truth, there are few privately owned landscapes (if any) not regulated in some way by a larger governing body.

With this discussion on centralized authority, we come to the end of our crash course in landscape studies. The best way to learn, of course, is through examples. Although the first two chapters provide plenty of often-unrelated examples to demonstrate various concepts, we can incorporate many of these geographical ideas into a particular case study that allows for some rather detailed elaboration. For this purpose, I have chosen Flagstaff's railroad corridor, currently owned and operated by the Burlington Northern Santa Fe (BNSF) Railway Company. The following two chapters are thus devoted to a geographical study of the railroad and its interrelationships with the community of Flagstaff. Generally speaking, Chapter 3 answers the first two of the three primary questions in geographical inquiry—that is, "What is where," and "Why is it there." Answering these questions requires a focus on the historical development of the transcontinental railroad that operates through Flagstaff and an understanding of how the railroad has variously impacted the town's human landscape. In Chapter 4, we turn to contemporary times to answer the third geographical question, "So what?" What are the various implications of having one of the busiest freight railroad corridors in the nation situated at the heart of a thriving and growing community? There are many implications, both positive and negative. First, however, we start in the beginning.

Part II

Flagstaff and the Railroad

Chapter 3

Origins of a Railroad Town

Flagstaff is in some ways a quintessential western town. Like many places in the rural West, Flagstaff's economy has historically depended upon extractive industries, ranching, and, to a lesser extent, tourism. The social and cultural characteristics of the town's population have reflected these economic activities since Flagstaff's early days. Some of its landscapes, however, reflect more of a Midwest influence than a western one. In some cases, Flagstaff's cultural patterns can even be traced further east to the New England and Pennsylvania culture hearths. It is not preposterous, therefore, to consider Flagstaff an all-American town, representing a geographical blending of American regional and national traits. Although it certainly exhibits important western qualities, Flagstaff is in some ways "in" the West more than it is truly "of" the West, and it can even be interpreted as a midwestern transplant. Towns that look like Flagstaff can be found in South Dakota, Texas, Illinois and Oregon. To comprehend this southwestern community as a product of the eastern United States, it is necessary to discuss the powerful influence of the nineteenth-century railroads and their relentless expansion into the West during that century. It is the technology of the railroad that effectively allowed the eastern half of the United States—its people, cultural traits, and economic initiatives—to diffuse into northern Arizona.

Prior to the American Civil War, hopeful speculators or investors chose to locate new townsites along navigable waterways or near other advantageous geographical features. The growth and survival of these pre-railroad towns depended much on their locations along a river or at the junctions of important overland routes. Santa Fe, New Mexico, for example, prospered long before it gained its own rail connection because of its status as the western terminus of the Santa Fe Trail. By the 1890s, railroad companies had created a dense network of rail lines across the Midwest, and five transcontinental rail lines connected the West with the East. The transportation geography of the nation was thus fundamentally transformed, as the opposite coasts and everything in between were effectively brought closer together through easier and cheaper travel. In short, the friction of distance between both coasts and throughout the interior was drastically reduced. A cross-country journey, once requiring months by wagon train, could now be traversed in a matter of days by rail.

Some railroad companies, especially those owning the transcontinental lines, became vast landholders themselves. The federal government had little money for subsidies to help pay for the construction of such expensive projects; what it did have, however, was plenty of land! The government therefore granted huge swaths of public land to the railroads that, in turn, could be resold to settlers, entrepreneurs, and many others interested in moving west. The railroad thus financed its construction in part through the sale of its land along the right-of-way. Most of the transcontinental routes, including the Santa Fe Railway between Chicago and Los Angeles via Flagstaff, were financed in this creative manner. The land grant concept was actually quite brilliant, from an Anglo-American perspective. The federal government readily encouraged settlement of the West as a way to enhance control of its vast western territories. The railroad companies maintained the financial and organizational resources necessary to conduct such an undertaking. Thus, the railroads became the mechanism through which the government encouraged settlement. In return, the railroads themselves enjoyed the revenues and profits that often came with settling new stretches of the American frontier.

Not only did the railroads become involved with real estate, but they also got into the business of town building. By the 1860s, entire towns were sited, platted, and promoted by the railroad companies themselves. The easiest way to standardize the platting of new towns was through the use of the rectilinear street grid plan that emerged in the Midwest during the early 1800s. Given the primary economic interest of the railroad companies to increase the volume of traffic on their trains, it made good sense to create entirely new townsites spaced at calculated intervals along their routes (Figure 12). In fact, the purpose of "town-founding," first and foremost, was to invent new trade centers for a growing farm population in the Midwest and South. The consequence of these goals, according to John Hudson (1990), was played out in the planned layout of each new town. Land directly adjacent to the tracks was usually not sold, but was leased to grain elevator companies, lumber yards, and fuel dealers who required direct access to the railroad (Figure 13). These businesses were actually owned, quite often, by national corporations whose headquarters were in large cities, far away from the rural townsite. Some companies based in Minneapolis, for instance, owned more than 100 grain elevators along the tracks of a single railroad company (Hudson 1990).

Figure 12. The railroad town of El Paso, IL, located along a branch of the Illinois Central Railroad. The railroad and its depot represented the gateway into towns like this one, indicated by the orientation of the streets and commercial buildings to the tracks. (Photo: Author's collection)

Figure 13. Grain elevator in Tolono, IL. This scene demonstrates a *break of bulk* point, where commodities are transferred from one mode of transportation to another for shipment to far-away markets. During harvest season, farmers sell their grain to elevator companies like this one, where the grain is stored and subsequently loaded onto awaiting railroad cars. This entire process is viewed here in Tolono. (Photo: Author's collection)

In the process of creating new towns throughout the Midwest and West, railroads usually adopted one of two common plans. The earliest plan consisted of a street grid oriented to the railroad itself with business buildings lined up to face the tracks on both sides. Eventually, railroads noticed the limitations of locating its tracks in the center of town where nineteenth-century versions of traffic congestion often reigned supreme. The second, most common town design was a T-shaped plan whereby the main business corridor, or main street, met the railroad at a right angle, with the necessary depot located at the intersection. In both plans, the railroad asserted itself as an agent of centralized authority with respect to the street layout. Not only was the railroad responsible for the original town plat and the layout of the streets, but the streets themselves were purposely oriented precisely parallel and perpendicular to the tracks. Although the surrounding countryside was aligned to the National Grid, the town's grid of streets was aligned with the orientation of the railroad. Such towns, therefore, are easily recognized based on the alignment of the streets. Flagstaff is one of them.

Railroad towns, as geographers refer to them, are also identified based on what is missing from their street plans. John Hudson has observed that "because commerce was concentrated in the heart of town, railroads rarely set aside any of this valuable property for parks, squares, or other amenities of urban design. Lots for churches, schools, and courthouses, as well as for parks were donated by the townsite company and were taken from unsold land at the margins of the initial plat" (Hudson 1990, 184). Both commercial and residential lots on the townsite were sold by railroad townsite agents, and it was the agent's task to promote the town to potential business interests. Settlers were "recruited by railroad companies that wanted their government land grants filled with people and their boxcars filled with grain" (Wishart 1990, 262).

The placement of the Coconino County Courthouse in downtown Flagstaff is one case in point. Its status as one of the community's grandest public buildings was not enough to reward it with a location more prominent than the regular city block on which it sits (see chapter 5). In today's compact downtown, cramped with historic and modern buildings, the courthouse remains nearly invisible unless one is almost right on top of it. Granted, the railroad-imposed street plan predated the formation of Coconino County—and the renaming of Flagstaff as county seat—by 9 years. Thus, the railway had no way of knowing about Flagstaff's future selection as county seat. Still, the effect in the landscape was the same. The courthouse and other significant public structures were demoted to the remaining city blocks not already occupied by commercial buildings. It was "first come, first served," per the rules of capitalism, and it was commerce that secured its position in the new downtown.

Unlike the traditional New England village with its Congregational church located prominently on the town green, Flagstaff's downtown was designed to promote commerce, not religion. This ideology of "commerce first" finds its precedence among the early trade centers of the Pennsylvania culture hearth, where America's first true business districts replicated miniature versions of William Penn's 1682 grid plan for Philadelphia. Characterized by a rectilinear street grid complete with a central "square" or "diamond," the *Philadelphia plan* was perfect for encouraging a business-oriented downtown. These central squares quickly became a convenient place for open-air markets used by local and regional traders. Predictably, the idea of the central square diffused into numerous towns settled to the west and south of that major port city. Early Americans and—later still, the westward-moving railroads—revealed their cultural preference for free-market capitalism by readily adopting variations of the Philadelphia plan for their new downtowns (Figure 14).

Figure 14. Intersection of Main and Market Streets at the central square in Lewistown, PA. Notice how the commercial buildings are set back, outlining the corners of the square which purposely resembles William Penn's 1682 plan for Philadelphia. The plan diffused quickly into new towns west of that city, demonstrating that downtown would be a place for commerce, not religion. These places were the forerunners to America's more familiar main-street commercial districts. (Photo: Author's collection)

In turn, these were the forerunners to America's nineteenth-century main streets in the Midwest, which have today become symbolic and almost mythical places. Geographer Don Meinig has even identified *Main Street of Middle America*, as he refers to it, as one of our nation's three most symbolic landscapes (Meinig 1979). It should come as no surprise that Walt Disney—himself having grown up in a small Missouri town—chose the setting of *Main Street USA* as the gateway into his famous Florida and California theme parks (Francaviglia 1996). Conversely, the tranquil village "green" or "common" of New England, with its open space surrounded by white clapboard houses and often a Congregational church, was essentially snubbed and ultimately rejected for commercial downtowns. With some exceptions in upstate New York and the northern Midwest (the region known as *New England Extended*), it was the landscape of main street with its rectilinear street grid that ultimately prevailed as the American model for town building.

The impact of the railroad on the morphology (shape and pattern) of late nineteenth century towns cannot be overstated. In South Dakota, for example, 140 towns of 278 settled by 1889 were railroad-developed. Not only were the town plats themselves designed by railroad agents in a rather standardized format, but the location and spacing of the towns were also the product of railroad decision making. Throughout the Midwest and West, numerous pre-railroad towns had already been settled, based on geographical advantages such as access to navigation, water, lumber, minerals, and so forth. The railroad, however, could decide to "place" a new town anywhere it wished along its route. The economic fate of a town settled prior to the railroad's arrival was often decided instantly, based on where the company decided to build its tracks. More often than not, the railroad bypassed existing towns in favor of a more efficient route, perhaps only 1–2 miles away. This often induced a local land rush along the railroad right-of-way at the new town site. Businesses and people would migrate to the new rail connection, causing the original town's population and economy to stagnate (Conzen 1990). The construction of U.S. highways in the 1920s and limited-access freeways after the 1950s produced impacts similar to those of the early railroads—bypassing original town centers and encouraging businesses to move out of the original downtown.

The spatial organization of railroad towns was by no means decided at random. Towns were spaced at equal intervals along the tracks to serve primarily as rural trade centers and grain collection points for surrounding farms. Along the western transcontinental routes, towns like Flagstaff were spaced apart more widely as railroad service centers, especially where little agricultural activity was taking place. Geographers today point to the fact that the railroads, in their drive for land sales and profits, actually overbuilt the urban network. Simply put, there were too many towns—especially throughout the Midwest—than what the regional urban system and population could support. In the Midwest, it is not uncommon to find towns spaced every 4 miles along the tracks. Standing in the right place, one can actually see from a distance four or five towns and their respective grain elevators all lined up on the horizon.

Further, these towns were established during the horse and buggy era, when travel was slow and cumbersome. Thus, each little railroad town served as a *trade center* for its own rural *hinterland*, extending only 6–8 miles out from town. Each trade center served as the urban hub for its small hinterland, providing goods and services to rural farm families as well as a market for their agricultural products. With a dense rural population and many small farms dotting the landscape by the late nineteenth century, most railroad towns remained modestly vibrant because the surrounding population depended on them for goods, services, and social venues. The twentieth century was not as hospitable to these places, however. The automobile allowed easy access to major cities for shopping, better roads were built, and the number of persons employed on farms steadily decreased. The average farm size had increased substantially due to large-scale mechanization, so that three out of four family farms of the 1950s no longer existed four decades later. The majority of the railroad towns had lost their status as important central places, losing much of the rural population on which they once depended. Many are characterized today by boarded-up storefronts, declining populations, and stagnant local economies.

Some railroad towns managed to survive and even prosper, however, due especially to more recent development spawned by forces other than the railroad. Flagstaff represents one such railroad town that not only continued to grow, but is now finding itself dealing with a variety of social and environmental pressures associated with rapid growth at the beginning of the twenty-first century.

Flagstaff and the AT&SF Railway

Flagstaff exemplifies a typical western railroad town, with its midwestern-type rectilinear street grid oriented to the tracks. Since 1882, the evolution and development of Flagstaff has occurred in tandem with the development of its parent railroad company, known popularly as "the Santa Fe." More accurately, the Atchison, Topeka & Santa Fe Railway Company (AT&SF) is the corporate organization most responsible for the town's initial period of settlement and growth. Just as the community has grown through the past century, so too has the railroad company and its network of track. To better understand Flagstaff's situation with respect to the Santa Fe Railway, we must first examine the company's role in the context of national settlement and westward expansion.

As early as the 1840s visionaries had promoted the idea of constructing a transcontinental railroad to link California and Oregon with states east of the Mississippi River. In 1853 Congress provided the U.S. Army with $150,000 to ascertain the most appropriate route for an eventual transcontinental rail line. Subsequently, four survey parties consisting of army engineers and civilian scientists set off on separate expeditions along four distinct east-west routes, along the 47th, 38th, 35th, and 32nd parallels of latitude (Sheridan 1995). The latter two transects involved Arizona, at that time perceived as merely a region of little significance, a place to "get through" on the route to California. Ultimately, all four of these scientific surveys resulted in the building of a transcontinental railroad, though not simultaneously.

Lieutenant Amiel Whipple commanded the 35th parallel survey party that trudged through the future site of Flagstaff on its way to the Colorado River. According to Thomas Sheridan, Whipple was "extremely enthusiastic about northern Arizona as a railroad route" (Sheridan 1995, 113). Whipple noted the numerous springs and streams on the southern slopes of the mountains, and the vast supply of lumber in what turned out to be the largest continuous stand of ponderosa pine forest in the world. Upon completion of the survey, Whipple's final report was the most comprehensive study of northern Arizona to date. In many ways, this was the most practical route for the nation's first transcontinental railroad, and it may have very well been the first—that is, except for Whipple's one major error. According to Sheridan, "he estimated that the railroad would cost a whopping $169,210,265 rather than the $93,853,605 that he later realized was the more accurate figure" (Sheridan 1995, 113). Consequently, the proposed route received much less attention than it probably deserved, and the first transcontinental railroad was built instead through Utah, roughly along the 38th parallel.

Of the five transcontinental rail routes spanning the nation by 1893, the northern Arizona route was the third to be constructed. The first was the Union Pacific–Central Pacific, which was completed at Promontory Point, Utah in 1869. San Francisco became its western terminus, given that city's status as the leading port and trade center on the West Coast. Recall that Los Angeles, now our nation's second-largest metropolis, was only a small town of about 15,000 people at the time of the railroad's completion in 1869. The second transcontinental railroad was completed by the Southern Pacific Railway, constructed through southern Arizona along the 32nd parallel. Because Arizona's portion of the line was constructed from California eastward, in 1877 Yuma became the first Arizona town to welcome a railroad.

It may seem bizarre that our third transcontinental railroad—the Atchison, Topeka & Santa Fe—carries the names of three towns or cities of relatively little economic or political significance in a national context. Initially the Santa Fe was just one of numerous small midwestern companies operating in Kansas. Originally, President Andrew Johnson chartered the Atlantic and Pacific Railroad to build from Missouri to California via northern Arizona. Congress was quite generous with its land grants, providing the A&P with 40 alternate square-mile sections of land per mile through the western territories (Arizona, New Mexico) and 20 alternate sections per mile through the states (Sheridan

1995). Even today, these alternating sections reveal themselves on regional topographic maps, and they have further influenced the pattern of development within those sections.

The A&P went bankrupt in 1875 after completing less than 400 miles of track. It was another regional, more obscure railroad company in the Great Plains that allowed the transcontinental route to continue. In January of 1880, the Atchison, Topeka & Santa Fe signed the Tripartite Agreement with the St. Louis & San Francisco Railway (known as the Frisco). The Frisco had been formed in 1876 to take over the ailing A&P. In short, the Frisco sold half of its stock in the A&P to the Santa Fe. In return, the Santa Fe agreed to allow the Frisco to access New Mexico and further promised to start building track immediately along the proposed transcontinental route. Thus, the Santa Fe was involved with building the rail line through northern Arizona from the start, but it is the A&P name that often shows up on early maps of the railroad.

It is interesting that the route of the Southern Pacific had passed through Spanish-settled towns well established prior to the railroad's arrival, including Yuma and Tucson. In contrast, no Anglo settlements of any significance existed in northern Arizona. Only a few sporadic Mormon villages had been founded along the Little Colorado River valley, along with a few small mining settlements to the west. Therefore it was the Santa Fe that initialized the entire settlement process for northern Arizona. On August 3, 1883, only 3 years after the Tripartite Agreement, the Santa Fe completed the bridge over the Colorado River and drove the last spike at Needles, California (Sheridan 1995). Northern Arizona was instantly tied to the rest of the nation, to both the East and West.

Reflecting the dominance of the railroad in the region are the place names of towns settled along its route. Many towns in northern Arizona, owing their entire existence to the nation's third transcontinental railroad, were named for a Santa Fe or A&P officer or engineer. Prominent examples include Kingman, Winslow, Holbrook, and Seligman;

having been settled barely prior to the railroad's arrival, Flagstaff became an exception. Still, the railroad not only dictated the permanent street layout of the downtown but also enabled various extractive and agricultural industries to thrive in the area—not the least being the logging, cattle, sheep, and tourism industries.

If the railroad did not provide Flagstaff with its name, then how did Flagstaff actually become "Flagstaff"? Technically, the initial settlement of Flagstaff predated the railroad by approximately one year, but it was a meager beginning. Local historian Platt Cline has written perhaps the most useful and popular explanation:

> It was at McMillan's place (near present-day Flagstaff Junior High School and Marshall School) that a group of emigrants, known to history as the Second Boston Party, camped for a few restful weeks to enjoy the cool climate, sweet water and abundant game. In commemoration of the nation's centennial on July 4, 1876, the travelers trimmed a pine sapling and raised it as a staff for the Stars and Stripes. It stood for years, and the area became known as "Flagstaff." By the fall of 1880, with a dozen ranchers settled in the area and railroad construction about to start, the Yavapai County Board of Supervisors established a voting precinct "Flag Staff"—the first official cognizance of the name—and it stuck. A post office was established in February, 1881, and at a meeting of the few citizens, it was agreed that it should be named Flagstaff, and so it was. (Cline 1994, 3)

The first train rumbled into Flagstaff on August 1, 1882, complete with a local celebration. Generally speaking, the railroad was viewed as a symbol of progress from an Anglo-American perspective, and it promised rapid growth and nearly instant prosperity for any town that could attract it. The grid of streets known today as downtown Flagstaff, however, did not comprise the first townsite. In 1880, railroad surveyors set up a camp at Antelope Spring on the southeast slope of what is today Mars Hill, just west of the current downtown area. No official railroad townsite was planned for that location, as the company had already decided to create Winslow and Seligman as railroad "division" towns (Woodward 1993). These places would serve as the primary hubs for the Santa Fe's operations throughout northern Arizona.

Despite the eagerness of railroad companies to invent new townsites, the A&P therefore showed little initial interest in developing a place called Flagstaff—that is, until it started to develop on its own without the railroad's direct involvement. In 1881 a merchant from Prescott, Arizona, Peter J. Brannen, erected a store near the spring, just north of the tracks. Soon, other entrepreneurs were building their own simple commercial structures adjacent to Brannen's. This original settlement is known today by Flagstaff locals as "Old Town." In 1976 archaeological excavations revealed the foundations of the original commercial structures, but none of the actual buildings survived (Woodward Architectural Group 1993). At its prime, however, the settlement included two general stores, two hotels, a blacksmith shop, a newsstand, a bakery, three eateries, and according to old-timers, no less than 21 saloons (Cline 1994).

It was a combination of topographical limitations and local entrepreneurial spirit that led to the town's eventual relocation and its classic T-shaped railroad street grid where it exists today. As a quirk of geographic fate, it turns out that the settlement at Antelope Spring was on a steep grade, making it difficult for trains to stop and then regain momentum to climb the hill. Consequently, the railroad decided to locate its permanent depot a half-mile to the east on flatter ground (Woodward Architectural Group 1993). In early 1883, the railroad's land commissioner, Col. T. S. Sedgwick, planned the street grid on which the "new" Flagstaff would be built. As Platt Cline somewhat humorously observed, "We can blame him for the narrow downtown streets that, with the coming of automobiles and the town's growth, have been troublesome" (Cline 1994, 11). We'll come back to Col. Sedgwick in a moment.

Soon thereafter, other businesses clustered predictably around the all-important depot built out of local Moenkopi Sandstone. Once again, entrepreneur P. J. Brannen was the first to construct a commercial building at the new townsite, on the corner of San Francisco Street and Railroad Avenue. For a brief period, the new and old towns coexisted, located only a half-mile apart, exemplifying the aforementioned tendency for a new railroad townsite to siphon off another's vitality. When a fire all but destroyed Old Town in 1884, however, the new commercial center along Railroad Avenue was recognized to be Flagstaff's new, permanent location.

The new settlement, with its wood-framed, false-front buildings was not immune to fire danger, however, as evidenced by a similarly destructive blaze in 1886. Following that event, new downtown commercial buildings were required to use brick or stone for their primary construction materials. This partially explains why Flagstaff's business blocks today do not exhibit the expected appearance of other Wild West towns. The original wood-framed buildings with their classic balconies and false-front facades lining Railroad Avenue lasted but a few years in the town's early history of development. What one sees in Flagstaff today, then, is essentially the third downtown. Still, this place is celebrated as a historic district and is often assumed by unknowing visitors to represent the original downtown landscape. As this new and permanent downtown was allowed to evolve through free-market forces between the 1880s and 1960s, the cultural tastes and values of easterners dominated, most of all in the form of the various Anglo-American architectural styles that had diffused into the West from eastern sources. Rather than Spanish pueblo architecture, therefore, one finds in Flagstaff's north downtown district a variety of Anglo-American styles, including neoclassical (Greek Revival), Tudor, Romanesque, and Queen Anne, all derived from English or early American precedents.

Consequently, we can view Col. Sedgwick as an insignificant role player in the larger process of railroad town building that had been established in the Midwest decades earlier. Contrary to what Platt Cline may have insinuated, Sedgwick did not invent the grid plan for Flagstaff. Instead, the street grid can be viewed as a product of nineteenth-century corporate standardization and centralized authority. More accurately, this landscape was created in the form we see it today by a political and economic process rooted in the federal government's desire to gain control of western territory. Recall, the railroad company served as the primary mechanism to achieve that goal. The landscape of downtown Flagstaff, therefore, is historically contingent. Its narrow street grid, alleyways, and direct orientation to the railroad were contingent upon the pre-existence of a standardized settlement pattern already in widespread use further east. It was also contingent on the railroad company's own capitalistic drive to build tracks across the continent to capture the lucrative trade of America's interior and West Coast. Had poor Sedgwick not drawn up the street grid for Flagstaff, someone else would have been blamed for it instead. All he created was yet another replica of a midwestern townsite, like hundreds that came before.

To understand the evolution of Flagstaff's entire nineteenth-century street grid, we must also acknowledge the role of the Township and Range survey system and the railroad's pattern of federal land grants. The city grid was developed in three phases—the Flagstaff Townsite, the Railroad Addition, and Brannen's Addition, in chronological order (see Figure 21). Each phase of development involved the planning of a new grid of streets, each linked to street grids already in place and influenced by the orientation of two pre-existing geographical features: the location of the railroad tracks and the square-mile sections of the Township and Range survey system. The end result was not unlike that of other towns across America that eventually outgrew their original railroad-oriented street plans. Often, the new grids were not aligned in the same direction or pattern as previous plans, resulting in the look of a jigsaw puzzle with its pieces not fitting together properly. This pattern defines Flagstaff's development as well, and we can clearly see its impacts in the landscape today.

This type of pattern is quite common in railroad towns that expanded beyond their original grid of streets. The expansion of streets usually did not follow the original railroad but instead was reoriented to the National Grid. To this day, the boundaries between railroad grid and national grid have engendered unconventional traffic patterns, bizarre intersections, and irregularly shaped lots of land in towns and cities throughout the country (Figure 15). Similarly, Flagstaff's own street grid resulted in part from two interrelated historical processes that developed well before Flagstaff was even thought of: the combination of railroad corporate town planning and federal land grants, and the pre-existing national structure of the Township and Range survey system. From there, local entrepreneurs, businessmen, and city leaders used their labor and financial resources to build and alter Flagstaff's original downtown landscape. For these reasons, geographers can interpret Flagstaff's downtown landscape as the result of a combination of processes related to (1) *centralized authority* (corporate decision making and federal enabling legislation), (2) *political economy* (the free-market process of individual decision making and investment), and (3) *cultural diffusion* (transplanted tastes and values from the eastern United States). We will revisit all of these concepts in more detail as we explore the human landscapes of downtown in the upcoming walking tour.

Figure 15. Downtown Las Vegas, NM. Irregular intersections like this one often result from a town growing beyond its initial street grid aligned to the railroad. The edge of the railroad street grid is viewed here on the right, with a subsequent street grid oriented elsewhere on the left. (Photo: Author's collection)

HISTORICAL GEOGRAPHY OF THE AT&SF

Just as Flagstaff's initial street grid and architecture reflected trends originating in the East, so too did the beginnings of Flagstaff's transcontinental railroad. The AT&SF Railway began as the dream of one man, Cyrus K. Holliday, a lawyer living in Meadville, Pennsylvania during the early 1850s. Already an advocate for the future potential of railroads in the West, Holliday wisely asked for stock instead of cash for his legal services. By 1854 he headed west to Kansas with $20,000 in his bank account. His dream from the start was to begin his own railroad somewhere in the West (Poling-Kempes 1989). At this time, Kansas was still frontier territory, and the process of town building was just beginning throughout the Great Plains. Holliday eventually envisioned the need for a new community. Consequently, he took it upon himself to plan and promote the new town of Topeka soon after his arrival in Kansas. Holliday became Topeka's first town president and eventually became a member of the territorial legislature.

Following a stint prior to the Civil War as a brigadier-general for the Union, he turned once again to his idea of building a western railroad. Specifically, he envisioned a rail line between Atchison, Kansas, and Santa Fe, New Mexico. Of course, Holliday wasn't the only one convinced that a railroad to Santa Fe would be profitable. Several railroad companies were being formed in Kansas, and many entrepreneurs like Holliday were setting their sights on Santa Fe, a major southwestern trade center. Fortunately for Holliday, he had acquired the experience to follow through with his plans, having initially been hired by the Pittsburgh and Erie Railroad in Pennsylvania to draw up their charter. His experience with the P&E served him well. Holliday wrote the charter for the AT&SF in only 2 days while staying at a hotel in Lawrence, Kansas. Yet another railroad had been born on paper, and Holliday hoped that it would one day be built in the direction of Santa Fe and eventually to the Gulf of Mexico.

Holliday's big dream quickly became the topic of jokes; many questioned the wisdom of building a line from the rural frontier into unsettled territory. Despite the snickering behind his back, however, Holliday's little railroad—said to "begin nowhere and go nowhere"—was legally incorporated in February of 1859. The next major goal was to acquire a land grant from the federal government, but that had to wait until after the Civil War. Finally, in March of 1863 President Lincoln passed the necessary land grant for Holliday's new railroad, at which time he was given 10 years to build the Atchison and Topeka to the Colorado state line (Poling-Kempes 1989). In that same year, the company changed its name to the now-famous Atchison, Topeka & Santa Fe (AT&SF) as a symbol of its eventual western goal. By 1868 the railroad had completed its first 7 miles of track, and in 1870 the town of Emporia was founded, providing a railroad connection with the Texas cattle trade. This provided the AT&SF with its first substantial revenue generator, that of hauling highly prized western cattle to satisfy the voracious appetites of easterners. It wouldn't be until 1882 that the railroad would reach the fledgling site of Flagstaff, having made its aforementioned deal with the A&P.

Although this is not the place to write a detailed history of the railroad's beginnings and accomplishments—numerous other publications serve that purpose—the railroad's early history is geographically significant for numerous reasons. Not only did the line successfully tie southern California and the Southwest into mainstream American society and the eastern economies, but it also served as a primary agent for town settlement, as discussed above. Further, the railroad's initial supporters, investors, and infrastructure all came primarily from eastern sources; in fact, the entire success of the railroad was dependent upon eastern financiers. The railway sold stock "back east," because federal land grants alone would not generate sufficient revenue for the railroad's continued expansion. During its construction, Holliday himself actually traveled back east to garner financial support and to convince eastern investors of the railroad's potential. He and his board of directors spent months at a time on the East Coast just to secure willing financiers for their railroad (Poling-Kempes 1989). Further, after its first year of revenue operation in Kansas, the headquarters of the new AT&SF was actually moved to Boston, where 3 of the 12 railroad's directors resided (Bryant 1974). Ten years later, in 1880, the *Boston Herald* described the railroad as the "splendid child of Boston energy and enterprise" (Bryant 1974, 142). By 1880 the headquarters had moved back to Topeka, Kansas, though Boston retained the railroad's executive offices. In virtually all aspects except its actual physical location, then, the Santa Fe Railway as we know it was an eastern railroad—conceived of and built by easterners, for easterners. Holliday himself embodied that very eastern legacy.

The railroad's second decade, that of the 1880s, witnessed incredible expansion along the railroad's system, especially to the west. The system's mileage increased from a mere 470 miles in 1879 to 2,620 miles by 1883. A significant portion of this expansion reflected the construction of the A&P's 35th parallel route through northern Arizona and Flagstaff. Likewise, the Santa Fe's inventory of railroad equipment increased substantially through the decade, from 5,530 pieces in 1880 to 32,293 pieces by 1895. During this period, railroad technology improved drastically, producing an impressive increase in the power and size of locomotives. Newer and larger engines pulled longer trains with freight and passenger cars of "ever-increasing length and capacity" (Bryant 1974, 145). All looked well for the entire Santa Fe system after its first two decades of existence.

The railroad's expansion program of the 1880s, however, nearly killed the transcontinental route through Flagstaff. One might assume that the A&P portion of the Santa Fe system would have been the most profitable due to its transcontinental status, but the reality could not have been further from the truth. It is important to keep in mind that the A&P, operating between Albuquerque, New Mexico and Needles, California, was only one of numerous branch lines throughout the AT&SF system at this time. The main lines included trackage from Kansas City to Denver, Albuquerque, and El Paso as of 1896. By the late 1880s the AT&SF was heavily in debt, in large part because of the expansion program and the operation of so many as-yet unprofitable branch lines like the A&P. Annual reports from the late 1880s reflected a continuing decrease in earnings and, more specifically, the burden of interest payments demanded by various branch lines including the A&P. Opposition by stockholders to the railroad's expansion program grew, and several law suits were filed in an attempt to prevent other expansion plans, such as the acquisition of the Gulf, Colorado and Santa Fe and the planned construction of a new line to Chicago (Bryant 1974). With the end of the expansion program of the 1880s, the AT&SF's debts totaled nearly $159 million, not including the additional debt owed by the A&P. In one year, the A&P branch alone lost more than $1.5 million for its parent company.

The poor condition of track and facilities along the A&P reflected its low status as a branch line. A detailed engineering analysis of the Santa Fe system in the early 1890s, for instance, concluded that although the main lines in Kansas were in decent shape, some of its affiliate lines, including the A&P, were in "dreadful condition" (Bryant 1974, 166). Annual deficits of the entire Santa Fe system peaked in 1893 at just over $3 million, and the A&P was responsible for a good portion, as "the A&P's 750 miles of wretched track continued to produce huge losses" (Bryant 1974, 165). A three-man committee was established to address the financial concerns of the Santa Fe's affiliated lines, and they recommended no less than dropping all of the affiliates entirely, except for the A&P, which maintained perhaps the best future potential for increased traffic. By 1896, however, some people were seriously advocating the total abandonment of the A&P through New Mexico and Arizona.

Were it not for the vision of the Santa Fe's president, E. P. Ripley, Flagstaff might have lost its railroad connection for good. Ripley dealt specifically with the issue of the A&P in a mid-1890s annual report, stating that if the A&P were to be abandoned, the AT&SF would amount to no more than just another regional railroad. Ripley envisioned—quite correctly—that California would continue to grow rapidly and would produce increasing traffic for the railroad. He viewed the ailing A&P as the future transcontinental link for the entire AT&SF system (Bryant 1974). As part of a massive corporate reorganization scheme, the A&P line was foreclosed for $12 million on May 4, 1897, and a new affiliate corporation, the Santa Fe Pacific Railroad, took control of the dissolved A&P. Flagstaff's transcontinental railroad would be saved, but only after intense planning and visioning for a wider railroad system that would emerge throughout Arizona.

The problems of the A&P in the last decade of the nineteenth century could be attributed to no less than three primary geographical situations: (1) competition from the Southern Pacific Railroad in California, (2) insufficient volume of local rail traffic, and (3) the unpredictability of Indian raids and train robbers, especially in New Mexico. All three were related, however, rooted as they were in the regional context of the poorly settled Wild West that the A&P crossed.

A major dilemma involved the Santa Fe's fiercest competitor, the Southern Pacific Railroad. Ever since the SP began building its own transcontinental route through southern California and Arizona, the SP and its steamship affiliates had successfully monopolized transportation in California. Only the AT&SF attempted to challenge the SP and its self-proclaimed territory, and SP's leadership fought vigorously to deny the Santa Fe its coveted access to the West Coast. Indeed, much of the historical development of the Santa Fe railroad in the Southwest was heavily influenced by the competitive efforts between these two companies. Much of Keith Bryant's (1974) book, *History of the Atchison, Topeka and Santa Fe Railway*, concerns the Southern Pacific as much as it does the Santa Fe because of the SP railroad's significant competitive influence on the Santa Fe's decision making.

For instance, while the A&P was still under construction through northern Arizona, the Santa Fe was constructing its first true transcontinental link through southern Arizona to the port city of Guaymas, Mexico. The basic intent was to provide a vital West Coast link for the Santa Fe while avoiding the domain of the Southern Pacific in southern California. Only in November of 1885 did the Santa Fe finally succeed in connecting the A&P with the much-desired southern California port of San Diego. A round of intense negotiations with the Southern Pacific eventually provided trackage rights for the Santa Fe over Southern Pacific rails into Los Angeles. Though still a fierce competitor, the Southern Pacific had lost its California monopoly by the mid-1880s. On November 26 of 1885, the first Santa Fe Pullman passenger train arrived in San Diego from Kansas City via the A&P, exclusively on Santa Fe-owned trackage (Bryant 1974). A true transcontinental link with California had been established, promising increased traffic along what was once a dead-end A&P route through northern Arizona. The Santa Fe's original rail line to Guaymas quickly became a financial disaster and was eventually traded away. Although the Santa Fe still had its California connection, the Southern Pacific controlled the lion's share of transcontinental traffic.

Despite the A&P's new access to California, the number of trains remained relatively few, and the Santa Fe affiliate continued to lose money as noted above. In short, the A&P suffered from a lack of local rail traffic between New Mexico and California. Although one might presume that a transcontinental line would create instant prosperity for its corporate owner, the reverse was actually true in this case. Even today, railroad profitability depends on volume of cargo transported, much of it to and from local businesses along the line. In lightly settled New Mexico and northern Arizona, however, few prospects for local traffic existed during the nineteenth century.

To make matters worse, the A&P's federal land grants were not producing sufficient revenue from land sales, also due to the lack of rapid settlement in the region. Although the A&P had received more than 14 million acres of land from the government, much of the property consisted of desert wasteland with some limited ranching possibilities. Between 1883 and 1889, the Santa Fe went so far as to offer free transportation for land buyers in the region, but to no avail. By 1897 the A&P had received only $3.8 million from all of its land grant sales. Further, by the mid-1880s public opinion about railroad land grants had soured, and Congress heavily debated the possibility of forfeiting the A&P grants altogether. On the flip side, however, had the A&P not received its land grants in the first place, the A&P might have actually been abandoned permanently by 1884, only 2 years after its celebratory arrival in Flagstaff (Bryant 1974). Thus, the land grants were at once a blessing and a burden for the ailing A&P.

AT&SF President E. P. Ripley understood the implications of not generating enough local traffic to make the A&P profitable through Arizona. Ripley's solution was to actually create a demand for the A&P in Arizona. Doing so required the construction of various branch-line tracks through central and northern Arizona, thereby connecting the A&P to potentially growing markets and populations.

One such line was already in demand by the late 1880s, prior to Ripley becoming president. At that time, Arizona's Territorial Governor pleaded with the Santa Fe to construct a branch from Ash Fork to Prescott, the territorial capital. The A&P's chief engineer Samuel Rowe studied the potential for such a line in 1889 and reported that, in Bryant's (1974, 184) words, "much heavy grading would be necessary," but "the copper mines near Prescott and the Salt River Valley at the town of Phoenix would generate considerable traffic. The climate of the Phoenix area allowed considerable production of winter produce, and the town already had some 7,000 people." Rowe envisioned that a rail line to Phoenix would generate tremendous growth in the area. By 1891, a Santa Fe affiliate company, the Santa Fe, Prescott & Phoenix Railway (SFP&P) was organized, and the first trains were running between Ash Fork and Prescott by April of 1893. The route was extended to Phoenix 2 years later, enabling the predicted economic boom. Soon thereafter, Phoenix replaced Prescott as the region's major urban center and as the territorial capital.

The "Peavine," as the SFP&P was known, due to its serpentine, winding route, enjoyed a steady increase in earnings after 1895, and President Ripley arranged for the Santa Fe to purchase the line outright in 1901. The Peavine became a sort of lifeline for the formerly ailing A&P, resulting in a rather ironic geographical situation: A largely unprofitable transcontinental route was essentially saved by the traffic generated by one of its connecting branch lines. Ripley continued his expansion program in Arizona with the creation of various other feeder lines, including a branch from Williams to the south rim of the Grand Canyon. A steadily growing number of tourists eager to experience that scenic wonder had not gone unnoticed by the Santa Fe.

Initially organized as the Santa Fe and Grand Canyon Railroad (SF&GC), construction began in 1899. After building 63 miles of track, however, the railroad collapsed financially in 1900 (Bryant

1974), but Ripley was determined to make it work, and he soon incorporated the Grand Canyon Railway and completed the line to the canyon rim. A detailed history of this now-famous branch line can be found in Al Richmond's (1995) book, *The Grand Canyon Railway.* Today the privately owned Grand Canyon Railway serves as a prominent tourist attraction and shuffles thousands of visitors between Williams and the Grand Canyon each year.

The stories above demonstrate well the process through which the AT&SF expanded its system during its first few decades. When a new rail line was to be built, the AT&SF would organize an affiliate, or subsidiary railroad company. The A&P, the Peavine, and the Grand Canyon Railway were three such affiliates in Arizona, although they remained under the control of the parent AT&SF. Over time, the affiliate companies were abandoned, sold, or purchased outright by the AT&SF. As for the parent company itself, the AT&SF retained the same corporate name until its merger with the Burlington Northern in 1995. Even in 2002, the railroad is still popularly referred to as the Santa Fe, and its various pre-merger logos, locomotive paint schemes, depot architecture, and luxurious transcontinental passenger trains are remembered nostalgically in the Southwest and throughout America.

One of the more memorable aspects of the railroad's heritage were the services that it offered, through an entirely independent partner to the AT&SF, the Fred Harvey Company. Fred Harvey operated numerous eating establishments, hotels, and concession stands along the Santa Fe route through the Southwest. As Lesley Poling-Kempes (1989, 30) has explained, the story of Fred Harvey and that of the AT&SF "are closely intertwined, because the success of one was directly supplemented by the success of the other." Most Americans are unaware of the important legacy of the Fred Harvey Company and the close business partnership it formed with the AT&SF, which lasted more than 70 years. Both of these companies made a significant impact on southwestern geography and are credited directly with inventing an entirely new image of the Southwest. Together, the AT&SF and Fred

Harvey companies were the first major actors to successfully theme the Southwest, primarily for the enjoyment of eastern travelers.

After arriving as an immigrant boy from England in 1850, Fred Harvey made a deal with the AT&SF in 1876 to provide food service for railroad passengers (Howard and Pardue 1996). The business grew rapidly in the next two decades, and after opening his first restaurant in the Santa Fe depot at Topeka, Kansas, Harvey's company ended up preparing food for railroad travelers at depot restaurants all along the line. To staff his restaurants and railroad dining cars on the trains, Fred Harvey hired young, single women from the East and Midwest to serve as waitresses. These young women became known as the *Harvey Girls*; they collectively became a symbol of the Southwest for many decades. Between 1883 and the 1950s, approximately 100,000 Harvey Girls moved west to work for the Fred Harvey system (Poling-Kempes 1989). Wearing full-length uniforms and starched, white aprons, the Harvey Girls provided assurance to travelers of a safe, clean environment, which the Harvey Company and Santa Fe railroad believed necessary to attract wealthy easterners into the remote Southwest (Figure 16). At the same time, the railroad made heavy use of Native American cultural symbols and Spanish Revival architecture in their advertisements to promise the traveler an element of adventure (Howard and Pardue 1996). Thus, the Santa Fe and Fred Harvey companies collaborated to encourage tourists to visit the Southwest, the true heritage of which was both exaggerated and manipulated in the name of increasing travel on Santa Fe trains.

Figure 16. The revived Harvey Girls of Winslow, a local group of women dedicated to keeping the history of Fred Harvey and the Harvey Girls alive. These women are demonstrating the typical Harvey Girl uniforms to a geography field class at La Posada Hotel in Winslow, AZ. (Photo: Author's collection)

Between the 1880s and 1930, numerous Harvey Houses were also built at prominent station stops along the line. The Santa Fe and Fred Harvey companies used the *Mission Revival style* of architecture for its Harvey Houses to reflect the Spanish heritage of the Southwest (Figure 17). This was the imagery that eastern tourists expected to see while traveling through the region, so the Santa Fe gave it to them by aggressively theming its infrastructure along the route.

The last and grandest Harvey House to be constructed was the elegant *La Posada* (the Resting Place) built in Flagstaff's neighboring town of Winslow, completed in 1930. Unlike several of the original Harvey hotels, this one still survives, and is being fully restored by its current private owners. Its construction began prior to the stock market crash of 1929, so the Santa Fe and Fred Harvey companies remained optimistic about its future. Because La Posada wasn't completed until after the Crash, however, it is said that the hotel never netted a profit for its owners, and it remained underused through its short life as a Harvey House. The *Fray Marcos*, another Harvey hotel, was built in Williams, 30 miles west of Flagstaff. Others were constructed in Gallup, Las Vegas (NM), Albuquerque, Santa Fe, and Grand Canyon Village at the South Rim (the El Tovar). The Fray Marcos in Williams is still standing, and is currently used as the depot for the revived Grand Canyon Railway.

Figure 17. AT&SF Railway depot at Kingman, AZ. Many depots, hotels and other buildings displayed the Mission or Spanish Revival style of architecture in one of the first large-scale attempts to construct a unified theme of the Southwest. (Photo: Author's collection)

One question remains: Why was there no elegant Harvey House in Flagstaff, a city today of more than 50,000 people? Winslow and Williams hosted Harvey Houses, but these are much smaller communities where growth and development are slow in coming. Why not Flagstaff? Part of the answer lies in the urban settlement pattern as it existed a century ago—somewhat different from today's geography of northern Arizona. Flagstaff in 1900 was an insignificant logging and ranching town, unlike Winslow, which actually served as the hub of northern Arizona and the true gateway to the natural wonders of the region. Winslow became the regional headquarters for the Santa Fe Railroad, and the railroad naturally expected Winslow to grow and prosper. Thus, the railroad and the Fred Harvey Company established their major activities and operations in Winslow—not Flagstaff. From here, the famous Harvey touring cars (Harvey Cars), marketed as the "Indian De-tours," fanned out to Indian reservations and natural wonders nearby.

Not that Flagstaff didn't try to capture a Harvey House of its own. After learning in 1905 that the Fray Marcos would be built in Williams, prominent Flagstaff citizens including David Babbitt pleaded with the railroad to bring a Harvey hotel to Flagstaff. Low county taxes and reasonably priced water were used as incentives to win over the railroad. Ultimately, though, the railroad's Harvey hotels were planned for major railroad division points or junctions, so the Santa Fe showed little interest in Flagstaff. Some Santa Fe passenger trains made stops at Gallup, Winslow, and Williams, and even at little Ash Fork, but they passed by Flagstaff without stopping (Cline 1994).

What about Williams? Williams is home to only 3,000 people, roughly the same population as in 1900. Williams enjoyed a locational advantage, however, serving as the railroad's own gateway to the Grand Canyon. The Santa Fe Railroad built its branch line from Williams in 1903 to the south rim of the Grand Canyon, necessitating the construction of a Harvey House at Williams Junction. Santa Fe passenger trains traveling between Chicago and Los Angeles often took a detour up the Grand Canyon line from Williams to the grandest Harvey hotel in the West prior to the 1930s, the El Tovar.

Even more significant was the cultural impact of the Santa Fe railroad on the Native American tribes of northern Arizona and New Mexico. The building of the railroad in the 1880s across this region reduced the friction of distance between these once-isolated peoples and the expanding Anglo society. Now, Anglo-American travelers were provided with relatively easy access to these native peoples and their homelands. The railroad and its tourists, therefore, represented the first dominant intrusion of the American cash economy into the subsistence-based Indian lands of the Southwest. It was not uncommon to see a train stopped at a station with eastern travelers hanging out the windows to purchase hand-made pottery, rugs, and jewelry from Native Americans who greeted the trains as they arrived.

Chapter 4

Living on the Transcon

The BNSF Railway: Moving Your World

On September 22, 1995, the Atchison, Topeka & Santa Fe Railway ceased to exist after maintaining the same company name for nearly 132 years. It was merged with the Burlington Northern Railway (BN), another railroad giant that dominated the northwestern United States. The product of this corporate mega-merger was the BNSF, or Burlington Northern Santa Fe Railway Corporation. As far as railroad companies go, this one is a monster! In 2001 the Web site of the BNSF boasted proudly of its status as "one of the largest rail networks in North America, with 33,500 route miles covering 28 states and two Canadian provinces." One of the BNSF's principal main lines is the *Transcon*, or transcontinental railroad that connects Los Angeles with Chicago by way of Flagstaff, generally following the route of the original A&P through northern Arizona.

Headquartered in Fort Worth, Texas, the BNSF employed some 44,500 people throughout its system in 2001, owned approximately 5,000 locomotives, and maintained some 90,000 freight cars. The company listed its total assets at $23.7 billion in its 1999 annual report. Confirming its status as a global corporate giant is the company's trademarked slogan, "We can move your world," used for customer relations efforts. Thus, the Flagstaff community now finds itself located along one of the busiest rail corridors in the nation, and along one of the BNSF railroad's foremost east-west main lines, which handled an average of 80–100 trains per day in the late 1990s. Indeed, much of the world now moves through Flagstaff on mile-long freight trains destined for Chicago, Los Angeles, Phoenix, and elsewhere.

These freight trains and the steel corridor beneath them comprise a rather unique feature of Flagstaff's local geography. To stand near the tracks in downtown Flagstaff is to experience a window of global transportation. Flagstaff's local community is now in many ways plugged in to the world's emerging global economy. Aside from the community's access to satellite, telecommunications, and Internet services, the railroad itself represents one of Flagstaff's connections to the rest of the world. Specifically, new technologies in transportation and communication systems have contributed significantly to the current round of globalization, especially through the integration of shipping, railroads, air cargo transport, and highway networks developed since the 1960s.

The advent of the *container era* has allowed these more efficient transportation networks to emerge, and this has revolutionized the long-distance transportation of cargo (Knox and Marston 1998). Quite simply, containers are large, metal shipping boxes of a standardized size that are used to carry consumer goods to practically anywhere in the world (Figure 18). This method of transportation is referred to as *intermodal*, in that containers can be transferred efficiently from one mode of transportation to another—usually from ship to train to truck, and vice-versa. Railroads also commonly transport tractor-trailer trucks on flat cars, referred to as TOFC traffic (trailer on flat car), another type of intermodal transport. An international standard for containers has been in place since 1965, providing a highly integrated global transport infrastructure. Before containerization, ships were required to spend, on average, one day in port for every one day at sea, due to the labor-intensive activity required for loading and unloading cargo either by the crate or by the pallet. With standard containers that can be loaded and unloaded quickly with large cranes, today's ships are required to spend on average only 1 day in port for every 10 days at sea (Knox and Marston 1998). As of 2002, the largest container ships in the world could be loaded or unloaded and sent back to sea in less than 48 hours (Plezia 2002).

Figure 18. A westbound intermodal train carrying containers and tractor-trailer trucks rumbles by the Flagstaff depot. The container and its associated infrastructure brought a revolution in the shipment of cargo around the world. (Photo: Author's collection)

Because the BNSF railroad does not operate in isolation from other global modes of transportation, it is hard to understand the railroad's operations and growth without also recognizing the shipping industry and the ports of Long Beach and Los Angeles. Much of the rail traffic through Flagstaff is either coming from or going to one of these two adjacent ports in southern California. As with many innovations that eventually change the world, the current era of shipping cargo with standardized containers can be traced to the initial ideas of one individual. In 1956, a New Jersey trucker, Malcom McLean, developed the first trailer-sized steel container that could be used interchangeably on trucks and ships (Port of Long Beach 2001). He proceeded to create the first container ship, a tanker called the Ideal X with a capacity of 58 containers. The idea of placing containers on trains would come later. McLean's innovation ultimately brought to an end the laborious practice of manually loading and unloading pallets of cargo at port facilities. Further, a new era of standardized global transportation of cargo had begun: by the early 1960s major world ports such as the ones at Los Angeles and Long Beach were adapting their facilities to handle the new container traffic. The first Sea-Land container ship entered the port of Long Beach, for instance, in 1962. By the 1970s, container traffic had become mainstream worldwide, and ports including Long Beach were constructing their first-ever terminals dedicated entirely to containers (Port of Long Beach 2000).

Since the 1970s, ocean-going container ships have only become larger and more impressive in their capacity. The earliest containers were only 20 feet long, and this size became the basis for the TEU measure. One TEU (20-foot equivalent unit) is equal to one 20-foot-long cargo container. Today's more common 40-foot containers equal two TEUs each. This is the measure used to describe the carrying capacity for ocean-going container ships. The first container ships of the early 1960s were built to carry little more than 200 TEUs. The first 1,100 TEU ship was produced in 1968, followed by a successive chain of ever-larger ships, including the first 3,000 TEU ship in 1972, the first 4,300 TEU ship in 1988, and the first 6,000 TEU ship in 1996. By the mid-1990s, shipping lines were regularly adding 5,000 TEU ships to their fleets. In 2001, the China Shipping Group went so far as to propose a new mega-ship with an amazing capacity of 9,800 TEUs (Port of Long Beach 2000).

As ships become larger in size and scale, however, port facilities are forced to adapt to handle these ships effectively. The Port of Long Beach, for instance, from which the BNSF Railway receives much of its transcontinental container traffic, was in the midst of a monumental master plan to overhaul and expand its docking facilities as of 2002.

The port's Gerald Desmond automobile bridge will be heightened to allow larger ships to move underneath it between the port's inner and outer harbors. In 2001 the container ships could barely fit under the once spacious bridge span. The port will also develop five container terminals requiring more than 300 acres each, and two other large terminals to keep pace with projected cargo growth (Port of Long Beach 2000).

One of the more impressive projects completed at the port, in June of 2002, is the Alameda Corridor, which consists of a 20-mile railroad cargo expressway linking the adjacent ports of Los Angeles and Long Beach to the transcontinental rail yards east of downtown Los Angeles. Billed as the "first consolidated rail link of its kind" by the port's promotional documents, the Alameda Corridor is among the largest public infrastructure projects of its kind in the United States. Running parallel to (and below) Alameda Street, the central part of the corridor consists of a rail line that descends into a trench that is 10 miles long, 33 feet deep, and 50 feet wide. The entire project eliminates some 200 street-level railroad crossings, and average train speed between the ports and the Los Angeles rail yards have increased from the former 5–20 mph to 30–40 mph.

You may be wondering how the Alameda Corridor project relates to the BNSF railway in Flagstaff. The BNSF and the UP (Union Pacific) railways both maintain extensive freight yards just east of downtown Los Angeles, but neither company enjoys access to the contiguous ports of Long Beach and Los Angeles. Instead, the ports have contracted with a separate company, the Pacific Harbor Line Railroad, to shuttle containers and other commodities between the ports and the BNSF and UP rail yards 20 miles away. This setup makes for a transportation nightmare in the heart of the LA metropolitan area. Until June of 2002 the Pacific Harbor Line trains had to snake their way carefully through the urban development south of Los Angeles, a very inefficient method for transferring cargo from the ships to the transcontinental rail lines. Further, only 25 percent of all incoming containers that left the Port of

Long Beach, specifically, were shipped inland by rail in 2002 (Plezia 2002). The rest left the port by tractor-trailer truck, one container at a time! This process makes for quite a hectic scene at the port facilities. Seemingly unending lines of trucks enter the port from the surrounding freeways to haul away their respective containers. The goal of the Alameda Corridor is to increase the efficiency of cargo traffic into and out of the ports, and a larger portion of this traffic will go by rail instead of truck. Specifically, the corridor promises to serve as a much more efficient link between the ports and the BNSF rail yard 20 miles inland.

This added efficiency will in turn allow the continuing growth in container traffic that is expected throughout the next two decades. Between the years 2000 and 2020, container movements into the ports of Long Beach and Los Angeles have been forecast to increase by 5.0 percent (low forecast) to 6.6 percent (high forecast) per year. To put this in perspective, the Port of Long Beach alone handled 4.6 million TEUs in 2000. Given this predicted growth in container traffic, the port will be handling between 12 and 16 million TEUs by 2020! Much of this traffic will necessarily make it to the BNSF rail yard and onto awaiting transcontinental trains—many of which Flagstaff residents will see whizzing through town. Clearly, the continuing globalization of trade is only increasing in intensity and efficiency with time, and it is all happening right before our eyes.

It wasn't long after the first containers found their way onto ships and trucks that the railroad industry began its own standardization program. It is perhaps not surprising that one of the leading railroad companies to successfully develop intermodal services and technologies was the AT&SF. As early as 1952, the Santa Fe began to experiment with "piggy-backing" truck trailers and, eventually, with the new metal containers on flat cars. The experiments were so successful that the railroad was already offering TOFC service between Chicago, the Gulf of Mexico, and California by 1954 (Bryant 1974). As TOFC technology progressed, the Santa Fe developed new and longer styles of flatcars with depressed decks to lower the center of gravity. Though enhanced over time, the basic technology remained the same in 2003, and train-watchers in Flagstaff could regularly see container trains speed through town with flat cars appearing to nearly drag on the ground. For such flat cars loaded with top-heavy containers (known as stack trains), the center of gravity must be as low to the ground as possible. Between 1968 and 1972, intermodal traffic on the Santa Fe continued to increase, with TOFC traffic increasing from 113,523 to 156,262 trailers between those years. During that same short period, the Santa Fe increased its handling of metal containers from 1,626 units to an impressive 22,749. Thus, a new era of container traffic had emerged on the Santa Fe by the early 1970s, mirroring the global trend (Bryant 1974).

With all innovations there are tradeoffs. For one thing, the geographical distribution of port facilities has been greatly affected by containerization. Because container traffic requires a high level of investment in ocean vessels, standardized railroad cars, and dockside handling equipment, this activity has become concentrated in a small number of major ports worldwide. In the United States, these ports have become the nation's primary gateway cities for global trade, most notably including Los Angeles, Long Beach, Seattle, and New York City. The BNSF's Hobart Yard in Los Angeles is credited with being the largest truck-trailer and container-handling rail facility in the world—yet another superlative. According to BNSF calculations, more than a million trailers and containers were moved through this facility in the year 2000.

Given its sheer expanse across much of the nation, it is probably easier to envision the BNSF as three railroads rather than one, based on regional specialties and locational advantages. The BNSF controls such a wide expanse of territory that the company focuses on transporting entirely different commodities through different regions of the nation. On northern routes between Montana, Minnesota, and Illinois, for instance, coal is king. During the month of January of 2000, the BNSF loaded 47 coal trains per day, which translates to 302 train sets attached to 1,121 locomotives (Frailey 2001). Formerly part of the Burlington Northern railroad system, the routes handling these trains consist of those radiating east and south from Wyoming and Montana toward Nebraska, Colorado, and Lake Superior.

Grain is another major commodity for the BNSF; most of it rolls on trains from the Midwest to Galveston, Texas and to Seattle and Portland in the Northwest. Much of that grain is going overseas, of course, to nations that regularly import U.S. corn and wheat. At any one time, some 35 to 45 grain trains are moving outward from the Midwest to global markets, though little grain is actually shipped on its southwestern route through Flagstaff. Similarly, coal trains are rarely seen in northern Arizona, except to supply various industries and coal-fired power plants in the region.

Instead, Flagstaff is located on the BNSF's "third" railroad, described by Fred Frailey (2001, 31) as the "high-speed Transcon—Chicago to California in 50 hours and Hail Mary." This southwestern route is dominated by high-speed intermodal trains. Estimates of the number of trains that speed through Flagstaff each day vary widely. In a personal interview with BNSF employee and fourth-generation railroader Mike McCallister, he explained that it is difficult to provide any specific number of trains on a given day. It is more reasonable to speak of average train *frequencies*—a number that McCallister confidently placed at 80–100 trains per day in 2001. Further, this statistic changes with the seasons; the busiest season for the BNSF through Flagstaff is the company's fourth quarter, between Thanksgiving and Christmas. "There are days in our peak season," said McCallister, "when we exceed 100 trains. We don't average that many, but there are days when we exceed that" (McCallister 2001). Putting this in perspective, McCallister estimated that roughly 25,000 trains roll through Flagstaff each year. Given that each train averages about a mile long, that's 25,000 miles of trains that snake their way through town annually!

Many Flagstaff residents wonder if the number of trains through town will continue to increase. Most likely, any increase in traffic volume along the Transcon will be slow but continuous. Geographically speaking, the BNSF Transcon is expected by industry insiders to continue benefiting from its strategic position as the shortest and fastest route between Chicago and Los Angeles. Of the seven principal transcontinental railroad routes that cross the nation's Continental Divide, the BNSF's Transcon has tallied the most rapid increase in tonnage since 1980; in 1980, freight tonnage along the Transcon between Williams, Arizona and Belen, New Mexico totaled 63 million gross tons (mgt), compared with 145 mgt in the year 2000, a 130 percent increase. The second highest increase in freight tonnage, by contrast, was only 78 percent throughout the same period, along the former Southern Pacific's Sunset Route through southern Arizona. Further, freight tonnage along Union Pacific's Overland Route, roughly the path of our nation's first transcontinental railroad through Utah, was nearly identical in millions of gross tons as the BNSF Transcon during the year 2002. Looking to the near future, the editor of *Trains* magazine, Mark Hemphill, explained that "Union Pacific's Overland Route, transcontinental tonnage champion throughout the twentieth century, by now may be surpassed by the Santa Fe. The Overland already has fewer trains, but has a higher proportion of heavy commodities, notably grain and soda ash" (Hemphill 2002, 63). Thus, freight traffic along the Transcon is likely to continue increasing as time progresses.

According to Mike McCallister of the BNSF, however, a rapid increase in activity is possible, but not likely. Freight-train traffic along the Transcon increased rather consistently throughout the 1990s and into 2000, a consequence of America's booming economy during that decade. The amount of freight carried by rail can serve as a rough indicator of the nation's economic growth as a whole. By the end of 2000, the economy had begun to cool off a bit and was not expected to grow quickly anytime soon—especially given the recession following the terrorist attacks of September 11, 2001. In turn, train traffic is not likely to expand measurably in the near future. However, despite tougher economic times, McCallister explained that the amount of freight traffic handled by the railroad has not changed much: "We've started to see it tail off in our revenues, but traffic volume has remained the same. As it becomes more competitive, you make a little less per ton. You try to do it more efficiently, so they expect some payback on the opposite end. So, revenues have fallen a bit, but I would say that gross ton miles have probably not diminished much" (McCallister 2001).

Increasingly aggressive competition from other railroad companies may further reduce the probability of seeing more trains through Flagstaff in the near future. In 2002 the decades-long trend of corporate mergers and consolidation in the railroad industry had come to a virtual halt, mostly due to a lack of consenting partners (Frailey 2002). In short, there are too few large railroad companies remaining in the United States to expect more mergers anytime soon. Only three giant railroad companies controlled the bulk of rail mileage in the West in 2002: the BNSF, the UP, and the Kansas City Southern (KCS).

The story of corporate mergers in the railroad industry represents a typical process within the political economic system of capitalism. Whether one is speaking of fast-food restaurant chains, big-box discount stores, automobile manufacturers, or railroad companies, the story is generally the same for one and all in a free-market economy. Small businesses that survive in the long term will continue to grow and expand their operations by either merging with or acquiring other companies. It is easy for Americans to sometimes conveniently ignore the fact that virtually all of America's large corporations began as small businesses that happened to grow and prosper with time, because of good business decisions and a bit of good luck. We have already examined the modest beginnings of the early AT&SF in Kansas. After growing to become one of the giant railroad companies of the West by acquiring numerous affiliate companies and competitors, the Santa Fe itself was finally dissolved to become one component of the BNSF in 1995.

The 1960s marked the beginning of the most recent era of railroad mergers in the United States. In that decade, railway passenger traffic steadily declined, and unprofitable freight routes were abandoned. Many railway companies thus found no other option than to merge with others in order to survive (Tayler 1996). This is probably not the place to provide a detailed history about railroad mergers, but a few major cases are worth mentioning to place the BNSF in a temporal context. At first, only the smallest regional railroad companies were lost to mergers, until 1963 when the Chesapeake & Ohio acquired the Baltimore & Ohio. In 1973, both of these former railroads, along with the Western Maryland, became subsidiaries of the new Chessie System. Larger companies were beginning to merge as well, a process that continued into the middle 1990s. One of the most renowned mergers occurred in 1968 between two big rivals in the East, the New York Central and the Pennsylvania Railroad. The Penn Central was the result, itself being merged with a variety of smaller regional railroads in 1976 to form Conrail (Consolidated Rail Corporation). Most recently, Conrail has been purchased by Norfolk Southern.

Other major recent mergers have included combining the Southern Railway with the Norfolk Western Railroad to form the Norfolk Southern, and the Atlantic Coast Lines with the Seaboard Air Line to form the Seaboard Coast Line. The Seaboard Coast Line then merged with the Louisville and Nashville to form Seaboard System, which in turn merged with the aforementioned Chessie System to form today's CSX Corporation. Following this? In the West, the Union Pacific acquired the Western Pacific and Missouri Pacific, only to be followed by a larger merger by the creation of BNSF from the AT&SF and the BN (Tayler 1996). Most recently, the Union Pacific purchased the Southern Pacific in 1996 but ultimately kept the UP name, apparently bringing to a close a four-decade era of railroad mergers in the United States. Thus, the BNSF and the UP now control Arizona's two transcontinental lines in the northern and southern parts of the state, respectively.

Railway mergers do not occur entirely without government regulation; the role of central authority has more or less influenced the railroad industry from nearly the beginning. For instance, the federal entity responsible for overseeing and handling proposed mergers is the ICC, or Interstate Commerce Commission. The beginning of the ICC can be traced back to the 1870s, when it became clear that a few major railroad companies were attempting to eliminate competition from other railroads by assembling major railway systems and monopolizing regional trade and freight rates. The aforementioned Southern Pacific, which vigorously attempted to deny the AT&SF access to California, exemplified this process well. By 1880, pressure had mounted nationwide for the federal government to intervene, which ultimately resulted in the passage of the federal Interstate Commerce Act in February of 1887. The ICC was set up by the Act to regulate all railroads engaged in interstate commerce, even if they were located entirely within one state. Currently, the Act has been broadened to apply to trucking, water carriers (i.e. river boats, barges, ferries), and freight forwarders.

Under the regulation of the ICC, railroads are forbidden to "give preference, advantage, special rates or rebates to any person, company, location or type of traffic" (Tayler 1996, 45). Over time, other acts of Congress have modified the responsibilities of the ICC, and railroads have found themselves more restricted, with increasing government regulations. In the 1970s, the Carter administration partially deregulated the trucking and airline industries, which consequently put more pressure on the government to do similarly with the railroads. In 1980 the railroads finally got their wish: the Staggers Act was passed (named for Rep. Harley Staggers of West Virginia), which significantly changed the terms under which railroads and shippers could determine freight charges. For one thing, railroads could offer volume discounts, which had previously been prohibited. Railroads and shippers could now negotiate their own contracts without interference by the ICC. Further, the 1980 deregulation allowed the railroads to increase their transport of coal, grain, automobiles, and intermodal containers—the latter of which has greatly affected the BNSF.

Perhaps most important, the Staggers Act encouraged a fundamental change in the geography of railroad transportation in America. A whole new class of railroad emerged, known in the industry as Class III companies. Generally, these consist of small regional and short-line railroads, many of which have originated since 1980. These companies could successfully operate rail lines that had previously been unprofitable. As Arthur Tayler (1996, 163) has explained, "The new companies could take on lines with low flow densities and operate them profitably because many of the old high-cost rules no longer applied."

Today, the ICC recognizes three broad categories of railroad companies: Class I railroads are those with revenues in excess of approximately $250 million, Class II railroads maintain revenues between roughly $20 million and $250 million, and Class III companies consist of the numerous short lines with annual revenue of less than $20 million. Since 1980, a combination of large corporate mergers and an increase in the number of Class III companies has produced a two-tiered hierarchy of railroad companies in America. At the top of the hierarchy are the seven remaining Class I railroads, the Union Pacific, BNSF, Amtrak, Chicago & Northwestern, CSX, Kansas City Southern, and Norfolk Southern. At the bottom end of the hierarchy are approximately 475 Class II and III railroads, many of which are quite small in terms of annual revenue and route miles (Tayler 1996). This means that there is still plenty of opportunity for small competitive railroad companies in the United States, despite the recent era of big corporate mergers. In this way, centralized authority—in this case the process of deregulation—has influenced the transportation geography of the United States, by changing the rules by which companies can do business.

As for competition, it is the recently energized Union Pacific that, at least in the short term, is giving the BNSF its share of headaches. The contemporary story of the UP and BNSF reflects the latest phase of corporate rivalry between the parent companies of Arizona's two transcontinental railroads. As the BN and SF were forming their mega-merger in the mid-1990s, so too were the UP and SP. What hasn't changed is the intense corporate rivalry between these two western giants. Just as Huntingdon's SP fought vigorously to prevent the AT&SF from gaining access to California more than a century ago, the UP today is proving to be a worthy competitor for transcontinental traffic.

Under the helm of a visionary CEO, Dick Davidson, the UP pursued in 2002 what Davidson calls "alliances" with other eastern railroads rather than new merger opportunities (Frailey 2002). These alliances allow faster transcontinental rail service by making mutually beneficial deals with other railroad companies. The result is some 60 trains per day exchanged by the UP with other railroads, so that these trains simply bypass previously time-consuming gateway terminals at transition points from one railroad to the next. Although new mergers are not out of the question for UP's future, Davidson's alliance strategy was making the UP stronger in the near-term.

In addition to its alliances in 2002, the UP competed effectively with the BNSF in other ways. Thanks to underbidding the BNSF in 2001, the UP was the sole transporter in the West for new automobiles from General Motors as of this writing. Also gained were some lucrative coal contracts, and the UP was also in the process of rebuilding its Golden State Route—its southern transcontinental line between Kansas City, El Paso, and southern California. Aside from these strategies, the UP was "grabbing every carload of traffic possible, even if it means worrying about profit margins later" (Frailey 2002, 35).

In response, the BNSF was working through more than 100 strategic initiatives, one of which consists of corporate downsizing. In early 2002 this downsizing promised to include a reduction of its total system by some 1,000 route miles, reducing its workforce by 400 non-union employees, and collapsing the number of operating divisions from 23 to 13 to improve efficiency.

While dealing with a new round of intense competition from its former SP neighbor, the BNSF is still concentrating on its dominant strength in the Southwest—that is, high-speed intermodal service. As many as three fourths of the trains negotiating the Transcon through Flagstaff are intermodal. Intermodal traffic continued to increase during 2000, spurred by a rising volume of containers transferred from ships at Los Angeles and Long Beach, and new business from truckload partners such as J. B. Hunt. That same year, intermodal revenue ($2.6 billion) became the BNSF's largest source of income for the first time, and the Transcon represents the core of the BNSF's intermodal network (Frailey 2001).

The issue of speed is also important when considering the operation of intermodal trains. Revenue from intermodal freight is measurably less than for other commodities shipped by rail. To compensate, the BNSF offers fast service between its major hubs. Unlike the former Burlington Northern Railroad, which generally attempted to operate all of its trains at the same speed, the former Santa Fe operated a "hot railroad" along the Transcon by allowing high-speed intermodal trains to intermix with slower freight trains of lesser priority. The BNSF continues this practice, and it is not uncommon to see a faster train literally passing a slower one within Flagstaff city limits, both moving in the same direction. This practice puts on quite a show for Flagstaff's visitors, who are not used to all of the train traffic.

With such an enormous railroad operation, how does the BNSF control its trains and monitor their locations on the system? Most of the answer is found in Fort Worth, Texas, home of the BNSF headquarters and center of operations. Although the trains may be a constantly visible (even if moving) component of Flagstaff's local landscape, the movement of these trains, the setting of track switches, and communication with train crews is all conducted from Fort Worth.

More locally, Winslow still serves as the hub for operations along the BNSF's Arizona Division, which includes the Transcon main line between Needles, California and Belen, New Mexico, just south of Albuquerque. Winslow is where the division superintendent's office is located, along with other railroad personnel. Train crews operate out of Winslow, and roughly a third of these crew members actually live in Flagstaff. When on call for the railroad, train crews drive out to Winslow to be assigned to their respective train and destination. Also, trains coming to or from Phoenix are "broken up" at Winslow's rail yard, allowing freight cars to be channeled to their proper destinations. Approximately 10 daily trains through Flagstaff originate in, or are destined for, Phoenix. Inbound trains to Phoenix travel from Winslow west through Flagstaff to Ash Fork, where they turn south on the aforementioned Peavine route.

The size of a typical crew operating these long freight trains has dropped by nearly half since the early 1980s, from four or five individuals per train to two or three. In an effort to make the railroad industry more efficient and cost-effective, railroads around the nation—including the AT&SF—had phased out their use of cabooses by the end of the 1980s (Figure 19). The caboose was typically the last car of the train and served primarily as an office on wheels for two or three of the crew members. Cabooses also included either a cupola or bay window from which the crew could occasionally scan the train in front of them for safety hazards or potential problems.

Figure 19. A railroad caboose on display in Las Vegas, NM. The typical caboose has a distinctive shape with its cupola designed so that crew members can sit above and scan the train for potential problems. Cabooses are now a rare sight on most railroads; many have been relegated to museum service in various communities. (Photo: Author's collection)

Railroad enthusiasts, or *railfans*, have lamented the loss of the caboose, given that the little red car at the end of the train had become the subject of much romanticism and folklore associated with railroading in America. In place of the caboose (and its two-person crew) on the rear of the train is now found an uninspiring little device known as an ETD (end of train device). Attached to the rear car, the ETD includes a flashing red light, a motion detector, and an air-brake-line monitor. Information about train motion and air brake pressure is transmitted from the ETD to the locomotive cab, reassuring the engineer that all is well at the end of the train (Tayler 1996).

Railroads across America had collectively acquired so many cabooses by the 1980s that it became another challenge to determine what to do with them all. Many cabooses have therefore been sold relatively cheaply to practically anybody who wanted one and could transport it off of railroad property. Other cabooses have been donated to museums, parks, and local communities along the line. They have also become collectors' items. Some of the Santa Fe's old cabooses can be seen dotting the landscape along Interstate 40 through Arizona and New Mexico, both in people's back yards and in local parks. One caboose, carefully restored by local enthusiasts, sits along Route 180, Fort Valley Road, outside the Pioneers Museum north of Flagstaff.

Although the long-distance freight trains understandably receive the most attention from people in town, the keen observer may notice another lesser-known activity, that of the *Flag switcher*. Communities that host a relatively large number of track-side industries are often assigned a special locomotive, the duty of which is solely to switch carloads of freight into and out of these local companies. In Flagstaff, this operation is known by BNSF employees simply as the Flag switcher. Its hub of activity is right here in Flagstaff and its territory covers about 25 miles out of town, east to Winona and the cinder operations there. The Flag switcher currently handles a half-dozen industries here in town, the largest of which is the Ralston-Purina plant located on the town's east side. Typically, freight cars with loads destined for one of these companies in town are dropped off onto a siding by a main-line train heading east or west. The Flag switcher crew is then responsible for "spotting," or moving, these cars to and from their respective businesses with rail sidings in town. The Flag switcher can often be seen with a few freight cars moving slowly through town, or idling downtown, patiently waiting for the busy main-line traffic to clear.

The Flag switcher and its crew currently operate 5 days per week, and sometimes on Saturday when necessary. Although this represents the most local type of railroad activity that takes place in Flagstaff, one might be surprised to learn that the switcher's weekly schedule is still crafted at the division headquarters in Winslow. Also benefiting from global communication technologies, its crew is constantly in direct radio communication with BNSF headquarters in Fort Worth. Given that all main-line train activity is controlled out of Texas, the crew of the Flag switcher must obtain permission from dispatchers there before it can occupy one of the main-line tracks in town. This process can be a tedious one indeed, given the heavy volume of main-line rail traffic.

The Flag switcher crew typically begins its day at 7:00 or 8:00 in the morning, but the length of its workday is determined by the time required to complete the day's switching duties. Mike McCallister described the unpredictable aspect of the Flag switcher's operation this way:

> They have to fight to get out to certain industries, especially if they have to utilize the main track. For the most part they can switch the downtown area without really bothering the main line. If they have to switch SCA Tissue, then they have to occupy what we call Main 2 South in order to do it because there's not enough room to clear. But they have to vie for time. Sometimes they sit around a lot, a good portion of the day, waiting for track and time, to get authority [from Fort Worth] to run on the main track and do the work they want to do. (McCallister 2001)

What are the implications of this frequent and constant rail activity for Flagstaff? The town happens to be located along one of the busiest rail lines in America, partly because this BNSF route serves as the shortest distance by rail between Chicago and Los Angeles. On a more global scale, Los Angeles is one of America's primary gateways to the entire Pacific Rim region. The ocean itself now serves as a virtual liquid highway for global trade between the countries that have access to it. Pacific Rim nations—especially Japan, China, South Korea, and Taiwan—export a wide variety of manufactured goods to the United States, and much of this traffic is funneled through Los Angeles and along the BNSF to points east. Some of these commodities even continue across the Atlantic Ocean to Europe, though BNSF container trains with Europe-bound cargo constitute less than 10 percent of the total (Plezia 2002). Given such cargo, however, North America can be interpreted as a *land bridge* for cargo to move across the continent from one ocean to the other. In turn, other commodities are shipped from the United States and Canada to the Pacific Rim in the other direction, including coal, grain, automobiles, and other manufactured goods and food products. For better or worse, Flagstaff has a front-row seat to this impressive show of global trade.

To watch a BNSF train rumble through Flagstaff, then, is to see a bit of globalization roll by. Aside from the common intermodal trains, the more traditional freight trains (known as manifest freights) exhibit a variety of freight cars that carry a wide range of commodities. The manifest freights are especially interesting to watch—these trains do not consist of one standardized type of freight car as do the intermodals. Typically painted on the sides of box cars, tank cars, and coal and grain hopper cars are the logos and names of their corporate owners—often other railroad companies from elsewhere around the nation. It is not uncommon to see freight cars owned by the Wisconsin Central, Norfolk Southern, Canadian National, Chicago & Northwestern, Illinois Central, and those of many other railroad companies. Other freight cars also serve as the last reminders of railroad companies that no longer exist—the victims of mergers or bankruptcy, including the Rock Island, Santa Fe, Conrail, Central Vermont, and many others. These rail cars and their paint schemes have outlasted their parent railroad corporations and reveal the colorful regional corporate geography of the rail industry prior to many of the larger recent mergers. I suggest that while you are stuck at the railroad crossing waiting for a train, you pay attention to all of the "geography" rolling past, and the time may go by much more quickly—perhaps more quickly than the train itself.

Incidentally, it is interesting to note that because the BNSF owns so many locomotives (from both pre-merger railroads), the company had not yet been able to paint all of them with the company's new paint scheme as of 2003. Thus, if you watch one or more trains cruise through town you will likely see an eclectic mixture of new and old paint schemes on the locomotives that represent the long history of the railroad. The old AT&SF used two common paint schemes in the past: the railroad's famous "war bonnet" silver and red pattern, or its other popular blue and yellow scheme. In contrast, the Burlington Northern (known affectionately by railroaders as "The Big Green") painted its locomotives with a forest green and black two-tone pattern. The new BNSF has been repainting its locomotives into a sharp-looking orange and green "pumpkin" paint scheme that makes symbolic gestures to the prior BN and Santa Fe designs.

Thus, the locomotives themselves have become veritable advertisements for their corporate owners, and the slogans used are designed to be memorable and to instill pride in the company. Emblazoned on the front of recently painted BNSF locomotives, for instance, is the famous cross-shaped Santa Fe Railway logo that has been adopted and modernized for the BNSF itself. The use of the cross by the AT&SF was originally intended as a symbol of southwestern Indian culture. Any given train is likely to include a mixture of locomotives that represent one, two, or perhaps all three of these various paint schemes.

A Bittersweet Relationship

A stroll through the heart of Flagstaff's downtown area might lead one to believe that the community is somehow obsessed with the railroad. The historic downtown is loaded with symbols, images, artwork, and railroad-related artifacts and buildings that reflect the heritage and accomplishments of the AT&SF Railway (and the lesser-known Central Arizona Railroad). At Heritage Square, you can sit on benches made with authentic railroad wheels or walk over a winding path made to look like the image of a railroad track through the use of in-laid brick. If that weren't enough, the town's recently completed Santa Fe Plaza, featuring Flagstaff's first permanent railroad station, is a virtual outdoor railroad museum including an old logging locomotive, a flat car (with logs on it, of course), a meticulously renovated sandstone depot, a life-sized sculpture of a railroad worker, and a plaque that details the importance of the railroad industry's vital contribution to the growth of Flagstaff. With all of this, you might surmise that Flagstaff's community is bursting with pride when it comes to the railroad. And you would be right.

For the community, however, the railroad remains a paradox. Although residents are more or less aware of the community's heritage and its strong association with the railroad industry, passionate sentiments against the railroad ring loudly through town. Many residents wish that the BNSF would simply go away, and take its main line with it. Not surprisingly by now, this situation is largely geographical in nature. The town and railroad have grown up together, one literally embedded within the landscape of the other. At the same time that Flagstaff is dealing with the positive and negative implications of its own rapid growth, so too is the BNSF. These are good economic times for large railroad corporations, and the BNSF is at the top of the heap. Now a North American giant, the railroad has learned to profit from the booming global economy, especially by capturing global intermodal freight.

At the same time, the corporation is attempting to deal with nearly inadequate infrastructure in handling the increased traffic. It owns and operates one of the busiest main-line railroads in the nation, and the railroad basically perceives that Flagstaff is in its way. And the feelings are mutual. It may be an exaggeration to say that "the railroad runs through the middle of the house," as the old song goes, but Flagstaff residents now often feel that way. Quite simply, if the BNSF operated only several trains per day through Flagstaff, as is common on many secondary routes, the railroad probably would not have evolved into the controversial issue that it has become.

The local issue surrounding the railroad revolves around three basic concerns, each of varying importance depending on who is doing the talking: (1) the incessant noise of the locomotive horns, (2) the role of the trains in causing traffic congestion, and (3) the ever-present danger of devastating train derailments and crossing accidents in town, given that the railroad regularly transports hazardous materials. All three concerns are directly related to the existence of Flagstaff's five at-grade railroad crossings, including (from west to east) Beaver, San Francisco, Enterprise, Steves, and Fanning. The crossings themselves have become an issue, especially with regard to train collisions with automobiles and pedestrians—a much too frequent occurrence in town.

The geographical layout of Flagstaff's street system, rooted in its historical development, contributes to the high probability that automobiles and trucks will become stuck on the tracks, only to be destroyed by a high-speed freight. And, the train always wins. Santa Fe Avenue, also known as Route 66, closely parallels the tracks through town, and the road serves as one of Flagstaff's primary east-west corridors for automobile traffic. Intersecting with Route 66 are the town's primary north-south streets that cross the railroad's main line just south of their respective intersections. Aside from one overpass on the east side of town and one underpass on the west side, all of Flagstaff's road traffic is forced to cross the tracks at one of the five congested grade crossings (Figure 20).

Figure 20. Railroad crossing at San Francisco Street in downtown Flagstaff. Drivers must often stop on the opposite side of the tracks while waiting for a traffic light at Route 66, as seen here. All five of Flagstaff's at-grade crossings present the same hazard. Route 66 parallels the BNSF main line the whole way through town. (Photo: Author's collection)

The railroad presents a veritable geographic barrier to the flow of north-south traffic. Because the crossings are so close to the intersections with Route 66, traffic typically overflows across the tracks. From my own observations, local residents have more or less adapted successfully to this quirk of transportation geography, by simply not stopping on the tracks while waiting for a long-winded traffic light. If traffic backs up to the other side of the railroad crossing, motorists judge in advance—sometimes poorly—whether there is room on the other side of the tracks for their cars. If not, they wait on the other side of the tracks until the light turns green. This appears to be learned behavior, however, and many visitors to town, including tourists and delivery trucks, are not aware of how many trains roll through each day. The trains themselves have actually become a tourist attraction, as entire families will stop what they're doing and watch the spectacle of the Transcon. I have seen this myself at various places throughout town. When at crossings, however, people may stop on the tracks while waiting for a Route 66 traffic light, or misjudge how much room is available after they cross the tracks. It is the ultimate death penalty for visitors to Flagstaff: the train sometimes takes them out with little warning.

Sergeant Gerry Blair of the Flagstaff Police Department explained that impatience is just as important a factor at railroad crossings as is lack of understanding of local geography: "We've had those accidents where it is heavily congested, people are in a hurry to get out of there, so they get as close to the light signal as they can, but they find themselves stopped on the tracks. Along comes a train, they get confused, and they get hit" (Blair 2001). During a recent public awareness event sponsored by the police department, the police and local media were watching the behavior of motorists at one of Flagstaff's notorious crossings.

> It was interesting, because the TV station was filming this, and there was this car stuck on the tracks, and we weren't there, we were at another intersection. And the anchor lady was crying

> because she thought she was going to witness an accident. Fortunately, the vehicle got out of there before the train hit it, but an officer did find that vehicle and the driver was given a ticket. The driver was incensed, saying that she was certainly not on the tracks. We told her to watch the news tonight at 5:00. She did, and she called us back and said "I plead guilty." So, using the media is good, and we use the media a lot. (Blair 2001)

The BNSF Railway and the Flagstaff community agree about one thing: they both wish to eliminate the at-grade crossings. From the railroad company's perspective, trespassers and pedestrians have always presented a serious hazard for train operations through town. Pedestrians waiting downtown at the Beaver or San Francisco street crossings will often not wait for the gates to go up after a train has passed. Walking around the gates, there is no warning other than the train's whistle if another train is coming in the opposite direction on the other track. The automobile crossings are a big issue for the BNSF as well. Says Mike McCallister, "we'd like to get rid of them." In an effort to reduce the hazards of grade crossings, the BNSF initiative is to do just that. In 2000 alone, the company closed off nearly 600 grade crossings throughout its system, and it has plans to close 500 crossings per year during the next few years. One of those crossings might end up being in Flagstaff. In return for the company's cooperation with constructing the Fourth Street overpass, the BNSF has requested that the city close one of its at-grade crossings, with Steves Boulevard a primary candidate for closure.

The city of Flagstaff is less enthused about closing Steves, however. Flagstaff's redevelopment manager, Michael Kerski, laughed at the idea when asked about it during a personal interview in February of 2002. Kerski explained the city's perspective, that the city would be forced to pay the bulk of the cost to close the crossing. In turn, the community would lose a critical street connection that would only exacerbate traffic congestion. According to Kerski, the closing of Steves amounted to no more than a "dream" of the BNSF. He further implied that the

BNSF was not yet willing to be responsible for its share of the project and that the negotiations between the BNSF and the city were entirely unfair as they stood at the time:

> We're spending around $10 million to move and improve their grade there because it's really bad. So the Fourth Street overpass will not only make a grade separation, but it will also improve the railway's ability to go through there. We told [the BNSF] that we're going to flatten that out for them, and they said, "Oh, while you're at it, close Steves." And we went, "I don't think so." In 10 years, if nobody's using that road, we'll take a look at it, but it's the only industrial corridor there. That would require all the trucks to go a half-mile out of their way, which is going to degrade the vehicular circulation at the new intersection. (Kerski 2002)

Based on the clear difference of opinion and perspective between local city leaders and the BNSF railway, it is safe to conclude that no Flagstaff railroad crossing will be closed anytime soon.

Still, in many cases the city and BNSF enjoy a successful working relationship with regard to various issues that affect both parties. When asked if the BNSF was essentially a "thorn in the side" of the city, Mike Kerski replied, "not at all—we work with them. It's an issue we have every 18 minutes, a train running through downtown. It impacts all the businesses. Still, I think it's an issue that can be dealt with" (Kerski 2002). Several projects—controversial in themselves—were being planned in 2002 by the city, each designed to potentially alleviate some of the railroad issues in the downtown area. One project may include a median in the center of Route 66 to prevent cars from turning the wrong way onto San Francisco Street and then being hit by a train (this happened to an older couple who got confused and were broad-sided by a train at San Francisco Street). Another project involves the construction of a pedestrian underpass to connect downtown with the South Side.

Another primary railroad-community issue involves noise pollution, caused by the seemingly incessant blowing of the locomotive horns.

Sound knows no barrier, so although locomotive air horns are directed to the front of the train with the idea of warning motorists, the vast majority of Flagstaff residents can hear the horns from their own homes and businesses. These horns are more of a nuisance during summer nights when residents typically have their windows open to allow in the cool mountain air. Few homes or apartments have air conditioning in Flagstaff because most of the time it just isn't necessary. Only occasionally do temperatures reach 90 degrees on summer afternoons, and the temperature drops relatively rapidly in the evening due to the high altitude.

Consequently, residents become the most annoyed with the train horns on summer evenings. For some, sleep is often disrupted, and household conversations are stymied by the relatively frequent blowing of the horns. According to a *Daily Sun* guest column written by Dan Frazier in 1995, "the noise from the trains has undoubtedly driven many a fine citizen to drugs." Another letter-writer agreed, asserting that "the train horns are absolutely deafening—especially when you are trying to sleep." Dan Frazier continued somewhat facetiously, "and the deafening blasts from the horns at all hours of the day and night would shake our homes to smithereens were it not for the special techniques and material used in their construction. This of course is the real reason homes cost so much in Flagstaff."

As a Flagstaff resident who lives less than a mile from the tracks, I can sympathize. In my own household, the horns may not be "deafening," but they have taken some getting used to. Through informal discussions with family and neighbors, an unscientific measure has been developed to determine how well we sleep through any given night, especially in the summer. If we hear two trains while in bed at night, it is declared a "two-train night," meaning that we slept pretty well. A "five-train night" signifies perhaps an average night of sleep. A "15-train" night is bordering on insomnia.

Sometimes, not unlike listening for the howl of coyotes on a summer night, we are lucky enough to hear the trains "talking to each other." This is how I refer to the not-uncommon event of two trains passing each other in opposite directions, both blowing their horns through town, seemingly carrying on a conversation with one another. For those musically inclined, the horns tend to be similar in sound quality, but no two horns are exactly the same, especially when moving in different directions. When the horns of two trains overlap, sheer cacophony is the result, quite an unpleasant experience.

The horn-blowing ritual of the railroad engineers puzzles residents, as indicated through numerous letters to the editor of the *Daily Sun*. "Perhaps long ago, when people were not so bright as we, train whistles were in order," reflects Dan Frazier. "But now that we have electronic sensors that automatically lower barriers and turn on flashing lights, why must trains go on incessantly blowing their horns?" Frazier ultimately hoped to determine "for whom the horns blow". Sometimes residents will blame the train engineers for the problem. One person compared the operation of trains with the driving of cars: "I couldn't agree more on how inconsiderate the engineers are who operate these trains. When we as vehicle operators approach an intersection with a stop sign or signal light, do we blow our horns non-stop until we cross the intersection?" Another resident asks, "Why do they need to blast those horns all the way through Flagstaff—isn't one toot enough?"

Actually, the answer to this last question is no. Although individual engineers certainly take some personal liberties with their horn-blowing habits, they are operating under a specific code that dictates precisely how the horn should be blown for any given situation. In fact, in the days before train crews had radios, the engineer often used the whistle to communicate with the crew. Many of these whistle signals are still used today by railroads throughout the country.

All American railroads use a standardized system of whistle signals, as spelled out in Section 5.8 of the General Code of Operating Rules. The system makes use of a combination of long and short whistle blasts. The most common horn signal heard by Flagstaff residents is the required sequence of two long blasts, one short blast, and one final long blast, which serves as a required warning for upcoming grade crossings. According to the General Code, an engineer is required to start blowing the horn "not less than one-quarter mile before reaching the crossing, if distance permits." The engineer is supposed to be good enough with timing so that the last long blast is sounded as the locomotive moves through the crossing. If the sequence is completed before the crossing is reached, however, the Code instructs the engineer to "prolong or repeat signal until engine occupies the crossing." Because trains move through town at a rather fast clip, however (usually 40 mph), and because the town's crossings are relatively close together in the downtown area, it can often sound as though the horns are being blown incessantly with little discernible pattern.

New technologies may eventually offer an alternative for communities plagued by train horns. Known as *wayside horns*, the concept essentially involves the placement of permanent train horns at the railroad crossings themselves. Instead of having the sound of train whistles blasting throughout the community, the wayside horn would send a blast of noise directly down the street from the crossing itself. This new warning system is still undergoing testing in Nebraska and elsewhere, and the BNSF has considered it for Flagstaff (McCallister 2001). When asked about the potential of this new system, Mike McCallister unfortunately expressed little excitement. Once again, the geographical layout of Flagstaff may be operating against it. "If you go to wayside horns," explained McCallister, "those actually blast down the streets in the community, so the people down those streets may get the blasts." Basically, too many of Flagstaff's densely populated neighborhoods are clustered around the crossings—another one of Flagstaff's historical contingencies.

An additional potential problem with wayside horns involves the impatience of pedestrians. Speaking mostly of the Beaver and San Francisco Street crossings downtown, McCallister claimed that after one train clears the crossing traveling in one direction, a short delay of a few seconds exists before the gates go up again. The gates may stay down if another train is approaching from the opposite direction. During those first seconds, however, it is hard to tell if another train is approaching or not. Pedestrians often walk around the gates, not knowing if another train is barreling toward them from the other direction. "If the trains were not allowed to whistle, we'd have people walking right out in front of the train" (McCallister 2001). Referring to the wayside horns, he continued, "The technology is out there, but what is the best way to control [crossings]? In high pedestrian areas, you've got to control the pedestrians." This situation presents one continuing challenge for a historic downtown area that is only becoming more popular for foot traffic.

Aside from the "air-raid sirens on wheels," as one resident called the trains, a related issue concerns the perceived traffic congestion created by the regular barrage of trains through town. For those who do need to cross the tracks regularly, it is easy to become frustrated. One writer to the *Daily Sun* took a common-sense approach to the problem, asking "Would you allow a clown to dance in front of your car for 10–12 minutes at a time? Then, tell me, why do we allow trains to interrupt our lives constantly, 24-hours a day for up to 10–12 minutes at a time?" Another writer told a completely believable story about how he sat at the Enterprise crossing for more than 15 minutes waiting while a train—presumably the Flag switcher—moved back and forth slowly across the road. After turning around to try another route, he ended up at a Route 66 restaurant with a view of the tracks, and "after 30 minutes saw the train finally moving." Clearly, many view the train-related congestion as a very pressing problem, and a major situation for the community.

Regardless of what scientific studies might reveal about the actual severity of the congestion problem, this particular community concern remains very subjective and open to personal perception. One person becomes impatient with sitting at the tracks for a few minutes, while another resident has absolutely no problem with it. For this reason, community members appear to direct their frustration at fellow residents as well as at the city council. For every letter to the editor that condemns the evil trains for negatively impacting their everyday lives, another writer supports the railroad and accuses others for not being responsible for their own actions. The following statement from one letter, for instance, suggests that the railroad is the main problem: "the man or woman who sits at Enterprise for 10–12 minutes while two trains go by is the same person who is going to speed up Milton mad as hell and run over your dog or ram the side of your Buick." From this perspective, the railroad—not the driver—would be responsible for such an accident that might occur on Milton Avenue.

Others are not so quick to blame the railroad. Challenging one anti-railroad letter writer, one person replied, "'unbelievable traffic snarle'? Our traffic jams last a few minutes at the most. Has [Joe Resident] experienced those of L.A.?" Less than sympathetic to those complaining about train-induced congestion, he continued, "I don't want any of my taxes going for unnecessary multi-million dollar overpasses so that [Joe Resident] isn't three minutes late to work one day a week." Mike McCallister of the BNSF agrees, stating correctly that the railroad is only one of numerous local contributions to the traffic congestion along Flagstaff's major roads. Multiple traffic lights downtown, a major interstate dumping into Milton Avenue, and a north-south oriented university blocking some east-west traffic are a few of the other geographical situations that contribute to traffic congestion. Believing the issue to be more of a psychological one, McCallister supposes that "you don't notice it as long as the train doesn't come, unless you're sitting in line and say 'oh, darn, here comes the train.' It's the most visible thing, and it's not a constant. It's an intermittent thing, so if you catch it at a time when a train is coming, it has a tendency to set you off psychologically. That's my take on it" (McCallister 2001). He has already expressed this thought several times at different meetings with the city.

Others actually enjoy stopping for the train, as one person has written, "Even today I appreciate the time out I am blessed with while waiting for a train to cross." Few would deny that the combined growth of the BNSF and the city of Flagstaff has exacerbated traffic patterns in town, but the severity of the problem is quite clearly in the eye of the beholder. For some, the railroad constitutes a vital part of "Flagstaff's soul," as one resident put it. "If the train leaves downtown," she wrote, "I will feel a heavy loss in my heart. As a kid, I lived near the tracks, and I was reassured, even comforted by the passing of trains. Sometimes after dark, I'd sit on a hill and watch an approaching train's headlamp search down the moonlit rails, its haunting whistle as always proceeding it." This resident expressed the romantic appeal of the rails, ultimately describing how the railroad enhances Flagstaff's sense of place. Without it, the town somehow would not "feel" the same.

With such a wide diversity of opinions, it is no wonder that finding solutions to these railroad-related issues is problematic at best. In theory, at least, the solution would be to change the geographical relationships in which they are rooted—those physical aspects of Flagstaff's landscape that are historically contingent on the development of the town. There is wide-ranging support in town for two basic proposals that would effectively separate the tracks from the city streets. The first is to move the tracks, in effect creating a rail bypass around the town. Both city leaders and Flagstaff citizens have seriously suggested relocating the tracks down the median of Interstate 40 or somewhere further out of town. The other dominant proposal, the application of which is actually moving ahead slowly, involves building overpasses at the critical intersections in town.

As one might suspect, both potential solutions would require exorbitant sums of money. As of this writing, only one overpass—at Fourth Street—has been planned and ultimately approved by voters in May of 2000. From my observations, however, no transformation of the Fourth Street landscape has begun more than 2 years following the vote, and city leaders made it well known that at least 7 years would be required to complete the overpass. Given Flagstaff's continuing rate of growth, some people suspect that a single overpass will make little if any improvement in the grand scheme of traffic issues in Flagstaff. Still, the city leaders and the community at large have taken action, and the town's human landscape will change once again because of it, many hope for the better.

A further concern surrounding the presence of the railroad involves the fact that—despite the consistent efforts of railroad maintenance workers—trains don't always stay on the tracks. Every so often a train derails near or within Flagstaff, producing not only an astronomical mess to clean up but also a lively though predictable community discussion revolving around railroad safety issues. As I write this, the BNSF is still cleaning up from a derailment near Ash Fork, Arizona, two towns to the west of Flagstaff. It is no touch of irony that the ill-fated freight train spewed more than 200 new SUVs around the debris site. It could have been hazardous waste. For 2 days no trains moved east or west; their whistles started up again at 2 o'clock this morning, indicating that a track had been re-opened. Of course, when something like this happens outside of town, Flagstaff residents notice it almost immediately. Silence. No trains, no horns. When an accident occurs in town, the implications are more serious. In the past decade several accidents have taken place within city limits, one involving the evacuation of residents from East Flagstaff. In 2001, one train rear-ended another at speed, killing one railway engineer just a few miles west of Flagstaff near Bellemont. In 2002, no less than three rail accidents occurred in or just outside of town within a period of several weeks.

Many consider it "just a matter of time before a train disaster occurs in downtown Flagstaff resulting in loss of life or a spill of hazardous substances," as one resident gruesomely—though not unrealistically—predicted. A more recent letter to the editor, following in the wake of the terrorist attacks on September 11, 2001, strongly recommended that all BNSF trains rolling through Flagstaff be inspected for suspicious loads before entering the town. In this sense, the railroad represents the recent downside of globalization for Flagstaff—the negative implications of being connected to the larger world and its trade network. Flagstaff residents are certainly not afraid of terrorist-related rail accidents in town, but it is certainly on some people's minds.

Although the idea of moving the tracks—literally—out of Flagstaff is not a new one, the idea emerged with a degree of seriousness in early 2000 during community discussions about options to relieve traffic congestion in town. County Supervisor and one-time Flagstaff Mayor, Paul Babbitt, lobbied heavily to relocate the railroad to the center of Interstate 40 just south of town. A feasibility study of the idea released in September of 2000 estimated a price tag for such a project at $300 to $380 million. Besides solving the railroad-crossing problem, Babbitt claimed that "the relocation will transform Flagstaff's downtown and provide an unprecedented opportunity for development of the railroad right of way." The chamber of commerce director, Dave Maurer, was less enthusiastic, noting that the cost alone of the business acquisition and relocation plan, in addition to the $380 million, made the project prohibitive. Further, given Flagstaff's sprawling growth to the south, I-40 now practically bisects the community, meaning that the railroad would still run through highly residential areas.

The public response to the proposal to move the tracks was mixed, as might be expected with such a subjective issue. "I just think it would take away from beautiful downtown Flagstaff," commented one person interviewed by the *Daily Sun*. She continued, "The train is part of the historical downtown area and it's a big part of Route 66." Another believed that "the trains are beautiful. I like seeing them. I think they add to the beauty of the town. I like hearing them at night." Clearly, the presence of the railroad and its 80–100 trains per day has invited arguments rooted in both practical reasoning and sentimental values. No doubt, the railroad has contributed significantly to the town's unique sense of place and heritage, and disturbing the tracks in such a way would mean the loss of yet another unique aspect of community life and landscape. Others wish to never see or hear another train again.

In any case, the debate over moving the tracks was little more than academic, given that the feasible transportation improvements voted for by city residents in May of 2000 did not include any option for moving the tracks. One resident maintained perhaps the most realistic prognosis: In response to the idea of moving the tracks, she claimed that "I'd be in favor of it, definitely, but it'll never happen, not in a million years." That might be a bit optimistic. Representing the BNSF perspective, Mike McCallister pointed out that the railroad operates through, and works with, hundreds upon hundreds of communities along its route. Thus, Flagstaff really does not present any problems for the railroad that they don't regularly deal with throughout their entire system. The railroad company, therefore, has no intention of moving its tracks, given that it has no good reason to do so (McCallister 2001).

One approach to dealing with railroad-related issues in Flagstaff has been provided by the Flagstaff Police Department with an annual program referred to as "Officer on a Train." Its purpose is dual, to crack down on impatient drivers attempting to beat the trains, and to educate the community about railway safety issues. Once each year, the department collaborates with the BNSF to place uniformed officers on a train that travels from one end of town to the other. The whole event is really quite a spectacle. Police vehicles with other officers are stationed at the town's five at-grade crossings, and the media is always invited to watch the show. Further, a video camera is placed inside the cab of the locomotive, with the intent of filming near-misses. Sergeant Gerry Blair strongly supports the program, stating that "it's really amazing to actually see what the [train] engineers see." Blair further claimed that aside from raising public awareness through the event, it serves as a learning tool for the police department so that it may redirect its enforcement efforts in the most effective ways. And, Blair continued, "The media love it. People are asking me every year, 'When are you going to do Officer on a Train again?'" (Blair 2001). The most dangerous crossings, with regard to auto, bicycle, and pedestrian traffic combined, are the two located downtown at Beaver and San Francisco

Streets. The Officer on a Train program will be effective, claims Blair, because "it shows that if you take enforcement action, you have the highest chance of changing people's behavior. And that's what police enforcement's all about, is changing behavior." From my own personal observations and the occasional local news story, however, evidence of success at changing behaviors has been hard to come by.

The paradox of the railroad continued in 2002. On one hand, the community appreciated the role of the railroad in Flagstaff's economic development and history, and its variable contribution to Flagstaff's sense of place. This is clearly evidenced in the downtown landscape as well as in the media. On the other hand, the geographic dilemma presented by the railroad's existence and the town's continued growth is very real, both for community peace of mind and for safety issues. At once, the train is celebrated and rebuked. Perhaps a *Daily Sun* reporter best summarized the paradox by writing in a 1999 news article that local politicians "are eager to find ways to make the railroad—a charming part of city history but a royal pain at rush hour—a less obtrusive presence." For the time being, it appears that this particular railroad town will keep its railroad, along with the lively community discussion surrounding it.

Part III

Flagstaff's America Tour: A Walk Through Town

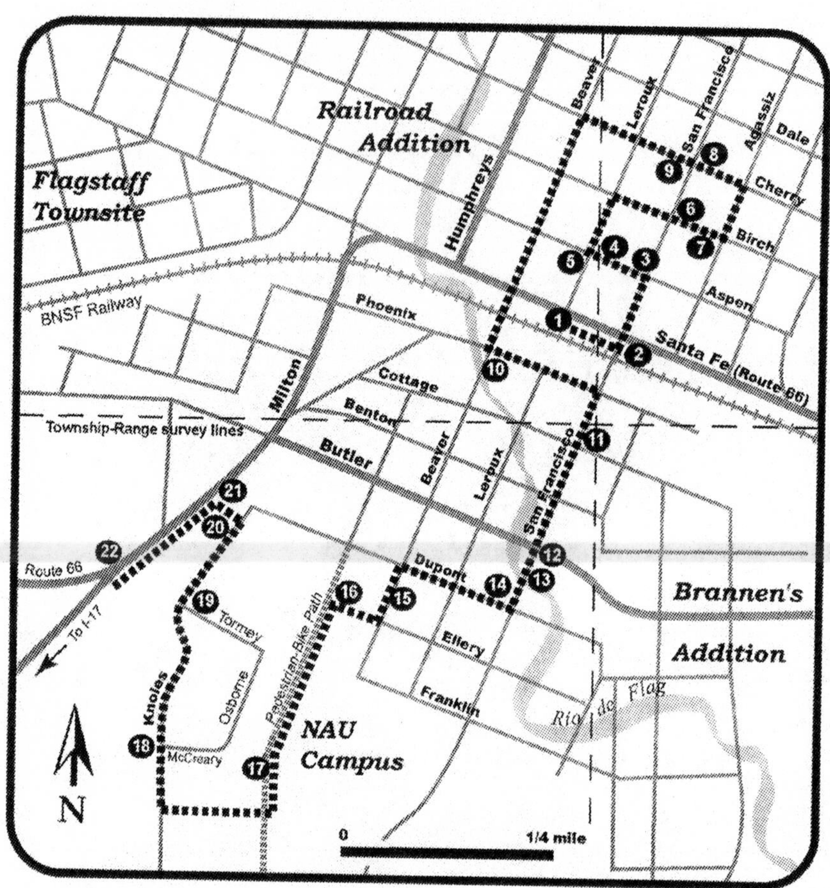

Figure 21. Route for Flagstaff's America Tour. Numbers refer to locations of stops 1–22 discussed in Chapters 5–8. (Map: Author)

Chapter 5

Flagstaff's *Theme Park:* The North Downtown

(Please refer to the route map for Flagstaff's America Tour in Figure 21. Additional color photos and related web links available at **http://jan.ucc.nau.edu/~twp/americatour**)

STOP 1
Depot: Flagstaff Visitors Center

Aside from a brief daily visit by Amtrak's transcontinental train, the Southwest Chief, the old brick platform skirting the Flagstaff train depot usually remains absent of human activity. Standing at this same location in the 1940s, however, would have provided a much different, and more active scene. Also known as "train stations" or "terminals" in larger cities, small-town depots were typically the most important building in their communities. For several decades following its construction in 1926, this impressive small-town depot served as the principal gateway into and out of Flagstaff. Thus, it makes perfect sense to begin a walking tour here at the depot, once representing the community's most vital connection with the rest of the world. Currently the depot symbolizes something different, namely Flagstaff's continuing transition into a new, postindustrial economy based primarily on tourism and services. As Flagstaff's Visitors Center, the depot is now the information hub for visitors who arrive mostly by automobile rather than train (Figure 22).

Figure 22. AT&SF Railway depot, constructed in 1926. The restored depot currently plays the dual roles of Amtrak station and Flagstaff Visitors Center. Its distinct Tudor Revival style of architecture makes it one of the most unique structures in northern Arizona. (Photo: Author's collection)

Whether large or small, grand or plain, the train depot in America became the hub of small-town life after the 1860s (Stilgoe 1983). John Stilgoe wrote the following about the significant role of the depot in American society:

> Around them developed businesses dependent on train transportation, and in them converged people anxious to learn the latest telegraphic news, to greet travelers from the corridor, and to depart

> from traditional life to the mysteries of Pullman sleepers and underground terminals. No longer did the general store, barber shop, and post office focus small-town life; instead the depot, the gateway to the corridor, attracted everyone interested in metropolitan excitement. (Stilgoe 1983, 193)

The corridor that Stilgoe refers to is more specifically the *metropolitan corridor*, or "the portion of the American built environment that evolved along railroad rights-of-way in the years between 1880 and 1935" (Stilgoe 1983, 3). No other term could adequately describe the human landscapes constructed by various railroad corporations to support the movement of their trains. Along the corridor "flowed the forces of modernization, announcing the character of the twentieth century, and abutting it sprouted new clusters of building" (Stilgoe 1983, 3). Through its luxurious passenger trains and its freight trains filled with the latest manufactured wares, the depot came to symbolize the intersection between small-town life and the energizing influence of the metropolis.

Today, much of the metropolitan corridor's supportive infrastructure has either deteriorated or been removed entirely. Gone are the large, wooden water towers necessary for the operation of giant, chugging steam locomotives. Gone are the coaling towers supplying fuel for the same locomotives, and it is the rare case where one can still find a surviving *roundhouse*—the circular-shaped engine maintenance facilities built especially for the needs of the railroad. Semaphore signals are also a thing of the past, as are signal towers, switch stands, section houses, and the metal hoops from which engineers would grab written orders from speeding trains. And now, even the caboose is a thing of the past. Much has changed on the metropolitan corridor in the past half-century. Only some physical remnants, and of course both of Flagstaff's old depots, can be seen here today.

Perhaps this is why train depots such as this one remain all the more important for communities attempting to hang on to some of their past. Across the nation, the depot has received perhaps the most attention of any other former structure along the metropolitan corridor—and Flagstaff is no exception, having now successfully restored two of them, both during the 1990s.

This depot is probably the most prominent landmark in Flagstaff; it was completed in 1926 to replace the old sandstone depot located one block to the east. This depot exemplifies the *Tudor Revival* style of architecture, named for its apparent connection with Tudor (early sixteenth-century) England. The primary features of the style are clearly evident on this depot: decorative (not structural) half-timbering on the exterior walls (large wooden beams), massive chimney, steeply pitched roof, prominent cross gables, and casement windows that open sideways like shutters. The Tudor name for this style is somewhat imprecise, given that the style is actually loosely based on later Medieval English building traditions (McAlester and McAlester 1997).

Accurate or not, Tudor Revival was one of several popular *period styles* of architecture in the United States during the time between the two World Wars, especially during the 1920s. By World War I, period-style architecture had become trendy across the country, so it made perfect sense to adopt such an exterior style for Flagstaff's newest depot. Numerous popular period styles were used for houses and other structures during this time, such as Neoclassical, Spanish Revival, Tudor Revival, Colonial Revival, Italian Renaissance, and Mission. There were other period styles as well, but they were less common (e.g. Egyptian Revival). Many of these styles often competed for attention within America's 1920s suburban neighborhoods, where one might find mixtures of Dutch Colonial, Neoclassical, and Colonial Revival houses adjacent to one another on the same street. These were collectively known as period styles because each style attempted to replicate architectural traditions representing a specific historical period and a specific place or region.

Apparently, the Santa Fe Railway adopted the Tudor Revival style for Flagstaff's new depot because it better represented a high-altitude, mountain town. Most of the railroad's other depots, restaurants, and hotels made use of the Spanish and Mission styles throughout the Southwest. The Flagstaff depot's exterior and interior exhibit recent efforts at historic preservation; it was restored during the 1990s to reflect its original appearance, and its "new" turquoise paint scheme caused quite a stir within the community, as we shall see.

In part, the train depot was restored specifically to serve as Flagstaff's new visitors center. For years community leaders debated the issue of the best location for a future visitors center, but ultimately it ended up at the heart of downtown. In historic preservation terminology, the conversion of this building (part of it, at least) from train depot to visitors center exemplifies the concept of *adaptive reuse*, whereby older buildings are adapted and modified for new, contemporary purposes. Probably the bulk of historic preservation projects throughout the nation have involved adaptive reuse, given that the original purpose of a building has often become obsolete. To justify the economics of saving it, then, one must invent for it a new, more acceptable purpose.

For Flagstaff, what could be more appropriate than converting its former gateway to the metropolitan corridor into the hub for visitor information? Although probably not thought of in this way by the local community, one interpretation might view this landscape as a product of shifting economic bases in the community and across the country. Today, tourism is the bottom line, and anything communities can do to attract more tourists, all the better—and for the local growth machine as well.

To every landscape there is the *unseen* story, or process, that describes its development and creation over time. This is no less true for the Flagstaff Visitors Center, located here in the heart of downtown. Initially, the goal of the Flagstaff Chamber of Commerce was to create a visitors center at one of the freeway interchanges on the edge of town. In a "State of the Chamber" address in early 1988, the chamber's president, Jack Duffy, promoted the idea of creating a new visitors center to increase tourist activity in and around Flagstaff. Even before 1988, tourism had been elevated to Flagstaff's number one industry, and Duffy commented in his address that, "there is a tremendous potential to develop it further." Clearly, the primary economic goal of establishing a visitors center was to streamline the tourism component of Flagstaff's local growth coalition. A *Daily Sun* editorial in 1988 promoted the idea, stating that "restaurants and lodging establishments could advertise their businesses at the center," and tourists could be further directed to the "Museum of Northern Arizona, Lowell Observatory, Northern Arizona University, historic downtown Flagstaff and highways to Wuptaki, Sunset Crater and Walnut Canyon national monuments." From an urban geographer's perspective, then, a new visitors center would contribute directly to the exchange value interests of Flagstaff's local and regional growth proponents. Consequently, the consumption of places and products would be stimulated through the process of directing and guiding visitors from a central location.

From that point on, initial celebration of the visitors center idea was transformed into a decision-making process regarding the location and funding of the new center. For some time the planned location of the center kept changing from one place to another. In early 1989, the city's Tourism Commission was focusing on the historic Dolan House for the new center, located along Riordan Road in the southwest part of town. Others suggested that the Milligan House, located on the western edge of the downtown area, could be used for the facility at least temporarily. At this point a tourism consultant, Amy Horowitz, came to town and recommended a site close to the I-40 and I-17 interchange. "Pick a property 1 to 1.2 miles within the intersection of I-17 and I-40," she advised, adding that any other site outside that zone should not be considered. Horowitz had gained respect for her considerable efforts with developing a tourism program in Durango, Colorado; this would not be the only time when Flagstaff would look to Durango for guidance on matters of development.

The Tourism Commission was still looking elsewhere for a new visitors center site. Not entirely abandoning the interchange idea, the commission seriously eyed the possible purchase of the well-known

Wienerschnitzel building on the corner of Route 66 and Switzer Canyon Road, just east of downtown. By June of 1989 the commission was recommending that the city purchase the property for use as the permanent center. Still, the commission was contemplating other possible sites, listed for the public in the *Daily Sun*. After the Wienerschnitzel site, the list consisted of, from highest to lowest priority: (1) 35 acres of property owned by NAU near the I-40 and I-17 interchange, (2) then-vacant land on the northeast corner of University Drive and Milton Road (the present site of Target), (3) a piece of city-owned property on the northeast corner of Airport Road and I-17, and (4) the aforementioned Dolan House, on the corner of Metz Walk and Riordan Road. No mention of the Santa Fe Railway depot was made.

The *Daily Sun*'s editorial board was seemingly also undecided, stating, "let's wait for the appraisal of the Wienerschnitzel building" before making a decision. The editorial continued with an attempt to solicit the public's input: "Meanwhile, it might be wise to let the city council know how you feel—either through direct contact or in a letter to the editor." One site the paper did not promote was the Dolan House, which suffered from its locational disadvantage, away from a "main drag." By August, all aforementioned sites had been eliminated as possibilities, and the favored site remained the NAU leasing option near the interchange.

It was at this time when the public learned of a new historic preservation project beginning in the downtown area: that of the deteriorated 1926 Santa Fe Railway depot. "Years of use and abuse have caused premature aging," read one *Daily Sun* article, "and passengers are now greeted with orange and green plastic chairs, a leaking roof and locked, antiquated restrooms." Just as it is today, the depot was being used for travelers arriving or departing on Amtrak's twice-daily passenger trains. At this point the year-old Main Street Flagstaff Foundation got involved, and its director, Kent Burnes, suggested in November of 1988 that the depot be renovated into the new Flagstaff Visitors Center. This was apparently the first public mention of the train depot idea. Meanwhile, the city moved ahead with negotiations to develop the NAU site south of town.

Credit for promoting the idea of the depot site should be given to the coalition of downtown merchants known as the Main Street Flagstaff Foundation. Not only did the foundation "urge the city council to find a suitable site within the downtown," but it also warned in the *Daily Sun* that "moving the visitors center and Chamber of Commerce from downtown puts the entire Main Street Program at risk." In early 1990, the Foundation recommended four of its own potential sites, all within the downtown area: the former Babbitt Department Store building, the Amtrak depot, the older Santa Fe freight depot just to the east, and the old Babbitt warehouse, located on the northwest corner of Verde Street and Aspen Avenue. By this time, letters to the editor were occasionally appearing in the *Daily Sun* with individual ideas for sites. Several of these letters supported a downtown site, which would presumably bring more visitors to the historic downtown. One writer argued that "if you want the most gain for the dollar, establish a visitors center near the center of town, which will reflect Flagstaff, not Wal-Mart." About the proposed expansive NAU site near the interchange, the letter continued, "The day Flagstaff out draws the Grand Canyon will be the time to build the Taj Mahal you envision." Thus, arguments for a downtown location were primarily appealing to aspects of local sense of place and the promotion of heritage landscapes in the downtown—as well as for the economic gains that merchants would realize from a visitors center site. Both the use values and exchange values of downtown were being promoted by those advocating a downtown center.

Meanwhile, in May of 1990 NAU President Eugene Hughes announced that the university was withdrawing its offer to provide land for the visitors center. Hughes commented that it was not the intent of NAU to create a controversy in the community, and that the offer was not designed to benefit NAU, as some had criticized. Simply losing patience with the process, Hughes pulled NAU out of the list of options. However, the train depot was still not on the short-list of final sites several months later. By July, the two sites recommended by the Tourism Commission included the old Trailways bus depot at the corner of Santa Fe Avenue (Route 66) and Humphreys Street, and the current Chamber of Commerce building across the street. For the first time, however, both potential sites were located in the historic downtown area.

Patience was already wearing thin when the Tourism Commission actually recommended in October of 1990 that the visitors center remain where it was already located temporarily, at the Chamber of Commerce building west of the depot. In the period of 2 years the debate had gone full circle, and now the recommendation was to simply enlarge the existing facility. In a front-page story, the *Daily Sun* hinted at the irony with its headline, "Visitors center solution: Stay put." Finally, however, there seemed to be agreement among Flagstaff's major growth interests. The Chamber's board of directors fully endorsed the plan, as did the Main Street Flagstaff Foundation. Main Street director Kent Burnes supported the idea, arguing that the project could be completed by the following summer tourist season: "Then we could quit bickering in the community about what to do about a visitors center," stated Burnes. For all intents and purposes, it seemed the issue was settled. That is, until the city council debated and ultimately nixed the idea in late October, citing safety and traffic concerns.

In a move that clearly demonstrates the role of local politics and decision making, it was the city council itself that finally pushed for the idea of converting the Amtrak station into a visitors center. At a work session a full year later—in October of 1991—five of six city councilmembers claimed to prefer the train depot over four other potential sites. From that meeting, the plan materialized rapidly. The council embraced the depot idea knowing full well that the city would have to negotiate first with a new player in this local process, the AT&SF Railway. The railway owned the building and leased space to Amtrak for its ticket and waiting services. The remaining space, according to Amtrak officials, would amount to 600–700 square feet for a potential visitors center. At the time, the council estimated that the center would need five times that much space, at roughly 3,500 square feet. Still, councilmembers appointed Maury Herman, president of the Main Street Flagstaff Foundation, to negotiate with the railway for more floor space. Another option was studied by the planning commission, that of purchasing the depot property outright, at a probable cost of about $1.8 million.

On March 10, 1992 the *Daily Sun* announced the plans for the depot, given the promising negotiations underway with the railway. Under a proposed floor plan drawn by an architectural firm, the city would be able to use about 1,700 square feet of space. Amtrak would retain the center of the terminal, and the city's new CVB (Convention and Visitors Bureau) would occupy the eastern end of the building. The actual visitors center would occupy the west end. Aside from some parking limitations that would have to be overcome, the city's planning commission estimated that the visitors center and CVB could move into the station by the summer of 1993. In November of 1992, the city officially announced its plan to purchase the depot property from the railway for a price of $480,000. The city estimated that the cost would be increased beyond that by $390,000 for the depot's renovation and for an additional parking lot. Apparently, the railway was pushing for the deal in part for its own corporate interest, that of getting rid of the train depot by the end of the year.

The controversy was not to end, however. With the visitors center in place and the renovations nearly complete, the community focused on an aesthetic issue—color. According to the architects involved with the renovation, the depot's exterior was originally painted with a light turquoise color, although the research that pointed to this original color is still highly contested. The main idea was to return the depot to its original, historic look, even though recent evidence has revealed that the original color may have been more subdued. Nonetheless, in the name of authenticity, the exterior beams and trim were repainted with a turquoise hue, creating an instant showpiece for a community not used to such "historic" colors. Since the 1920s, cultural tastes have changed drastically, and whether or not the original depot sported a turquoise hue, this was not a popular choice of color in 1994 Flagstaff. The building quickly became the laughing stock of the town. If a building's feelings could be hurt, this one certainly took a beating.

After first learning about the planned paint scheme, the *Daily Sun* opened community discussion with a humorous editorial titled "You can't miss Visitors Center." According to the editorial, "This building is going to take some getting used to." It continued in a less-than-diplomatic way: "We confess that our initial reaction to the Visitors Center color scheme involved shock and disbelief. Nausea, too, if we're brutally honest." Then the editorial actually promoted a community debate on the issue, stating, "Upon reflection, if tradition is to be followed, the color scheme probably should be controversial. For years, city officials argued about where the Visitors Center should be located, with suggestions ranging from a spot near interstates 40 and 17 to an eastside location. So maybe it's only appropriate that the debate should rage on." Rage on it did.

Upon seeing the depot's new colors, the town's letter writers got busy. Letters poured into the *Daily Sun* revealing either praise or disgust for what they saw. The first round of letters began with titles including, "Fries with that map?" and "Enough already" and "Out of control," and "Where's the pool?" The *Daily Sun* then conducted an informal call-in poll of reader opinions, in which respondents "voted" by a 3-1 margin against the turquoise paint scheme. During the 2-hour call-in session, more than 400 people expressed their opinions, and many more were upset with missing the opportunity. Cultural tastes and values are strong, and these values often carry over to our own human landscapes. That which is visible to the public eye maintains a very important place in American culture, so even though the *Daily Sun* admitted to its surprise over the huge response, the whole thing does make sense. The train depot is centrally located and represents an important part of Flagstaff's heritage. It has further been described as perhaps the most unique architectural piece in town, with its Tudor Revival styling. It comes as no surprise, then, that a paint scheme could cause such a stir.

Personally, I was somewhat sad to see the turquoise trim go away in the summer of 2002 during its most recent paint job. It seems that by the late 1990s the community had "grown into" the bright station—at least more than it had originally. Citing new evidence from interior paint chips that the original color was in fact a forest green, the controversial visitors center underwent its latest aesthetic makeover in June of 2002. Aside from one news article in the *Daily Sun*, the changeover was done quietly and without fanfare.

STOP 2
PUBLIC ART: SANTA FE PLAZA

Santa Fe Plaza is a tribute to the railroad's role in the settlement and development of Flagstaff. Although it may seem that the entire plaza was created as one large project, just the opposite is true. This little urban park actually evolved over time in an ad hoc fashion, each element of which maintains its own interesting story.

The most prominent feature consists of Flagstaff's first permanent train depot, constructed of locally quarried Moenkopi Sandstone (Arizona Red) in 1889. Now a popular restored landmark in downtown Flagstaff, the old depot was actually slated for removal by the railroad company in 1988. A 1998 *Daily Sun* news article explained that the "railroad has asked the building be removed because of lack of funding for building maintenance or personnel to man the now boarded-up sandstone building." Owned by the railroad itself and considered by the company to be obsolete, it was a wholehearted effort by local individuals and organizations that succeeded in having the building saved, for historical and sentimental reasons.

Early plans for the old depot included a variety of options that were discussed seriously, including its relocation—stone by stone—to the Coconino County fairgrounds, or next to the current train depot. Obviously, such relocation efforts did not prove successful or necessary in the long term.

In late 1994, the city of Flagstaff received good news—it had been awarded a half-million dollar federal transportation grant to purchase and renovate the old depot. Citing safety concerns, however, the AT&SF Railway balked at the offer, stating that the company was hesitant to sell unless the building was moved elsewhere. In no small amount of bad luck, however, the removal of the building would make the necessary federal grant null and void. The city was stuck between a rock (or railroad) and a hard place, and the old depot remained boarded up.

In another, more favorable twist of fate, the AT&SF merged with the Burlington Northern in 1995, creating the giant BNSF Railway Corporation discussed in Chapter 4. This corporate merger was the saving grace for Flagstaff's old depot. In a 1997 *Daily Sun* article, Mike McCallister explained that the former Santa Fe Railway had expressed no interest in keeping the depot, for the reasons mentioned above. Thus, "it became both a civic eyesore and a public health and safety hazard." McCallister continued, "Then the merger came along and we [the BNSF] had the need to put more people in Flagstaff and no place to put them." The railroad then became much more interested in saving the old depot.

After ironing out the details between the city and the railroad, the city sought and secured a $123,000 grant from the State Historic Preservation Office to aid with the building's restoration. For its part, the BNSF contributed some $95,000 to renovate the interior in order to convert it to railroad office space. Additionally, the city provided $152,000 in beautification funds from the city's bed, board, and booze tax. Completing the renovation was the BNSF's investment of $160,000 to reconfigure the railroad's downtown freight yard, provide a parking lot for the renovated depot, and provide space for the city's planned extension of its Route 66 bike path and streetscape project. The city could then obtain the $500,000 it expected earlier from the federal ISTEA grant to complete the bike path and streetscape. All of these projects were completed by 1997.

The transformation of the old depot and its surrounding landscape into a centerpiece of downtown redevelopment resulted from a combination of factors originating from both inside and outside the community. The organization and funding for the entire project came from a variety of local, state, and federal sources—not unlike many sizeable historic preservation projects around the nation. Local efforts to restore historic structures for the benefit of the community are most often supplemented by a variety of enabling circumstances from outside the locale.

In this case, a major railway corporation ultimately made the project feasible because of the railway's own self-interest. In the end, everybody won with this project, including the railroad company and local preservation enthusiasts. The community now enjoys yet another historical attraction for visitors and local residents, aiding the city's overall efforts to revitalize the downtown.

A more recent addition to Santa Fe Plaza came in 2000 with the dedication of a special piece of artwork placed just west of the depot. Now the visual centerpiece for the plaza, the sculpture known as *Gandy Dancer* seeks to honor the working-class heritage of railroad workers who constructed the nation's transcontinental railroads (Figure 23).

Figure 23. The *Gandy Dancer* sculpture at Santa Fe Plaza. The 1926 depot is seen in the background. (Photo: Author's collection)

The local process that made *Gandy Dancer* a reality was no less complicated than that of saving and restoring the old depot. Previously, the Flagstaff Public Art Advisory Committee had been responsible for choosing two other works of public art, ultimately placed at two locations along the Route 66 corridor through Flagstaff. Both of these attempts resulted in veritable public relations disasters for the committee. Composed primarily of accomplished artists and art teachers, the committee was established to provide the city council with advice on the purchase of public art for Flagstaff. In the words of one committee member quoted in the *Daily Sun*, it is a "group of people knowledgeable in various aspects of the art world and well qualified to give leadership to the community in the choice of art work for various sites." It was apparently their very knowledge that gave them trouble.

The committee came under fire from the public not once but twice for commissioning two abstract pieces of art along East Route 66. Since their construction, the pieces have endured a relentless barrage of insults from Flagstaff locals and visitors. These first two pieces were described diplomatically in 2000 by the *Daily Sun* editorial staff as "less than runaway hits." In a word, *Solar Calendar* and *Timeless Apparitions* are abstract, and therefore may be a challenge to understand by the majority of the public, including this author. Though certainly appreciated by a segment of the community, it is more common to hear rather humorous descriptions of the sculptures, comparing them to "alien outhouses," "lipstick farms," and "beef jerky."

Being a geographer, I had personally questioned the locations of these sculptures as well as their respective meanings. Both of them are perched at prominent Route 66 intersections east of the downtown, where the only time allowed for viewing occurs while waiting behind other cars at the stoplights. There is little time for reflection or meaningful analysis, especially given that both streetlights are often green for Route 66 travelers. One must pay careful attention to traffic at the intersection while zooming through, rather than risk a hazardous glance to enjoy *Solar Calendar*. Although mine represents only one opinion, I might have placed them in pedestrian-oriented public places where they may have been more appreciated.

Seemingly trying to redeem itself, the Art Advisory Committee wisely solicited public input for the third piece of public art to be placed along Route 66, this time at Santa Fe Plaza. The committee first narrowed down "a goodly number" of sculpture submissions to three finalists, miniature versions of which were placed on display at the Flagstaff Mall and public library. During this viewing period, the committee welcomed comments—essentially counted as votes—to determine which piece the public preferred.

The three finalists included *Gandy Dancer*, a statue of a lone railroad worker hammering ties into place, *Iron Men*, which depicted two men preparing to lay a rail, and *Iron Horse*, consisting of a life-sized horse standing on all fours and clad in iron plates. Indicating a relatively high level of interest in the community, a total of 536 votes were cast, only 9 percent of which favored *Iron Horse* over the other two choices. *Gandy*

Dancer received the most support, having acquired approximately 40 percent of the vote. Some 35 percent of voters favored *Iron Men*, and 10 percent claimed to have no clear preference. The remaining 5 percent were not pleased with any of the three choices.

Given that the public had spoken in an acceptable democratic process, the choice of *Gandy Dancer* seemed assured. Instead, however, the Art Advisory Committee snubbed the public's voice and recommended *Iron Horse* to the city Arts and Sciences Commission and to the City Council in a 5-3 vote of its own. The city council would make the final decision to accept or reject the committee's recommendation. And thus the controversy began. Why had the committee rejected the public vote?

To make matters worse, certain committee members defended their choice in what was perceived by many as an arrogant and condescending attitude, even if that was not their intent. In the first newspaper article printed following the informal vote, for instance, one committee member claimed to reject both *Gandy Dancer* and *Iron Men* because "they're just so literal. They're just so boring. We've seen these things before." She continued to explain how the individuals portrayed in both winning sculptures were Caucasian, which risked being insensitive to various ethnic minorities—a justifiable concern. Another desired to see a minority represented in the sculptures, and others claimed that *Gandy Dancer* and *Iron Men* were less than historically accurate. In the latter, the workers were carrying the rail by hand, without the more commonly used tongs. Further, the two men were shirtless, another historical inaccuracy (though one could certainly find occasions where railroad workers were not wearing shirts and not using tongs). As for *Iron Horse*, committee members preferred this sculpture because it represented what one called "the mechanization of nature," and the term "Iron Horse" itself reflected the Native-American term used to describe the railroad's steam locomotives. Thus, the sculpture would recognize more than the Anglo-American perspective.

No less than 10 letters to the editor expressed opposition to the committee's choice of *Iron Horse*, and some hoped to see the city council overturn their decision. Perhaps taking seriously the numerous letter writers looking forward to the next local election, city councilmembers ultimately sided with the public sentiment. First, the Flagstaff Arts and Sciences Commission made its own decision to overturn the Art Advisory Committee's recommendation, after which the city council unanimously approved in January of 2000 a $50,000 contract with artist Clyde "Ross" Morgan to install his *Gandy Dancer* sculpture at Santa Fe Plaza. The council was apparently "quick to approve" the recommendation of the Arts and Sciences Commission. With the saga concluded, the full-sized *Gandy Dancer* sculpture became the centerpiece of Santa Fe Plaza. Not just incidentally, it was BNSF employee and fourth-generation railroader Mike McCallister who was asked by the artist to pose as the model for the sculpture.

Making the "museum" setting of Santa Fe Plaza complete is an old artifact from earlier railroading days, a *steam locomotive* on display just east of the old depot (Figure 24). You can walk along the bike path to view this locomotive more thoroughly. Not just any old steam locomotive, *Old Two Spot*, as it is affectionately referred to, served its operating days on the Central Arizona Railroad right here in Flagstaff and in the forests south of town. For many local residents, the locomotive and the flat car behind it serve as nostalgic reminders of Flagstaff's early extractive economy based on the logging industry. The fact that Old Two Spot is sitting on display rather than working the forests south of town is testament to Flagstaff's changing local and regional economic situation.

Figure 24. Old Two Spot steam locomotive, displayed downtown along Route 66. Industrial relics like this one are now often celebrated for their heritage appeal in America's increasingly amenity-based economy. (Photo: Author's collection)

This relatively small steam locomotive was built in Philadelphia by the Baldwin Locomotive Works in 1911. Soon thereafter it was purchased by Timothy and Michael Riordan in 1917 for use in their lumber operations in and around early Flagstaff. Over the years the engine saw service for numerous lumber companies, including the Arizona Lumber and Timber Company, the Greenlaw Lumber Company, the Saginaw and Manistee Lumber Company, Southwest Lumber Mills, and finally, Southwest Forest Industries. In 1966 Southwest discontinued railroad logging operations, and Old Two Spot was replaced by more versatile and less expensive trucks. Local historians believe that this engine was perhaps the last one to remain in service up to that time. In the heyday of logging railroad operations around Flagstaff, as many as 30 trains hauled timber from the forests around Happy Jack to lumber mills in Flagstaff. Like most railroad companies in the waning days of steam trains, however, most of these engines were sold for scrap during or after World War II. Old Two Spot is one of two engines that survive in the area. The other, larger steam locomotive still surviving has been restored by local railroad enthusiasts and is on display along Route 180 in front of the Pioneers Museum north of town.

If you're wondering how Old Two Spot earned its name, the engine officially bore the number 25, painted on the side of the cab. Throughout many years of heavy use, water bags dangled outside the locomotive window, and gradually they wore away the 5; hence the "spot" where the 5 once was. Since then, Flagstaff residents have affectionately referred to the locomotive as Old Two Spot.

By 1966 when this particular locomotive was retired, most railroads in the United States had already abandoned steam power for newer diesel-electric locomotives. I would be willing to bet that few younger Americans today understand the basic mechanical principles of these older locomotives on which the entire national railroad network once depended. How do these strange-looking contraptions actually work? Basically, this locomotive and others like it are little more than giant water boilers, or tea kettles on wheels. The entire locomotive is built around a giant, cylindrical water boiler placed horizontally above, and supported by, the wheels. Water in the boiler is heated to above the boiling point, converting the water to steam, which expands to a volume some 1,700 times greater than its equivalent in water. The pressure inside the boiler forces the steam into a series of cylinders with pistons. The steam pushes the pistons, which in turn are linked to a system of rods connected to the drive wheels. The higher the pressure exerted by the steam into the pistons, the faster the pistons move back and forth, and the faster the locomotive moves. The series of eight large wheels (four on each side) on Old Two Spot consist of the "drivers." The used steam is exhausted into the smoke-box and up the chimney on top of the locomotive.

For steam locomotives like this one, the fuel of choice to heat the water was usually coal. Earlier steam locomotives burned wood, and later models, in the twentieth century, used oil. The fuel is stored in a small car trailing directly behind the locomotive, known as the "tender." The engineer is responsible for operating the locomotive, and the fireman shovels coal (or controls the flow of oil) from the tender into the firebox beneath the cab, thereby keeping the fire hot enough to boil water to create the necessary steam pressure. As one might imagine, the maintenance and fuel requirements are immense. Steam engines cannot travel far before they require a fresh tank of water and a new supply of fuel. The water was usually supplied by large water towers built at regular intervals along the railroad right-of-way. One such tower existed next to the old train depot here, until diesel power in the 1960s rendered it obsolete. In short, this is the locomotive technology and its supporting infrastructure that the nation's transportation system depended on for more than a century, mostly prior to the automobile era. The Grand Canyon Railway, based in Williams, Arizona still uses a steam locomotive during the summer months to shuffle thousands of visitors to the Grand Canyon's South Rim. Old Two Spot, then, serves as an important reminder of the railroad technology that allowed the rapid expansion of the United States into the West, and the settling of Flagstaff.

Not unlike the renovation of the old depot and the creation of the *Gandy Dancer* sculpture, there remains an unseen story that explains how Old Two Spot made it to its current resting place for display. Generally speaking, the salvaging and restoration of this locomotive was due to the tireless efforts of local individuals, clearly reflecting how the decisions and values of regular people maintain the power to transform their own landscapes. After its retirement in 1966, Old Two Spot sat for decades outside the offices of its owner, Stone Forest Industries, along Butler Avenue. When the company planned to cease operations of Flagstaff's last lumber mill in 1993, however, the fate of the old locomotive remained uncertain. It wasn't long before the media and various local residents took notice. The Northern Arizona division of the Arizona Historical Society was one group interested in saving the locomotive because, as the group's director explained in the *Daily Sun*, "it could help preserve a part of Flagstaff's lumber mill heritage." The lumber industry in Flagstaff was coming to an end, more than a century after it began, with the closing of the town's last lumber mill operations, then located on the now-empty tract of land at the corner of Butler Avenue and Lonetree Road. The company's mill and property were for sale, and local residents and historical enthusiasts feared that the locomotive would disappear as well.

Numerous ideas were discussed locally about how to save the locomotive, and once saved, where it should be placed on display. Letters to the editor of the *Daily Sun* began to appear, including one that envisioned a future for Old Two Spot that actually came to pass. In part, the letter read, "Stone Forest has a beautifully restored lumber train that, according to an article in the *Daily Sun*, they haven't decided what to do with yet. I think it would look great sitting next to Route 66, perhaps on the spur line that is already in place in front of the old depot building. Funds for the train could be raised by donations. It would be a shame to let something that represents Flagstaff so well be moved away from here. After all, aren't we trying to spruce up the downtown?" For this letter writer, downtown still represented the obvious display location for the locomotive, during the 1990s when the city was in the process of revitalizing its historic business district.

Ideas incur no financial cost, but actual implementation of those ideas is a different matter. One initial estimate valued the locomotive at $250,000. How would the city of Flagstaff be able to raise this much money to purchase the locomotive? This question was answered in late 1994 when a group of seven businessmen in town were inspired to act on their own. Flagstaff was about to lose its locomotive for good because Stone Forest had just sold it to a California buyer who agreed to have the train off of company property by February of 1995. These seven individuals then successfully purchased Old Two Spot from the buyer in California. In this way, the engine was saved for the Flagstaff community, but not before it was almost lost for good. Malcolm Mackey, one of the purchasers, was quoted by the *Daily Sun* as saying, "All of us have agreed it's the right thing to do…for the whole community." Mackey made a presentation to Flagstaff's Tourism Commission, where he asked the city to reimburse the businessmen for the locomotive and to move it to an appropriate place for display. One of the other purchasers, Jim Babbitt, promoted the locomotive as a potential centerpiece for a railroad theme park in downtown Flagstaff. Babbitt would become more influential in later years with the development of Heritage Square and the railroad-related imagery that ultimately appeared there.

The challenge of saving Old Two Spot for Flagstaff did not end there, however. The seven investors wanted reimbursement from the city rather promptly after their own purchase, but this was not to be. Policy dictated that no city money for the locomotive could be allocated until the budget session in May, 1995. No money had been allocated for the locomotive in the current fiscal year's budget, even though the city and its mayor, Chris Bavasi, expressed support for eventually purchasing it. By March, four months had passed since the businessmen had purchased the locomotive, and the Flagstaff investors encouraged the city to speed up the process of reimbursement or risk losing the locomotive to another buyer. The Flagstaff businessmen had paid $61,500 to the initial California buyer, and the city of Flagstaff was expected to cover this cost entirely. Patience was running thin by March, however, and the businessmen announced that they would consider selling the locomotive elsewhere if necessary.

This news spawned a flurry of letters and articles in the *Daily Sun* from various residents and organizations urging the businessmen to be patient and to wait out the city's budget process. The locomotive's role in enhancing Flagstaff's sense of place was of utmost importance. The writers of one letter to the editor commented that "now it seems the train is about to be sold. Once bought, it could be transferred out of state, where the original historical association with Flagstaff would be lost forever." Another letter writer compared the significance of Old Two Spot with surrounding parks and monuments: "The old locomotive is as rare and precious to our community as Walnut Canyon, the Mount Elden Pueblo ruins or any of the other reminders of our past…Please let us keep a part of Flagstaff's reason for existing—logging—from slipping away from us."

These sentimental arguments were supported by the *Daily Sun*'s editorial board as well, as expressed in an editorial that pleaded within its title, "Keep the brakes on Flag's train." In part, the editorial read, "Nobody in Flagstaff wants to see Old Two Spot leave town…The city needs to do whatever it can to quickly provide some sort of commitment to the train buyers." In the end, the editorial encouraged public participation to persuade the city to commit to purchasing the locomotive: "What the train's fate depends on more than anything else is how you Flagstaff residents feel about it. If people tell councilmembers it's a priority to them, it will be to the council, too. So if you want Old Two Spot to stay around, it's up to you to blow the whistle."

The saga of Old Two Spot finally ended happily in June of 1995 when the city of Flagstaff agreed to purchase the locomotive from the businessmen for the full amount of $61,500. Fortunately, in this case the Flagstaff businessmen hung on to their investment long enough for the city to incorporate the locomotive into its budget and ultimately save it for the public good.

STOP 3
ANCHOR: BABBITT BROTHERS DEPARTMENT STORE

The Babbitts are perhaps the most prominent and well-known family in Flagstaff. You may have heard their name in several contexts, even if you have had little experience with the town. Notably, Flagstaff native Bruce Babbitt served as the secretary of the interior under President Clinton until 2001. He was also politically prominent as governor of Arizona until 1988, when he made an unsuccessful run on the Democratic ticket for president. Bruce's brother, Jim Babbitt, has been responsible for numerous historic preservation efforts in Flagstaff. A third brother, Paul Babbitt, was serving as the Coconino County Supervisor as of this writing, and he was once mayor of Flagstaff. Overall, the entire Babbitt family has played a significant role in shaping the history and geography of both Flagstaff and northern Arizona since the first members of their family arrived in 1886 from Cincinnati, Ohio.

By the 1890s David Babbitt and his four brothers had established a major livestock operation, and it continued to grow until they owned more than a million acres of ranchland throughout northern Arizona and other states. Sheep and cattle ranching was one of the few economic activities that could be successful in this dry, high-altitude climate, given that the frost-free season around Flagstaff is too short for agricultural crops to be profitable. Thus, Flagstaff's first primary economic base was as a trade center for sheep and cattle ranches around the region, combined with the logging industry and Flagstaff's lumber mills. The Babbitt family became involved in merchandising and retailing as well, and these buildings on the northwest and southwest corners of this intersection are products of their efforts.

In 1888 David Babbitt constructed this brick and Moenkopi Sandstone building on the northwest corner of Aspen Avenue and San Francisco Street (Figure 25). This was Flagstaff's first two-story building with a refined style of architecture (Jackson 1999). Its tall, arched windows and the heavy, bracketed cornice on its roofline are indicative of a simplified Italianate style, still popular during the late Victorian era in Flagstaff. Victorian styles remained popular nationally until just after 1900, so it makes sense that such styles would be adopted for some of Flagstaff's early buildings.

Figure 25. The Babbitt Brothers Department Store, corner of San Francisco Street and Aspen Avenue. (Photo: Author's collection)

In 1957, a year after the last of the five original Babbitt brothers died, the facades of the Babbitt buildings on the north side of Aspen Avenue were enclosed with a metal framework and hidden for decades with tan stucco and aluminum siding. Such modern, metal facades were commonly applied over original main-street buildings throughout the 1950s and 1960s in towns and cities throughout the country. This was done not just to give the buildings a modern appearance, but also in hopes of attracting shoppers back to decaying downtown business districts. During this time, modern styles were "progressive," and older nineteenth-century facades were viewed as obsolete and behind the times. We will discuss America's "modern era" more thoroughly later along the Tour.

Since the 1970s, America's historic preservation movement has made it economically and socially acceptable to show off our historic buildings once again. The Babbitt building here exemplifies this trend. Restoration of this building began in 1990, led by Jim Babbitt, a grandson of the original Babbitt brothers. The distasteful aluminum sheathing and stucco were removed, and the entire original structure was restored to its earlier appearance. It is now once again a centerpiece and an excellent example of historic preservation efforts in Flagstaff's business district.

The Babbitt building further represents an important commercial tradition once found in America's downtown business districts, the department store. Our largest cities, including Los Angeles, New York, Chicago, and San Francisco, all had their famous, upscale department stores located at the heart of their downtown cores. Smaller towns and cities boasted their own department stores, albeit not as grand as their large-city counterparts. The Babbitts owned and operated their own department store in this building (known as the Babbitt Brothers Department Store) until it closed permanently in 1987. The Babbitts actually added a second department store at the Flagstaff Mall, though it too ultimately failed. This store served as a landmark in downtown Flagstaff for decades and as an *anchor* store for surrounding businesses that depended on it to attract large numbers of shoppers to the downtown. After it closed for good, letters to the editor were written in the local newspaper revealing how the store held a special place in the community's collective heart. The closing of Flagstaff's last downtown department store seemed to symbolize the darkest point in the business district's steady decline after the 1960s, made only worse by the opening of the Flagstaff Mall in 1978 on the east side of town.

Like most traditional business districts in America, Flagstaff's own downtown was adversely affected by increased retail competition developing on the periphery of town. At first, the "periphery" wasn't all that far away. The first major blow to downtown came not from the familiar invasion of Wal-Mart, Kmart, or any other big-box discount retailer, but from the construction of the Plaza shopping center at the north end of Humphreys Street in the late 1960s, only blocks away from the historic downtown area. Jim Babbitt, longtime owner and operator of the Babbitt Brothers' Department Store downtown, recalled in a personal interview the rough timeline of events that led to one business after another vacating downtown. About the Plaza shopping center, Babbitt remembered, "That was the first thing that started to take major businesses out of the downtown. Sears left, and the old Tissaw's store went up to [the Plaza on] North Humphreys." As I spoke with Jim in his second-floor office above the old Babbitt Department Store, he lamented the slow loss of businesses from downtown, and he told the story of how the downtown continued its economic and social decline during the 1970s and 1980s.

> Penneys, which had been located across from where Maloney's is now, was kind of looking to leave. And then my family, because we were a big property owner here and had a big interest in it, got together with Penneys and built the building next door with the parking ramp on top for Penneys relocation. That worked okay from, I guess, the mid 1960s until the Flagstaff Mall came along. And the mall was really the downtown killer, it really just killed downtown. Sears left the Plaza and went to the mall. Penneys left this store downtown and went to the mall. But it was all kind of downhill from there for the downtown. And the late 70s and early 80s were very grim down here. We kind of had our department store, which hung on and was sort of the anchor of what remained downtown through the early 80s. But even then we could see that it just wouldn't work [to compete] with the mall. I think in about 1986 Dillards came to the mall, and they were directly competitive with what we did in the old building here, so we hung on for awhile. Then we moved to a space in the mall ourselves, but it wasn't any good. It was too little too late. We were dead, and we closed this store. It went dark, and I think the downtown was pretty well boarded up by 1980 or so. It was pretty grim. We were kind of the final blow, when we moved out there. That's when people really saw that something needed to be done downtown, and that's when the Main Street Program was actually initiated here. (Babbitt 2001)

Babbitt's recollections are easy to confirm, given the abundance of *Daily Sun* articles devoted to the final days of Babbitts' Department

Store. The first front-page headline, "Babbitts to sell department store chain," appeared in the *Daily Sun* on August 9, 1987. The president of Babbitt Brothers Trading Company, William Galis, confirmed in a statement to the newspaper that the company's department store division had been losing money for years, and that the new Babbitt store opened at the Flagstaff shopping mall less than a year earlier, had not proven successful. The Babbitt Brothers Trading Company had operated a total of eight stores in the region: two in Flagstaff, and one each in Page, Winslow, Prescott, Cottonwood, Kingman, and Yuma. All were scheduled to be closed by October of 1987.

For a community accustomed to the Babbitt name and merchandise, the announcement of the store's closure came as quite a blow. Not only are long-time regional retailers important to a local economy, but they tend over time to become social fixtures in the community that generate their own sense of place. The Babbitt store in downtown Flagstaff had operated at this same location—the corner of Aspen Avenue and San Francisco Street—for almost a century, since 1891. In a *Daily Sun* article titled "Stores' sale means end to Northland tradition," reporter Paul Sweitzer understood well the special meaning that the store held for the Flagstaff community. In short, Babbitts' had become a special place in the downtown area, and consequently was viewed as an important symbol and fixture of the downtown as a whole. In part, Sweitzer wrote, "'I got it at Babbitts' generally meant you bought the item, whatever it was, in that store; sometimes helped by someone you had known there for years." In a *Daily Sun* editorial titled "Babbitts: the end of an era," its writers explained, "The Babbitts store was a part of Flagstaff's heritage. Even those who may be recent arrivals and who may not have shopped regularly at the familiar department store recognized the Babbitt name as a proud tradition in the Northland. The store and the family have been a part of Flagstaff for longer than most can remember."

Not only did the store's closing symbolize the end of an era for a family business, but it also highlighted the reality that the downtown would never again be the central place for commerce that it once was. For many longtime residents, the day Babbitts' closed its doors was the day downtown died.

Meanwhile, the Flagstaff community was compiling its new Master Plan, the text of which recognized that Flagstaff's business district would probably never again serve as the community's primary retail hub. Also known as the Growth Management Guide 2000, the new Master Plan in 1987 admitted, "Downtown Flagstaff has been undergoing a transition from being the regional shopping and trade center to being a regional center for finance, office uses, and government." That the new Flagstaff City Hall, the Coconino County Administrative building, and the new city library had been built downtown was evidence, according to the plan, that "governmental functions are staking an investment in the future of downtown for years to come."

The plan had yet to mention anything about tourism development in the business district, envisioning instead that the downtown would become dominated less by local retail stores and more by "finance, culture, and government." This coincides with the views of County Supervisor Paul Babbitt, who served as Flagstaff's mayor throughout the process of building the new city hall in 1983. In a personal interview, he explained how the decision of where to locate the new city hall related to the changes taking place downtown:

> That combination of Penney's leaving, Sears leaving, plus the addition of all these people at the mall who had not operated before in Flagstaff [contributed to the decline of downtown]. Simultaneous with that, there was a considerable amount of strip development. Safeway went into some new facilities, Bashas' came to town a little later. Anyway, there were some dislocations, some consolidations—it was really rearranging the retail activity in town, by and large, out from the downtown. At the same time, and I was mayor at the time, we started talking about developing the new city hall. And, we ended up placing it in the downtown, thinking that it would signal to developers and the community that we really wanted it downtown, and we set about that project. And there was

> some competition from other sites, but in the final analysis, we took four blocks on the west side of downtown and turned it into what you see: a park, two blocks of city hall, and a reserved space for the library. (Babbitt 2000)

Aside from the loss of traditional retailing, the old business district was literally crumbling to pieces. This was nowhere more evident than on the sidewalks, considerably old and cracked and in much need of maintenance or replacement. Broken curbs and gutters were the reality for downtown, and the sidewalks themselves were generally in poor condition during the 1980s. These conditions not only presented a hazard to pedestrians and wheelchairs, but also diminished the effectiveness of storm water drainage. Combined with numerous deteriorating historic buildings and vacancies, the poor maintenance of the sidewalks conspired with curbside litter and trash to make for quite an eyesore.

City Manager Dave Wilcox recalled the physical conditions of the downtown area as he perceived them in 1992. That year, Wilcox had replaced City Manager Frank Abeyta who had served as Flagstaff's top administrator for 11 years. Hailing from Beloit, Wisconsin, where he had been actively involved in that city's downtown redevelopment efforts, Wilcox had prior to that helped revitalize the downtown of Missoula, Montana. Essentially, Wilcox jumped into the fire during his first year in Flagstaff, as the downtown redevelopment process was well underway, with numerous challenges for the city yet to come. Wilcox reflected on his initial impressions of downtown Flagstaff:

> Prior to my arriving, from what I had heard, in the 1970s downtown was a pretty rugged area with a lot of transients and indigent people hanging around. It was quite a wild area, a lot of bars, it wasn't necessarily the students—it was really the transients and alcoholics, and a lot of vacancies. When I got here in 1992, it wasn't so bad in terms of business vacancies although the business mix was pretty lackluster, which I think is doing better, but the physical infrastructure was just terrible: it was dilapidated and it

> was actually difficult to walk on the sidewalks. It was in desperate need of being reconstructed. Of course the streets were in bad shape, the city infrastructure was in pretty bad shape. So that's what I found. (Wilcox 2001)

Sergeant Gerry Blair, a Flagstaff native who remained in town to become a respected citizen and police officer, supported Wilcox's stories. Given his law enforcement perspective, however, Blair focused more on the social concerns of downtown, including the challenges of public drunkenness during the 1970s and 1980s. For instance, a number of bars existed along what was known then as Front Street (Santa Fe Avenue), several of which remain as of this writing. From a policing perspective, one of the dominant challenges was the attraction to downtown of chronic intoxicants who regularly frequented these bars. "It wasn't uncommon to drive into the downtown area," Blair recalled, "and see people passed out on the sidewalks" (Blair 2001). At one time it was against the law to be intoxicated in public, though this law was eventually rescinded, or decriminalized. Additionally, downtown played host to a detox center, to which police officers would regularly take intoxicated individuals. This system failed to solve the rampant problem of public drunkenness during this time, however, because police officers would "pick up the intoxicated individual causing a disturbance off the sidewalk and take him to the detox center," Blair explained. "Because public drunkenness was decriminalized, though, we couldn't really hold them there. So they'd get there, get cleaned up a bit, and would then beat us back down to the bars" (Blair 2001).

The physical and social deterioration of downtown did not go unnoticed by the community at large. In 1987 one resident wrote to the *Daily Sun*, having previously visited several of Arizona's ghost towns, "never suspecting that historic downtown Flagstaff might soon join their ranks." Although downtown had traditionally been home to a variety of shops selling hand-made Indian jewelry, rugs, and southwestern crafts, this writer perceived that businesses were fading away in similar fashion to the larger establishments already gone. She perceived that downtown "has been degenerating in the past few years and the process has speeded up recently." Others claimed that the city government was responsible for the deterioration, arguing that various façade renovations completed by the private sector would not be enough to spark a revitalization effort. "Is it enough that the private sector cares enough to do this," another writer asked in 1987, or "is it possible that the spirit might increase if city officials would present a positive attitude rather than the apathetic one now displayed?" Even after the process of downtown redevelopment was well underway—or at least in the planning stages—another writer claimed that "every time we go downtown and try to walk the streets, we have to watch every step we take and try not to step into dog excrement, potholes and cracks in the sidewalk!" A decade later one would find no such letters with such descriptions of downtown.

Of course, the degree of deterioration by the late 1980s into the early 1990s was in the eye of the beholder. President of the Downtown Flagstaff Association, Roxanne Boehl, responded tersely to the above letters in support of the progress being made downtown. She claimed in the *Daily Sun* that the downtown was actually gaining small businesses, not losing them. "Sure, we've lost some important businesses downtown, yet the number of losses to gains is small comparatively. Change has not been bad," she claimed, "but instead has improved the diversity of downtown shopping." No matter the perception, the old business district was about to receive a whole lot more attention than it had during its previous half-century of development. During the 1990s Flagstaff's tired business district was effectively transformed through what some have described as a veritable downtown Renaissance. The vast majority of historic buildings underwent various amounts of renovation throughout the 1990s, the city successfully implemented a striking new pedestrian-oriented "streetscape" project throughout the district, and perhaps most important, the downtown gained an impressive and inviting public space that came to be known as Heritage Square.

STOP 4
PUBLIC PARK: HERITAGE SQUARE

Heritage Square embodies perhaps the most intriguing story of redevelopment efforts in Flagstaff's downtown business district (Figure 26). In what has become one of Flagstaff's most popular public spaces, the square represents many aspects of Flagstaff's local and regional heritage. It is quite enjoyable to walk around the plaza in search of various themes and symbols that reflect Flagstaff's environmental and human heritage: from the flagpole with its base representing the rock layers of the Grand Canyon, to the words "Empress Theater" emblazoned on the amphitheater floor. There are many others. For this reason, Heritage Square succeeds at helping community members and visitors become more aware of Flagstaff's diverse roots, its links with the past, and its place in the regional environment. Before its completion in 1999 this space was a dirt parking lot, and before that it was a row of historic commercial buildings that included the Empress Theater. For some time many of these older buildings were fused together into the enlarged Babbitt Brothers Department Store discussed earlier. Only recently, in this era of downtown revitalization, have towns and cities been reclaiming some of their parking lots for the purpose of redevelopment projects. In an effort to increase pedestrian activity and community interaction, communities are working to de-emphasize the automobile in their downtowns following decades of bulldozing buildings and creating parking lots. Heritage Square is a good example of this trend, one of people-centered development.

Figure 26. Heritage Square and the new A.G. Edwards Building on a chilly fall day in 2002. Notice the amphitheater in the foreground, the former site of the Empress Theater. The benches are constructed with railroad wheels and axles. The Square has become a popular public space in the recently redeveloped downtown area. (Photo: Author's collection)

The "square" actually includes the A. G. Edwards retail building set back from the corner of Leroux Street and Aspen Avenue, an enlarged replica of Flagstaff's first city hall. The original city hall existed one block south on Leroux Street until it was demolished sometime in the 1970s (Babbitt 2001). Further, from a political economic perspective, the building's construction was necessary to generate rent from various offices and businesses that in turn would help defray the cost of the plaza's development and maintenance.

Like the vast majority of urban redevelopment projects across the nation, the landscape of Heritage Square and of the downtown as a whole is the product of a capitalist-driven, Anglo-American process dominated by the male gender. This is not necessarily a criticism, nor is it an opportunity to bash white males. It is the geographer's job to understand who is creating our human landscapes, for what purposes, and with what meanings attached. It is necessary to acknowledge that our human landscapes are often created and designed by people of rather specific cultural, socio-economic, demographic, or gender backgrounds. This is why places are decidedly different in their appearance, character, and function. We do not live in a homogeneous world, nor do we live in a world where everybody's perspectives are equally represented in our human landscapes. Knowing more about who actually creates these places helps us to better understand and appreciate our human landscapes, and also to be more conscious about whose values these places best represent.

A celebratory railroad-oriented theme park, like that found at Santa Fe Plaza or here at Heritage Square, is most likely a place designed and conceived by a dominant Anglo-American perspective that cherishes the values of progress, technology, expansion, and economic growth (see Chapter 2). For the Anglo-American, embracing the technological and economic significance of the railroad embodies these cherished values.

Aside from other representations of Flagstaff's heritage, it is the railroad theme that dominates the imagery in this newly created public space. The railroad is an important symbol of America's optimism in the technological and economic progress afforded by the industrial revolution during the nineteenth century, and America's continued growth and expansion throughout the twentieth.

Ask many American Indians, however, what their choice would be for a heritage theme, and I do not imagine they would embrace the railroad with equal enthusiasm. For many indigenous people, the railroad has represented no less than the destruction of their cultures and their forced assimilation into the American mainstream. For some of these people there is little to celebrate about the railroad's arrival in Flagstaff, in northern Arizona, or in the entire West.

Images of the railroad—specifically of the Santa Fe—appeared frequently in the promotional literature of the Fred Harvey Company around the turn of the twentieth century. In much of this literature the eventual conquest of Native Americans is portrayed as inevitable (Dilworth 1996, 104). A powerful example of this is found in a painting titled *The First Santa Fe Train*, by Frank P. Sauerwein. The painting appeared on a postcard as early as 1908, on the back of which the caption reads: "Indians watching the first Santa Fe train crossing the continent, whose advent meant so little to their minds, and so much to the white man. The picture is from a famous painting" (Dilworth 1996, 94). Leah Dilworth expressed the power relationship between train and Indian in her book, *Imagining Indians in the Southwest* (1996, 105):

> The introduction to *The Great Southwest*, which reproduced this painting on its cover, depicted the history of the Southwest as waves of European conquest: the Conquistadors, the Jesuits and Franciscans, the Americans, and the railroad: "Finally came the railroads—the greatest open trails—and with their coming time alone was required to reclaim the wilderness." In conjunction with the Sauerwein painting, this sentence compressed that history: the train conquered the Indians. The conquest was easy because Indians were perceived as ruins, already gone. In the simple juxtaposition of train and Indian, the power relationship is clear; the Indian could not comprehend, much less resist, the transforming energies of the railroad.

Would an American Indian perspective on the railroad be welcome in a dominantly Anglo-American downtown landscape? It is difficult to tell, as to my knowledge nobody has attempted to create an alternative representation of the railroad within the historic district, except for, perhaps, the aforementioned effort to install the *Iron Horse* sculpture at Santa Fe Plaza. Therefore, it may be unfair to presume that a variety of multiple perspectives regarding the railroad would not be embraced in Flagstaff.

Given its cultural context, the process of transforming Heritage Square into a public park required a full decade of planning and cooperation among various parties in both the public and private sectors. Just as many redevelopment projects take place through joint public-private partnerships (that is, city government and private business), Heritage Square was envisioned and ultimately created due to the combined efforts of the city of Flagstaff and local developers and property owners. To recall, all parcels of land in a capitalist system maintain *use values* and *exchange values*. Land will typically be bought and sold based on its market value as well as the value of land parcels surrounding it. Thus, the main players in the transformation of a downtown business landscape over time consist primarily of property and business owners, who treat their properties as commodities for the creation of wealth and profit. On the public side of the public-private relationship is the city government, which actually maintains little control over the free-market processes that shape downtown business districts like this one. If the city wishes to exert its influence, hopefully for the public good, it must do so by playing within the rules of the capitalist system. The creation of Heritage Square required precisely this type of process. Thus, we cannot hope to explain the material existence of Heritage Square and its unique variety of cultural symbols without first understanding the political economic process that helped to produce it.

The economic perspective of exchange values was exemplified well by Maury Herman, a long-time Flagstaff resident and downtown property owner. During a personal interview, Herman explained how the free-market system actually works within a downtown business district like this one. From a real estate investment perspective, there are decisions one must make before purchasing a commercial property, as Herman explained: "Basically, you look at what your down payment's going to be, and then you look at the characteristics of the property. What will your net rental income likely be after you've paid all the expenses associated with the property? Let's say hypothetically that you're buying a property for $100,000. You put $25,000 down and then you owe $75,000. Then you look at what the property's going to make."

By this, Herman referred to the ability of a building on the property to generate rental income, from a business whose owner rents a commercial space for its operations: a retail store, restaurant or office, for instance. From this exchange-value perspective of property, then, commercial buildings are viewed for their ability to generate income for their owners. Herman continued with a simple example:

> If the property's going to earn $1,200 a month after expenses, and the debt service on the $75,000 investment is $700 a month, then you're making $500 a month or $6,000 a year on an initial down-payment investment of $25,000. That's an extremely good return. On the other hand, if you're going to have a building where you invest the same $25,000, and you're going to make $75 a year, it's not a good return. Here, the buildings we looked at [to purchase] had rents that were low even in the depressed market that existed then, and we thought we could raise those rents. (Herman 2001)

Herman also considered various geographical factors when deciding which properties to purchase in the downtown area:

> This is a university town, and it's at the intersection of two major highways, and it's a tourist area. Each of those factors contributes something to the local economy. The university contributes a payroll, the students are very good customers, the faculty are good customers, and the fact that we're in proximity to the Grand Canyon and to other world-class tourist locales draws a lot of people. None of those people are particularly interested in visiting Wal-Mart. They have a Wal-Mart or equivalent where they live, so that's not of interest. (Herman 2001)

Whether the smallest of towns or the largest of cities, whether small parking lots or 100-story office towers, the decision-making process to invest in such properties is one and the same, rooted within our capitalist economic system.

Similar types of factors, both economic and geographic, were considered in development planning for the space now occupied by Heritage Square. For many years, this entire city block was owned by the Babbitt family, and a good portion of the block was occupied by an enlarged Babbitt Brothers Department Store, discussed earlier. In 1988 the "Babbitt Block," as it is still referred to today, consisted of several large buildings, namely the department store lining Aspen Avenue, the Babbitt Garage, which has since been renovated as lawyers' offices on the northeast edge of the plaza, and the J. C. Penney department store building on the corner of Leroux and Birch. In 1988 the Babbitts were in the process of selling many of their property holdings in Flagstaff and around northern Arizona, and the Babbitt Block was purchased in its entirety by a local developer, Steve Vanlandingham. Initially, Vanlandingham had planned to construct a parking lot along Aspen Avenue after demolishing the Babbitt Department Store buildings. "The parking structure," claimed a *Daily Sun* article in 1990, "which will feature landscaping and old fashioned light posts, will provide parking during the week and a community center on weekends."

The creation of a parking lot, however, required the demolition of the Babbitt Department Store building, including the original structure. As the building was being carefully dismantled to avoid damage to surrounding businesses, Vanlandingham and the work crews uncovered a historical reminder of Flagstaff's past. While supervising the demolition, Vanlandingham found another building hidden underneath the once-renovated department store, which turned out to be part of the old Empress Theater. The Babbitt building had been expanded along Aspen Avenue since the 1890s, and the expansions had been built right over the top of the original structures. When he saw the work crews tear into the old theater, he immediately halted the work until they could determine precisely what they had found.

What they found was a small building constructed by the Babbitt Brothers Trading Company as a garage around 1910. In 1912, the Babbitts built a much larger garage on the northeast corner of the lot (today the Aspey, Watkins & Diesel building) that included three floors for housing automobiles. The older garage was then vacated until the building was pressed into service again in 1916. In that year, a snowstorm caved in the roof of the Majestic Theater (later the Orpheum), located next to the Weatherford Hotel. While the Majestic was being rebuilt, the old Babbitt garage became the new Empress Theater, which housed various Flagstaff entertainment and theater productions. After 1917, the Empress ceased as a scene for local entertainment when the Majestic (Orpheum) was repaired. In following years, the expanding Babbitt Brothers Department Store engulfed the Empress, and the entire Babbitt building received the aforementioned modern façade in the 1950s. As a reminder of the short-lived Empress, today's Heritage Square includes a small amphitheater inscribed with the words "Empress Theater," indicating where the building once stood.

Vanlandingham's historic find caught the attention of the community as well as the local media. Ultimately, the old Empress building was demolished with the exception of the building's cement-arch entryway with its original sign that read, "Empress Theater." In a personal interview, Vanlandingham recalled the events of the day of the discovery:

> The Empress Theater was kind of at the center of the block, facing Aspen Avenue, and it had two or three different facades put over the front of it for different uses. We had a track hoe in there tearing it down, and on that particular day we were working on the front of those buildings, and I was concerned that debris might fly across the street through some of those plate-glass windows. So, I was really careful, and we had people stationed over there to watch. I was actually standing on the other side of the street, and all of a sudden here comes a couple of facades right off the front of it, and there's this concrete structure that says "Empress Theater." I ran over and stopped everything. I mean, everybody shut down and turned off everything, and we were like, "I don't know what this is, but this is cool." And we did a little bit of research and found that it was in fact a theater, a theater that was used in 1916. I couldn't afford to stop work for very long, so I said, "protect this basic structure." It was basically four concrete posts with a concrete roof. I left that up for a couple of years, until the city bought it, [saying that] it was a hazard and tore it down. They just wanted it out of there. (Vanlandingham 2001)

Vanlandingham's initial decision to raze the older Babbitt buildings and replace them with a parking lot reflected solid economic logic with regard to property ownership. With the three-story Babbitt Garage and the department store all vacant, Vanlandingham was receiving very little return on his investment in the Babbitt Block, and he desperately needed to do something with the property that would generate revenue. He recalled, "That was early, very early, shortly after I bought it. I was thinking that the downtown needed more parking, and these buildings can't be rented, so let's just tear them down, because the office and government sectors were so strong. So I said I'd essentially land-bank the block and receive income generated off of a parking lot" (Vanlandingham 2001). Following his announcement that the Aspen Street buildings would be razed, Jim Babbitt and the Babbitt Foundation asked to purchase from Vanlandingham the original Babbitt building on the corner of Aspen and San Francisco so that it would not be destroyed. Then, Vanlandingham sold the three-story Babbitt Garage to the law firm of Aspey, Watkins & Diesel. The law firm, the Foundation, and Vanlandingham all agreed to cooperate on the development of the entire Babbitt Block. Then the city became involved, with its own idea of building an underground parking lot. In a 1991 *Daily Sun* article, Vanlandingham explained, "The last player to join the group was the city, and all of us were in place by the spring of 1990." The group worked with yet another organization, the Main Street Flagstaff Foundation, which hired architects to help design a development project that combined offices, stores, bars, underground parking, and open areas.

In September of 1990 it appeared that the city's plans for redevelopment might be delayed indefinitely due to legislative guidelines the city was required to follow. Waiting for a return on his property investment, Vanlandingham could not afford to delay any longer. He then withdrew his proposal to the city to help develop the lot. The city had been negotiating with Vanlandingham for more than a year on such a project when Vanlandingham reluctantly announced that he could "no longer afford the time and money that would be necessary to continue work on this project," as his letter stated to the city. With the necessity to create revenue from the lot in a hurry, he decided to begin the parking lot project without the city's help.

To make a long story much shorter, the city eventually decided to purchase the property from Vanlandingham so that a new public-private partnership could be forged with a developer of the city's choice. Further, it seemed that while Vanlandingham would continue with his plan for a street-level parking lot if left up to him, the city had other ideas, specifically for a major redevelopment project including an underground parking garage and a pedestrian plaza of some kind. Thus, in November of 1991 the city council voted 4-1 to purchase the 33,000-square-foot lot on the corner of Leroux and Aspen, the site of today's Heritage Square. The city paid Vanlandingham $425,000 for the lot.

This decision was not without its critics, including one councilmember, Nat White. White argued that the city was jumping into a deal before it knew what it would eventually do with the land, and even before the land could be fully appraised. Further, the purchase was speculative, in that the city only assumed that the property would be developed at some point in time. The majority of the city council, however, including Mayor Chris Bavasi, argued that the purchase was wise because it would give "the council an opportunity to turn downtown into a beautiful area, something it hasn't been for the past 25 years," as one *Daily Sun* article reported in November of 1991. Regardless, the city jumped into the game of real estate speculation with the hope of continuing its vision for redevelopment on its own accord. In March of 1992 the city had the old Empress Theatre arch demolished, citing safety concerns. Although Vanlandingham would have preferred to keep it intact, the city's Historical Sites Commission could not justify keeping it standing because it was only one small part of the original building, and it would thus probably not be eligible for listing on the National Register of Historic Places.

The idea to replicate the old city hall is credited to Jim Babbitt, who also opened a sporting goods store in the old Babbitt Department Store building. He and a few other local individuals and couples, including Steve Vanlandingham, formed a foundation to help pay for the completion of Heritage Square. Although generous to the tune of more than a million dollars, the foundation's goal was political, in that it agreed to help pay for the park's construction as long as the city allowed them some control over the park's design. In this way, Babbitt and the others secured some local control over a downtown project they feared would not represent an appropriate amount of local input if the city had its way.

Thus, Heritage Square and its various landscape elements were partially designed by influential local individuals, especially Jim Babbitt. The square has become a veritable theme park, displaying a wide variety of images and symbols that represent the aforementioned Anglo-American perspective of Flagstaff's heritage. Images of the railroad include an inlaid brick railroad track, and benches made from old railroad wheels (Figure 26). Jim Babbitt explained the origin of the idea for the benches, as well as other ideas for theming within the park:

> The railroad benches came from my wife and I being in New Zealand—Nelson, New Zealand, in a city park there. We saw these great old benches made out of railroad axles, and thinking, well, the railroad is kind of the key, it's the reason why Flagstaff is here at all. So we came back and designed the railroad benches with these little historic themes on the back: ranching, skiing, forestry, observatory and all that stuff. It was just people around a table for many months thinking about heritage themes and how to execute those themes [throughout Heritage Square]. (Babbitt 2001)

The benches, therefore, represent a classic case of cultural diffusion through imitation—in this case straight from New Zealand to Flagstaff. The various themes and images found at Heritage Square are similar to those found throughout the historic district. In one sense, the historic district has become Flagstaff's veritable theme park, whereby businesses and local residents are increasingly applying themes and images to the landscape in an attempt to enhance the local sense of place, to promote Flagstaff's identity with its local surroundings, and especially to encourage consumption of merchandise by visitors. This type of theming is not just a local trend, but a national one gaining the attention of geographers and other social scientists. Several books have been written about the trend to theme our human landscapes, including *The Theming of America*, by Mark Gottdiener (1997). One need not travel any farther than to downtown Flagstaff, however, to witness a wonderful example of this national trend.

Aside from its themed landscape, Heritage Square is important for another reason. This place represents a new *public space* for all to use and enjoy as they wish. Few public spaces are being created today, and geographers have lamented for decades the continuing loss of public spaces throughout America. By public space, I am referring to areas of a town or city that are not owned, managed, or policed by private businesses or corporations. Since the 1950s the ratio of *private space* to public space has been increasing steadily and shows no sign of abating.

Many places that we think of as public are actually private, in that they are controlled and policed by the corporations that own them. All shopping malls, theme parks (e.g. Disney World), and even many housing developments (with their private drives and neighborhood associations) are private spaces. Shopping malls and department stores, for instance, maintain their own security systems, video surveillance cameras, and business hours. "Big Brother" is always watching. Public spaces, however, are those where people are free to gather, protest, parade, eat lunch, stroll, socialize, people-watch, or do anything else that doesn't break a law or negatively impact other people. The streets of this downtown area represent a traditional public space, and today this space includes Heritage Square. During all months of the year, local community events are planned and held at Heritage Square, making the downtown a sort of hub once again for social activity in town. Many geographers, planners, and community leaders around the country are arguing that we need more public spaces like Heritage Square, not less. In this case, the creators of Heritage Square and the Flagstaff community as a whole can be proud of this local success story.

STOP 5
RESTORATION: WEATHERFORD HOTEL

The histories and geographies of all places are shaped in part by certain influential individuals. John W. Weatherford was one of Flagstaff's own. Weatherford arrived in 1886 and purchased a couple of lots on Gold Avenue (now Leroux Street) with the money he earned from selling his horse and buggy (Mangum and Mangum 1993). He tried his luck at several businesses, namely the Parlor Saloon, a *livery stable* (from which horses and buggies could be rented), and the Gent's Furnishing store. He built the south half of this building as a store in 1898 and added the north half of the building a year later, constructed with none other than Flagstaff's own locally quarried Moenkopi Sandstone.

He then converted the whole building into a hotel that opened for business on January 1, 1900 (Figure 27). With hot and cold running water, electric lights, and fine dining, this quickly became Flagstaff's premier hotel, gaining a regional reputation across the Southwest. It competed heavily with the *Commercial*, Flagstaff's first prominent hotel originally located directly across from the train station on Route 66. The *Commercial* burned down in 1975.

Figure 27. The Weatherford Hotel, with reconstructed steel, earthquake-proof balcony. The meeting rooms of the hotel have become a sort of hub for business leaders who have crafted downtown redevelopment plans and discussed the future of downtown. Also housed here is Charly's, a popular social venue for NAU students and other local residents. (Photo: Author's collection)

Flagstaff hosted as many as four *railroad hotels*, including the Weatherford, up through the 1940s. Railroad hotels were most often constructed within walking distance from a city's railroad depot, given that many visitors arrived by train right up through World War II. These hotels were usually the most lavish places in town, often featuring amazing services like running water and separate bathrooms. The Weatherford itself was quite luxurious in its heyday, prior to increased competition from newer motels after the 1920s—several of which we will encounter shortly.

Famous guests at the Weatherford Hotel included William Randolph Hearst and Theodore Roosevelt. It is interesting, though, that the guest most spoken of in Flagstaff is Zane Grey, who wrote his famous book, *The Call of the Canyon*, while he stayed at the hotel. Local historians Richard and Sherry Mangum have written about Weatherford's later adventures and contributions to the Flagstaff community in a downtown tour guide of their own. According to them,

Weatherford apparently embarked on a personal building boom after determining that his hotel would be a success:

> In 1909 he constructed the office for the first telephone company in Flagstaff. From this he went on to build Flagstaff's first cinema in 1911, the Majestic, rebuilt in 1916 after snow collapsed the roof. Finally, he embarked upon the building venture that was to be his crowning triumph, the Weatherford Road. The Weatherford Road was a scenic auto toll road to the top of the San Francisco Peaks. Weatherford secured Forest Service permits for construction but was short of funds. He tried to raise money by selling stock to local residents but the stock sales were meager. Doggedly, he carried on with his own money. After years of effort, he completed the road in 1926. When the Great Depression hit, Weatherford had over-extended himself, borrowing against his other properties to finance the road. As a result, he was wiped out through mortgage foreclosures in 1932 and died almost penniless in 1934. (Mangum and Mangum 1993, 35)

For its own part, the contemporary appearance of the Weatherford Hotel is a product of the historic preservation movement, as is the entire downtown business district of Flagstaff. The goal of many historic preservation enthusiasts is to restore buildings to their original appearance if possible. The white balconies that wrap around the Weatherford building were constructed in 1998 by the current hotel owners, Henry Taylor and Pamela (Sam) Green. The original wooden balconies had burned in a fire and were removed permanently by 1929; the building thus lasted almost 60 years without a balcony, and this is how many Flagstaff locals remember it. The hotel also featured a Victorian era turret on the roof (also known as a "witch's cap"), located over the northeast corner of the building. The current owners are planning to reconstruct the turret as well, and they have already reopened the building as a hotel and restaurant—both of which are once again popular attractions for visitors and local residents.

The story of the Weatherford's restoration provides a glimpse into the process of historic preservation. We all see "restored" buildings, with their fresh paint and maintained brick or stone, but how do they get that way? Often the process is a long one, and certain individuals necessarily invest grand amounts of time, money, and energy into such revival. The Weatherford presents an excellent case in point.

One of the hotel's owners, Henry Taylor, is by training a rehabilitation therapist who has lived in Flagstaff since 1975. At that time, he needed to find more space to house the mentally and physically disabled people with whom he worked. At the time, the Weatherford was suffering from benign neglect and was slated for eventual demolition. Thus, he purchased the building to save it and to provide housing for his patients. Some people in town were actually unwilling to go near the place due to the assumed instability of its new residents. In 1977 Henry opened a coffee shop on the ground floor, and began plans to restore the building's former balconies (Taylor 2000). In the 1980s the building's function shifted once again to a youth hostel. Today the structure is being used for its original intent, as a hotel, whose rooms are booked solid weeks in advance.

Henry knew nothing of the original balconies until his brother showed him a photo of the old building. Since then, it has been the goal of he and Sam to entirely restore them to their original splendor. As of this writing, the balconies remain incomplete, as they will eventually be extended across the entire north face of the building.

Just as many historic preservation projects are funded, Henry obtained a grant from the State Historic Preservation Office, in this case worth $100,500, to assist with the $300,000 balcony restoration project. He further took advantage of the downtown streetscape project in the mid-1990s, when the streets and sidewalks were torn up in front of his building. At that time, he installed the foundations for the future balcony posts, basically consisting of concrete footings built into the sidewalk itself. Today, these foundations can be seen on the north sidewalk, where eventually the final balconies will be installed.

Building codes have changed since the 1920s, necessitating a change in building materials as well. It is interesting to note that, when it was built, the Weatherford was the first structure in the downtown to comply with a city ordinance requiring all new structures to be built of iron or stone—an effort to prevent further conflagrations from destroying the business district. Since then, building codes have only become stricter. The balconies are therefore not constructed of wood like the originals, but of steel, standing on their own. Today's building codes in Flagstaff require all new construction to be earthquake proof as well as fire resistant. In a personal interview, Henry joked, somewhat seriously, that "if an earthquake hits, the hotel will collapse but the balconies will be in good shape" (Taylor 2000).

Today, the hotel is a centerpiece in the downtown district and a primary entertainment attraction for students and other local residents. The establishment houses the popular Charly's Restaurant and Bar, claimed by its owner to be the first social establishment to attract students to the north downtown in the 1980s. Since then, the downtown area both north and south of the tracks has become host to nearly two dozen alcohol-serving establishments, a mixed blessing at best. Henry Taylor himself has expressed frustration with the occasional intoxicated students who become disorderly and smash their fists through his windows and walls.

As downtown has made great strides toward economic and social revitalization, the district may be gaining too much of something else, according to some—that is, downtown bars and their patrons. By 1996, the downtown area north and south of the tracks had become home to no less than 17 bars located within a third of a mile from the Flagstaff Visitors Center. In comparison, Tucson's downtown area had only 12 bars within a similar radius at that time. The primary concern with the increase of drinking establishments in Flagstaff has revolved around the impaired judgment of bar patrons who may not drink responsibly. "Whenever you get a high concentration of bars, you get people milling around whose judgment is impaired to some degree," explained Flagstaff police spokesman Sgt. Gerry Blair in the *Daily Sun*. In 1996 this issue became prominent south of the tracks because of the collegiate clientele supplied by the 15,000-student campus of NAU. "You have a large number of people who are maybe inexperienced drinkers and don't know their limit," Blair continued, mentioning however that not all college students are "raving maniacs" after a couple of Kamikazes.

By early 1997 the downtown "imbibement industry" had grown to 20 bars with more on the way. The issue was considered serious enough to warrant a community forum organized by the Main Street Flagstaff Foundation and the Flagstaff Police Department. Approximately 50 people attended the forum, many holding a stake in the downtown or Southside area. Displaying a map of downtown, Chief of Police Pat Madden explained that "the whole image of this area has changed," as he showed all the red dots representing establishments with one of six types of liquor licenses. And it wasn't just the increase in bars, but restaurants with liquor licenses as well. Twenty-five years earlier, downtown had been through a period "rife with crime," including regular assaults, strong-armed robberies, and rapes. Realizing that a change of image was necessary, storeowners stopped selling pint bottles, and an alcohol treatment center moved out of the district to the east side of town. A further result of that crackdown of sorts was that "a lot of bars went out of business," according to Madden.

Few would disagree that the bar and restaurant scene on both sides of the tracks plays a key role in the social and entertainment component of Flagstaff's "new" downtown. The redeveloped historic business district today is a comfortable and safe environment with few problems during regular business hours and even into the late evening. Still, the biggest problem with this most recent revival of drinking establishments has involved public disorder, including fights and disturbances especially after midnight and on weekends. More reports of graffiti downtown and increased litter outside bars were also cited by individuals at the forum. Several business owners wrote a series of letters to the editor during the time when the number of bars and restaurants was gaining increased community attention. The assistant manager of the Monte Vista Hotel claimed in the title of her letter that, "Businesses don't appreciate noisy bargoers." She described in the *Daily Sun* the growing problem in her own words:

> Every weekend night, and sometimes during the week, the downtown area becomes an insane congregation of screaming adolescents and drunken bar hounds. At 1 am, when the bars close, people wander the streets yelling at full tilt. As front desk clerk, I have to bear the brunt of Saturday/Sunday morning complaints from angry guests who were kept awake all night by the yodelers on the street below…This problem is keeping the downtown from becoming a world-class downtown.

In 2003 the issue surrounding irresponsible bar-goers continued with no easy solutions in sight. Although the vast majority of students from NAU behave responsibly and contribute in many positive ways to the downtown area, it is the irresponsible few who give NAU students a bad name. In a personal interview, City Manager David Wilcox summarized this "love-hate" relationship between the downtown business community and NAU:

> I think the impact of students in the downtown is significant, both negatively and positively. I think there is a negative impact of students downtown—drinking, raising hell—their behavior is sometimes abominable, just really atrocious. It includes the damage to property and the things that one shouldn't do in public, and I believe that some businesses downtown that primarily cater to students kind of drag the rest of the business community down. I don't think that has a positive impact on the rest of the businesses. But I think that will upgrade over time. (Wilcox 2001)

Sergeant Gerry Blair described Flagstaff's new downtown as having more of a nightclub atmosphere than it has had in the past. Being very careful to not place a stigma on the university, Blair still admitted that the primary clientele for the downtown bar scene consisted of NAU students. During a personal interview, Blair repeated his 1996 statements, saying that students have a greater propensity to be inexperienced drinkers, who aren't yet familiar with their individual limits, and this situation creates some unique social issues and enforcement challenges. Not only do drunken students have a greater chance of committing criminal activity, but they also have a greater likelihood of being victims of crimes themselves. In this impaired state, "you're less capable of taking care of yourself" (Blair 2001).

One consequence of this situation is the relatively high number of alcohol-related traffic accidents in the downtown area. The Flagstaff Police Department makes between 1,000 and 1,200 DUI arrests annually within the city limits. Although exact numbers are hard to come by, Blair is confident that a high percentage of these DUI arrests take place in the downtown area, including the areas both south and north of the tracks. Prior to the 1990s the South Side area served as the "college bar district" and the business area north of the tracks was largely ignored by students. Since then this bar district has expanded to include the north downtown. This additional policing challenge has been met in recent years by increased bicycle patrols in the downtown area as well as walking patrols, or the "street beat." "A lot of times when there is a high police presence, it serves as crime prevention," explained Blair. Recently, the Flagstaff Police Department was further awarded a "Safe Streets" grant so that both NAU police and city of Flagstaff police could be encouraged to work overtime together to patrol the downtown area specifically. The ability for NAU police to work with their city counterparts is important given that "a lot of the people we have to deal with downtown are the same ones that the NAU police have to deal with on campus" (Blair 2001).

When asked how the downtown businesses have responded to this increased, and integrated, police presence, Blair responded, "they love it." Some businesses downtown are less tolerant with the destructive behaviors of some party-goers than others. Many retail businesses that are open during the day derive little benefit from the night-time bar crowd, but the merchants arrive in the mornings occasionally to find beer bottles and other trash scattered in front of their properties. On the extreme side, one barber shop located next door to a prominent downtown drinking establishment has had its plate-glass window smashed in several times by "having people thrown through it" as a byproduct of late-night street brawls (Blair 2001). One merchant had continuously complained about the bars for a long time until, according to one police officer, she finally gave in and opened up a bar of her own. Further, there tend to be more complaints from residences in the South Side area given that both homeowners and renters are intermingled within the South San Francisco Street business corridor. These people often call in complaints related to loud music and damage caused to people's vehicles parked in front of their homes.

The increase in bars and liquor-serving restaurants downtown reflects more than any other process the free-market economy at work. With the entertainment component of the downtown economy growing the fastest, entrepreneurs have been responding to the demand for these social places. Even former Main Street Director Jeffe Aronson agreed in 1997 that little could be done to prevent a new bar from moving in if it is economically viable for the property owner. This was the city council's position as well, though city council member Norm Wallen commented in the *Daily Sun* that "if there's a way to legally stop it, which is unlikely, I certainly would." Mayor Chris Bavasi at the time seemed content to allow the market to sort itself out through increased competition, stating that he had heard the argument of too many bars downtown since his coming to Flagstaff in the 1960s, and therefore the issue did not consist of an immediate crisis.

The issue surrounding the number and impact of downtown bars and restaurants was emblematic of the larger issue simply stated as *free-market capitalism* versus *centralized authority*. To what extent should city (or state or federal) government regulate the "imbibement industry," if at all? In one sense, Flagstaff's downtown business district may have been using pedestrian-oriented unifying devices in its new streetscape, reminiscent of suburban shopping malls, but shopping malls are strictly regulated and planned in advance by their respective managers, including the specific mix of business establishments, their spatial layout within the mall, and even the storefront displays of various retailers. This type of coordinated regulation does not exist in the free-market setting of a business district. Property owners may rent their spaces to whomever or whatever they wish. Despite the wide variety of city ordinances that provide limited rules and regulations pertaining to how a piece of real estate may look and function, a free-market economy allows private property owners to do pretty much what they want. In 1996 the *Daily Sun* quoted one new downtown bar owner as bluntly saying, "You can make a lot of money running a bar. It sure beats running one of those retail shops, but it's a lot more work." The bottom line for the bars in Flagstaff, according to this business owner, was the "bottom line."

Overall, the owners of alcohol-serving establishments expressed what appeared to be the general consensus of the 1997 Main Street forum: Let the free market take care of itself and the "bar situation downtown will settle in time." A *Daily Sun* editorial in 1996 agreed, stating that "left to its own devices, the market in spirits and food downtown will undoubtedly find its own level." Still, the editorial acknowledged the question of whether or not the market should have the final say. In part, its writers further expressed the significance of Flagstaff's historic business district as being "the last bastion of face-to-face democracy," consequently allowing for the argument that "public servants are elected to protect and enhance public resources, and Flagstaff's downtown is one of this community's most precious public commodities." Some form of limited city regulation, therefore, would not necessarily be uncalled for in this case. In 2003, however, the editorial's opening question, "Has downtown served its limit?" remained unanswered.

On the flip side, the student body's "rediscovery" of downtown—with Charly's on the vanguard of that trend—has assisted in the economic rebirth of the district. Students spend a lot of money here, and business owners including Henry Taylor at the Weatherford seem willing to put up with a few troublemakers in order to reap the economic benefits of increased patronage. Today, the downtown attracts a diverse array of people including students, permanent local residents, and visitors from elsewhere, helping to make the downtown area come alive once again. Today's image of downtown—aided by numerous individuals and their various historic renovation projects—is a far cry from the cracked sidewalks, crumbling buildings, unsafe lighting, and vacant storefronts that characterized this entire district as recently as the late 1980s.

The Weatherford has further become Flagstaff's hub for public celebration on New Year's Eve. Reminiscent of New York City's famous Times Square celebration where the nation rings in the new year with the lowering of a glowing crystal ball, Flagstaff lowers an object of its own—in this case, a giant pinecone—from the northeast corner of the Weatherford's roof and balcony. The pinecone drop represents a clear case of hierarchical diffusion, given that a small town has adopted a popular big-city idea. Rather than attempting to replicate Times Square precisely, however, Flagstaff's pinecone version reflects this community's environmental distinctiveness and local "mountain town" identity.

The pinecone was lowered for the third straight year on December 31, 2001, an event sponsored by the Downtown Business Alliance, an organization of downtown merchants formed following the demise of the Main Street Flagstaff Foundation. Following the terrorist attacks of September 11 only 4 months earlier, New York City was on everyone's mind, this time not just because of its traditional crystal ball. Consequently, the 2001 pinecone was decorated with red, white, and blue, as was the entire downtown area for the New Year's festivities. Further, the pinecone was dropped not once, but twice—first at 10 pm local time, coinciding precisely with the ball-drop at Times Square, and second at midnight local time.

More than an imitation of a national tradition, Flagstaff's own New Year's Eve festival aims primarily to attract people back to its downtown business district. The festivities are advertised heavily by local media, and the pinecone drop is one of numerous attractions. A local band plays at Heritage Square to entertain the hardy revelers, party favors and sodas are sold to passers-by, and in 2001 a giant video screen with laser projection was hung over the Animas Trading Company property to display the countdown to the new year. With this new and creative annual festival, the Downtown Business Alliance has not only carried on the promotional goals of the former Main Street Program, but has further contributed to the enhancement of the community's sense of place for downtown.

Directly west of the Weatherford Hotel is the Orpheum theater, built in 1916. The Orpheum represents a typical small-town theater located in the heart of downtown. It replaced the Majestic Theater, which originally sat on the site. On New Year's Eve of 1915, a huge snowstorm struck Flagstaff, caving in the roof of the Majestic. Its original builder, John Weatherford, immediately built this new theater and renamed it the Orpheum (Mangum and Mangum 1993). The current façade, or front face, of the theater is not its original, however. The actual architectural style was Neoclassical, another period style that remained popular roughly between 1910 and 1930. Its front façade therefore resembled a simplified classical Greek temple. Years later, as tastes changed, it received a modern makeover, still visible today.

Today our society is grasping onto any aspect of its past that it can. Consequently, many of the metal slipcovers that hid the shameful old facades in the downtown area 20 years ago have been removed to uncover the older architectural beauty underneath. In fact, the Orpheum is one of the few buildings still retaining its modernist makeover, now considered historic in its own right. Still, it would not be surprising to see this modern façade removed to reveal its true neoclassical self, continuing the trend of historic renovations that are taking place throughout the downtown area.

Today the Orpheum appears to be obsolete for another reason, related to the *decentralization* of traditional downtown functions as they shifted to the periphery of town. By the end of the 1990s, Flagstaff played host to no less than six different movie theater complexes, one of which was the wide-screened Orpheum. By 2000 all had closed except for the new Harkins Cineplex on the west side of town. Many communities have lost their traditional downtown theaters due to competition from the periphery of town, though sometimes a wealthy local couple, for instance, will purchase an old theater and ultimately restore it. This scenario is playing out at the Orpheum as well. In July of 2002 a fledgling company, called Orpheum Presents, headed by several local residents, worked out an agreement to lease the theater from its new owner. Renovations have since begun to transform the old theater into a multi-use performing arts center suitable for movies, theater, dance, and other cultural activities. The group envisioned a grand reopening for sometime in November of 2002. If successful, such a renovation will no doubt only contribute to the continuing revitalization efforts within the downtown area.

STOP 6
COURTHOUSE: HUB OF COCONINO COUNTY

This old sandstone courthouse represents the geographical and political hub of the second largest county in the United States. At 18,540 square miles, Coconino County includes the south and north rims of the Grand Canyon, the isolated town of Page and neighboring Glen Canyon Dam to the north, Sedona to the south, and two of the nation's largest national forests. Flagstaff has been fortunate to serve as the hub for county government, represented from the beginning by this impressive courthouse building constructed in 1894–95 (Figure 28).

Figure 28. Coconino County Courthouse in 2002, following substantial renovations. (Photo: Author's collection)

To provide some perspective on scale, only California's San Bernadino County is larger than Coconino in area, covering 20,164 square miles. Entire European countries are smaller in geographical area than Coconino, including Switzerland (15,941 square miles) and Denmark (16,629 square miles). Israel, a nation of much concern to its Middle Eastern neighbors, is less than half the size of Coconino. Finally, nine U.S. states are smaller than Coconino County, with diminutive Rhode Island only one-eighteenth its size.

The catch is that the county is almost entirely composed of rural places, with Flagstaff by far its largest city. In 2000 the county's population numbered only 116,320 residents, and roughly half of them lived in or around Flagstaff. Still, the county's growth rate was rather high, registering a 20.4 percent increase in population between 1990 and 2000, according to the U.S. Census. In terms of population density, the county maintains an incredibly low 6.3 people per square mile. Coconino County may be one of the largest in the country by area, but its population density also makes it one of the most rural.

The first courthouse, still in use today, is in itself a geographical paradox. Despite its importance as a central place for both local government and community, the building was seemingly just shoved aside, onto just another city block. Recall from Chapter 3 that the railroad company left few, if any, provisions in its standardized street grid plan for institutional buildings. Still, when constructed, it was by far the most elaborate structure in Flagstaff, signifying its importance as the hub of county government. At that time it was also highly visible, as the downtown district had yet to build up densely around it. The community was bursting with pride for its new architectural gem. The building represented progress and growth—two intertwined American ideals. Symbolically, the new courthouse indicated that Flagstaff was no longer just a frontier outpost or a rural stop along the railroad, but instead was a permanent and economically viable town that would continue to grow. As county officials moved into the new courthouse in 1895, editorials in the *Coconino Sun* celebrated with comments including this one: "Coconino County has as handsome and well-arranged a courthouse as there is in the Territory." The town's new status as county seat gave the community more reason to be optimistic about its future.

Aside from the role of the railroad, cultural geographers would interpret the location of the courthouse as indicative of America's deep-rooted interest in mobility and independence. Railroad or no railroad, the efficient grid-plan streets of many cities and towns allow a smooth flow of traffic with few impediments. Unlike in Europe, where significant and elaborate structures often serve as monumental centerpieces of their communities and cities, American architecture tends to "stand to one side," to use Craig Whitaker's words (Whitaker 1996, 31). That the courthouse "stands to one side" of San Francisco Street, then, not only indicates the efficient reproduction of a simple street grid by a railroad corporation, but also symbolizes America's real goal, that of unimpeded mobility. Indeed, a courthouse "square" with roads radiating out from it would only get in the way. Of course, this tendency to improve mobility on the ground continues everywhere, with the widening of two-lane streets, the construction of bypasses around congested cities, and the smoothing out of formerly irregular intersections. In larger cities, pedestrian skywalks connecting two or more buildings add further to auto-mobility by eliminating the pedestrians from the streets.

The space outside and around the courthouse plays a central role in a variety of social and political functions enabled in turn by our nation's democratic system of government. The courthouse door has been the place for important public speeches, ceremonies, swearings-in, debates, protests, and first-hand announcements about the results of various trials taking place inside (Clay 1996, 13). The courthouse itself is the historic center of both political, and in early times, military control. This place is clearly the hub of centralized authority in the county. The local power structure, consisting until recently of an all-male world, was also centered on the courthouse square. Within a 10-minute walk in most county seats, one could see everybody who counted. Even today in Flagstaff, a good number of the community's most prominent lawyers, business people, interest groups, and politicians are found congregating in offices and lunchrooms within blocks of the courthouse. Occasionally the city mayor himself is seen eating with friends and colleagues at one of many eating establishments located downtown.

Still, the county courthouse as a special place in American society is not what it once was. Following the suburban "white flight" after the 1950s, county governments grew larger and required more space. Courthouse annexes often appeared at the edge of town, the county jail would often be enlarged and relocated outside of town, and necessary county functions involving auto licenses, hunting and fishing licenses, tax payments, and voting registration also went elsewhere. Like many other traditional downtown functions, those of the county seat have been decentralized, moving to cheaper and more expansive land parcels on the edge of town (Clay 1996). In most counties, the proud old courthouse could not handle the new requirements and necessary enlargements; consequently it is common to find these buildings converted into a town museum or, worse yet, into a parking lot. Fortunately, although Flagstaff's county courthouse has taken its hits and has literally been engulfed by a series of additions, it still remains today in good enough condition to allow its careful restoration. It survived urban renewal and has managed to maintain its intended function right up to the present day. In August of 2002 the finishing touches were put on the building's impressive restoration, highlighted by the expansive grass lawn once again encircling it.

The courthouse further provides an excellent lesson in the evolution of American architecture. As cultural tastes and values have changed in America since the nineteenth century, so too have our architectural styles. Although the long reign of Britain's Queen Victoria lasted from 1837 to 1901, it was during the latter decades of her reign when *Victorian* architecture became popular in the United States (McAlester and McAlester 1997). Although it is common to speak of Victorian houses or commercial buildings, Victorian is a somewhat general term that encompasses a variety of distinct architectural styles. The most popular styles during the Victorian Era in the United States were, in roughly chronological order, *Second Empire* (1860s–1870s), *Stick Style* (1860s–1890s), *Shingle Style* (1880–1900), *Romanesque Revival* (1870s–1890s), and *Queen Anne* (1880s–1900). Most of these were heavily influenced by the Medieval period of European history. They tended to include polychromatic (multicolored) walls, strongly asymmetrical facades, steeply pitched roofs, occasional towers and turrets, and roof gables facing in multiple directions.

The Coconino County Courthouse exemplifies a small-town version of the *Romanesque Revival* style, still quite trendy for grand public buildings at the time of its construction. The style is immediately recognizable by a few dominant features found on this building, as heavy masonry construction, cavernous window and door openings, an impressive square tower, and most important, round-arched windows that reflect the Roman architecture of Europe. These arches are usually heavily emphasized through the use of stone materials or patterns different from the rest of the facade. The impressive arched entryway to this courthouse is probably its most distinguishing architectural feature.

Although the courthouse was constructed here in 1894, American architects had in fact experimented with the Romanesque styles as early as the 1840s and 1850s, especially for churches and public buildings. These early structures represented excellent attempts at replicating pre-Gothic, or Roman, architecture in Europe, commonly used for the impressive Romanesque cathedrals on that continent. The original Smithsonian Institution building on the Mall in Washington, D.C. is an outstanding example of this early era Romanesque Revival style in America.

Then along came the powerful influence of Henry Hobson Richardson during the 1870s and 1880s. Richardson is credited with creating a second interpretation of Romanesque Revival, ultimately making it a uniquely American style. Born in Louisiana, Richardson studied at Harvard prior to attending the prestigious Ecole des Beaux-Arts (School of Fine Arts) in Paris. After the Civil War, he returned to the United States and opened an office in New York, and finally in Boston. Unlike the earlier and more architecturally correct Romanesque Revival, Richardson borrowed his architectural ideas from numerous sources. For instance, he made use of the earlier Gothic Revival style's multi-colored walls, and his arches were frequently not Romanesque, but Syrian, an early Christian form in which the rounded arch originated from ground level and not from supporting pedestals.

In most cases in architectural history, the original prototype buildings—that is, the first true examples of a particular style—were grandiose projects attempted by cutting-edge, prominent architects, located within the most prominent cities. Similarly, Richardson's first dominant architectural work consisted of one building that established the style's future popularity. His 1872 design of Trinity Church in Boston won a prestigious architectural award at the time. If a unique piece of architecture becomes popular as did Trinity Church, its style then often diffuses to other cities, and eventually to small towns and rural areas. This process is referred to as *hierarchical diffusion*, whereby a cultural idea or element spreads down the urban hierarchy, from large urban centers to smaller towns. Often, 10 or more years were required during the nineteenth century for a particular style to reach rural areas and small towns, given that information about new trends and fashions required a longer time to make an impact elsewhere. This is precisely what happened in Flagstaff. An 1894 date for a Romanesque courthouse in northern Arizona is just about right, given the amount of time required for ideas and people to move westward a century ago. While the Romanesque style may have been losing favor in America's eastern cities, it remained popular in the rural West probably right up to the turn of the century.

The Romanesque revival style was however rarely used for houses. Instead, the style was favored for churches, university buildings, railroad stations, and courthouses like this one. Thus, towers were often a part of their designs, given the desired prominence of such public buildings. For instance, Richardson himself designed Pittsburgh's Allegheny County Courthouse and Jail (1884–1888). More than Trinity Church, it was this building that influenced many towns downstream of Pittsburgh along the Ohio River and points west. In the Midwest, and even as far as Arizona, numerous—albeit simplified—county courthouses can be found that are patterned after this building; Flagstaff's is clearly a variant of the Pittsburgh model. If there is a better example of cultural diffusion in Flagstaff, I don't know what it is.

Although its style borrows heavily from cultural precedents in the eastern United States, the courthouse's principal building material provides a distinct regional identity. Notice the reddish color of its thick stone walls. Along with the courthouse, numerous structures in town have been built with locally quarried rocks that represent the fascinating geology of the Colorado Plateau. The stone used for this building's construction is (and was) locally known as *Arizona Red*, because it consists of deep-red Moenkopi Sandstone (Jackson 1999). In her informative tour book of Flagstaff's stone buildings, Marie Jackson (1999) discussed the origins of this building material in Flagstaff. In 1888 a sandstone industry was established in town, and thick chunks of Moenkopi Sandstone were quarried about a mile east of downtown, near the current intersection of Enterprise Road and old Route 66. The distinctive stone became known throughout the West as Arizona Red, and the sandstone quarry served Flagstaff as the second most important industry after logging between 1889 and 1892.

Aside from its popular use in downtown Flagstaff between 1888 and 1900, Arizona Red was shipped by rail all over the West. More than 500 boxcar loads of the rock were shipped to Los Angeles for its own county courthouse construction in 1889. Some of the colorful rock actually made it onto buildings surrounding the plaza at Santa Fe, New Mexico. However, one physical concern with the stone was its relative softness; the stone holds up well in relatively dry climates like that of Flagstaff, but tends to deteriorate rather quickly in more humid and rainy locations. For instance, the Brown Palace Hotel in Denver and the Whittier Mansion in San Francisco "flaked, chipped, and disintegrated so badly as to require replacement in the case of the Brown Palace and years of repairs to the Whittier Mansion" (Jackson 1999, 38). Flagstaff continued to use the stone, however, through the 1940s, primarily for new buildings on the north campus of what is today Northern Arizona University.

As additional buildings were added to the courthouse complex, the styles changed as well, reflecting the architecture that was popular at the time. Early renovations and additions to the original courthouse were completed in 1925 and 1940, both times staying true to the original style of the building. However, it was the 1956 addition to the west side that has probably elicited the most community discussion, both then and now.

By the 1950s the Coconino County Board of Supervisors determined that they needed more office space. The end product was an International-style addition, sporting a very modern appearance: lots of plate glass, a flat roof, beige sandstone, and some apparently Native American—inspired designs just below the roof line, described by locals as "hieroglyphics". For the 1950s this addition was right in style, as many Americans and professional architects had fallen in love with "modern" architecture (Figure 29). Still, personal tastes in architecture and other cultural trends are highly subjective and therefore lend themselves to intense controversies and discussions—not everyone appreciated the 1956 addition. After its construction a county supervisor encountered a woman on the street who "entertained serious thoughts about using dynamite on the new addition."

Figure 29. Coconino County Courthouse with its modern-style addition, viewed here from San Francisco Street in 1998. This addition has been removed as part of the overall courthouse restoration project. (Photo: Author's collection)

Community discussion continued to focus on the appropriateness of the intrusive addition right up through the 1990s. "What stands today on the corner of Birch and San Francisco," claimed a *Daily Sun* news article in 1991, "is an architectural mish-mash that causes both residents and visitors alike to pause and shake their heads in dismay." In yet another touch of geographical irony, you can no longer view here the 1956 addition to the courthouse. The modern "mish-mash" has been replaced with the aforementioned grass lawn and a more historically sensitive addition on the northwest corner of the square.

Surviving on the northeast corner of the courthouse block is another International-style addition dating from the 1970s. As you walk eastward along Birch Avenue and continue around the block, you will view this modern addition to the county complex. In fact, as you walk counterclockwise around the block, you will be moving through a succession of architectural styles that represent the past century of architectural history in America. This city block itself, then, serves as a sort of architectural clinic. Making your way around to the corner of Cherry Avenue and San Francisco Street, you will see the latest additions to the county complex, on both sides of the street.

By 1993, the county was once again desperate for more space. With an increase in the county sales tax in September of 1993, the county hoped to raise $4.8 million to assist with future additions and renovations. By 1995 plans were well underway to construct a brand-new county facility to house various services such as the county assessor, treasurer and recorder, the public defender, the county attorney, and the elections department. Prior to the new building's completion in 1999, all of those offices had been housed in the old courthouse. This new and imposing county administration building can be seen just north of the courthouse at the corner of San Francisco Street and Cherry Avenue. Its own architectural significance is discussed later.

It is instructive to note why the county government decided to retain many of its services in the historic downtown area rather than moving out to the periphery of town. Both newspaper articles and personal interviews have helped to answer this question. For one thing, the decision was based on financial practicality. The factor of cost was significant, given that very little property had to be purchased for expansion just north of the old courthouse. Beyond cost, however, was the importance of being centrally located, still vital even in this day of suburban sprawl and decentralization. The fact is that the county had been rooted in the downtown area for a century; not only could patrons take care of their county business in one stop, but a sizeable number of law firms had already invested heavily in the downtown area specifically to be close to the courthouse. This clustering of professional firms in the downtown area plays out considerably on the landscape, as older commercial buildings and houses just north of the business district have been converted to lawyers' offices and other professional businesses.

Had the courthouse "up and left" the downtown, not only would some lawyers have to commute *from* the downtown—the direct reverse of the traditional pattern of suburban commuting—but a substantial economic base for the downtown area would be lost as well. Harold Watkins and his law firm, Aspey, Watkins & Diesel, exemplify the importance of proximity. When asked why he and his firm had decided to remain downtown and renovate a historic building, he explained without hesitation:

> The main attraction of this building for us is that it's cattycorner from the courthouse. And as lawyers, that means we're across the street from where we do most of our business, and where people expect us to be. I think a lot of professions tend to be in downtown areas, even if a lot of downtown areas at 6 o'clock turn out the lights and no one goes down there. We just thought, okay, here's a building that would give us room to expand, we could probably do something with it, and it's cattycorner to the courthouse. (Watkins 2001)

Not only has the courthouse and adjacent facilities attracted numerous county employees and an associated accumulation of lawyers and clients, but many of these people support downtown retail businesses as well. In total, they all increase the demand for downtown businesses and services. Whatever the primary motive was for staying downtown, the county's decision was a very wise one for the continued revitalization of the downtown area—Flagstaff's efforts to bring the community "back to the center."

Despite having a variety of the county's services and facilities located elsewhere in town, the base of operations for Coconino County still remains at the heart of the historic downtown. In one sense, the courthouse serves as a necessary anchor in the downtown area—that is, a major attraction that encourages other businesses and community activities nearby. According to County Supervisor Paul Babbitt, the county "kind of played the major pieces in the downtown and said, well, a mall effect is worthy of doing, so we'll anchor the west side of the downtown, we'll anchor the northern border with another public building, we'll eventually re-do this building, and we're doing the historic courthouse project" (Babbitt 2000).

This "anchor" approach to downtown revitalization is somewhat ironic. The idea for the indoor shopping mall in the 1960s and 1970s, with department stores typically anchoring each end, was not a new invention but a spin-off of America's traditional main street landscape—albeit more climate controlled and antiseptic. Today, the reverse has occurred. Main Street behaves more like a shopping mall with anchor establishments, business coalitions organizing downtown merchants much like a mall manager, and trendy building facades, streetlights, and sidewalk ornamentation decorating the streetscape. Main Street America has come full circle, a situation clearly evident in downtown Flagstaff.

STOP 7
OFFICE TOWER: BANK OF AMERICA BUILDING

This somewhat intrusive structure is the closest thing to a skyscraper that can be found in Flagstaff (Figure 30). Though not 100 stories tall, this office tower maintains all of the ingredients of the modern era skyscrapers built in larger metropolitan downtowns between the 1950s and 1970s. Constructed sometime between 1960 and 1962, depending on the source, the Bank of America building presented then as it does today a stark contrast with its older surrounding brick neighbors. What type of process could have been responsible for allowing this glass structure to intrude on an otherwise "historic" downtown business district?

Figure 30. The International-style Bank of America building on Birch Avenue. Located across the street from one another, the Courthouse and this building essentially represent the beginning and end respectively of the historic era of Flagstaff's downtown development, roughly between 1890 and 1960. (Photo: Author's collection).

Changing cultural values in America hold part of the answer. Roughly between the 1940s and 1970s, America looked to the future, reflecting our nation's rise as a global industrial and military power in which Americans took pride. Known as the *modern era* of American history, these decades were characterized primarily by a lack of interest in the past and a growing enthusiasm for anything that somehow represented economic and social progress, technology, and modernization. American lifestyles, along with the built environments that housed them, became dominantly utilitarian, ahistorical, and functional. The lackluster, cookie-cutter suburban ranch house of the 1950s and 1960s—with its origins in southern California—thoroughly embodied this ideology. A nation that had been transfixed with historical precedents through the Victorian era of the nineteenth century had come to view history instead as obsolete and of little value in the new, modern America. In this light, the architects of the Bank of America building most likely viewed their new creation here as an aesthetic improvement in an increasingly aging downtown.

Where did these modernist ideas come from? Like most cultural fads, modernism emerged within an initial core area, this time in Europe, and later diffused across that continent and into North America, where modernist ideologies hung on into the 1970s. Specifically, geographer David Lowenthal has traced the roots of modernism to northern Italy, where Italian cities such as Turin, Genoa, and Milan were transformed by industrialization in only a few short years. "The bizarre survival of antique and Renaissance forms in a landscape of radical technological change may help to explain Futurist manifestoes against the past" (Lowenthal 1985, 380). He continues, "Why 'waste all your best powers in this eternal and futile worship of the past?' asked the poet Marinetti." Marinetti boasted of "having 'provoked a growing nausea for the antique, for the worm-eaten and moss-grown' in seeking 'to free this land from its smelly gangrene of professors, archeologists, ciceroni and antiquarians." By the start of the twentieth century, the concept of history itself was resented in Europe for "binding men to antiquated institutions, ideas, and values" (Lowenthal 1985, 379). Many rejected the past because of its apparent opposition to the new and modern hopes spawned by the industrial revolution. Industrial society demanded the training of technicians rather than humanists, and modernist European societies increasingly favored originality over anything bound by established rules inspired by the past.

The concept of modernity formed the core of progressivist visions oriented to a technological future. *Progressivism*, as the modernist ideology is referred to, became central to urban planning after World War II. At the core of progressivist planning was the goal of reducing all urban spaces to their basic functions. According to Le Corbusier, a leading progressive architect following the war, the city should be conceived as a "machine for living"—a sort of tool that would enable continued progress and technological advance. Urban architects took this progressivist ideology to an extreme with their designs for buildings. To promote efficiency, the popular mantra became "form follows function." The primary goal when designing the interiors and exteriors of buildings was to "stand in the service of efficient work and movement in the new environment" (Gottdiener 1997, 30). Clean, geometric forms became the norm for modernist architecture, and the progressivist vision as a whole led to profound implications for America's cities and their urban landscapes.

The legacy of progressivist planning in America's post-war cities is profound. In Le Corbusier's 1940s vision for the city, transportation would be dominated by the expansion of automobile traffic and the superhighway. The chaotic and poorly planned city street would be abolished, and the construction of planned, high-rise apartment blocks would replace the former low-density housing. The practice of zoning would become paramount, so that work zones would be separated from residential zones, and residential zones would be separated from civic centers or recreational areas. And just as important, all symbols of tradition and sentimentality within the city would be eliminated.

Architects as well as planners came to adopt this progressivist thinking by launching a movement among architects around the globe. Known as the International School of architecture, their progressive movement was infused into every aspect of urban architectural design and planning throughout much of the world. Nearly every downtown center of nearly every major city around the globe "surrendered to the geometric rectangular boxes of high-rise buildings advocated by Le Corbusier. Superhighway construction demolished old neighborhoods and picturesque sections of the city in the obsessive promotion of 'efficient' automobile traffic" (Gottdiener 1997, 31). Although these ideals of progressivism had by the end of the 1970s apparently reached their peak of popularity and began a steady decline, they still appear to be driving many decisions affecting urban development to this day. The good citizens and city leaders of Phoenix, Arizona and its suburbs, for instance, still enjoy a somewhat regular pattern of celebrations for the opening of new freeways and lane additions throughout the metro area, apparently unphased by mounting evidence that freeway building can actually lead to increasing volumes of traffic (Duany, Plater-Zyberk, and Speck 2000).

A further implication of modernist thought was the rendering of all past architecture as obsolete. Only the creation of original, new architectural styles could adequately express society's growing interest in the future. Consequently, the spread of modernist ideology and its associated International School created a strong bias against almost any aspect related to the past. This notion of looking to the future coincided with America's building boom following the end of World War II. It is instructive to recall that—between the famous Stock Market Crash of 1929 and the end of the war in 1945—Americans had added very little to their built environment. Soldiers returning home from the war found a country that had changed little in nearly two decades. America's post-war human landscapes were still dominated by the construction and optimism of the 1920s. With the ideologies of modernism in full swing by the 1940s and 1950s, however, America's new landscapes came to be dominated instead by well-developed modernist and futurist tendencies that had not materialized earlier. Thus, the timing was nearly perfect for modernism to explode onto the American landscape with the coinciding post-war period of economic growth.

Trashing the historic while embracing the modern has held numerous implications for American society, still being felt today. Nearly two generations of modernism have led to the loss of much collective knowledge about the past. In 1985 David Lowenthal quoted Cecil Elsom as saying, "Forty years of the modern movement have left us with virtually no architects less than 60 years old who have been brought up with a knowledge of classical architecture—a knowledge necessary to cope with the current pressure of conservation of buildings" (Lowenthal 1985, 381). Primarily in the years between the 1920s and 1970s, therefore, America became mired in a sort of Dark Ages of modernist thought, where much historical knowledge and interest was apparently lost.

Modernism began to make its mark on the American landscape by the 1920s and into the 1930s through the use of "streamlining," whereby passenger railroad trains, buses, neon signs, and entire buildings were sheathed in a veneer of shiny chrome and metal to indicate America's new visions of a highly technological future. *Art deco* and *art moderne* styles became trendy during this early phase of the modern era, when buildings and their facades were adorned with simplified geometric shapes, smooth, rounded corners and rooflines, and chrome or copper trim. Some of this early modern architecture can still be seen in downtown Flagstaff; it is now celebrated somewhat ironically as being historic. Examples include the Federal building on San Francisco Street (art deco) and the retail building on the northwest corner of San Francisco and Route 66 (art moderne).

By the 1950s, those early modern stylistic attempts were being replaced throughout America by a new version of modern architecture known simply as *International style*, based on the aforementioned International School. In one sense, this style of architecture isn't really a style at all. The whole point of International-style was to exhibit the simplified forms of modernism without the use of excessive ornamentation and historical stylistic trends. A purposely simplified, functional blandness was the very trademark of this anti-style. As its name implies, its popularity rapidly spread and became international in scope, originating in Europe during the 1920s and making its way to America primarily following World War II. For all its popularity and incessant applications up through the 1970s, however, many Americans today can't wait to tear it down—a strong indication that the modern era, in a cultural sense, is now essentially over. Turning the table entirely from the teachings of the International School, this recent trend of viewing modern architecture as obsolete has materialized in Flagstaff's own downtown with the recent demolition of the county's 1956 addition to its courthouse, discussed earlier. Based on current plans for further downtown redevelopment projects, Flagstaff is likely to lose more of its modern era buildings in the future.

In smaller towns and cities throughout America, including Flagstaff, the modern era was often marked by the occasional construction of an International-style bank building or commercial storefront if the town was fortunate enough to be attracting new investment through the 1960s. Most often, however, the ideology of modernism and progressivist planning materialized in the human landscape by the eradication of older historic buildings in the downtown area. If these obsolete structures were not torn down under the guise of *urban renewal* (see Chapter 6, Stop 14) to make way for parking lots and the automobile, they were otherwise covered with some form of aluminum or plaster sheathing. During this period, storefronts were often remodeled or modernized while upper floors typically became vacant and converted to storage space. Aluminum siding also became popular during the 1950s and 1960s, as "siding salesmen worked their way through the small towns selling material with which one could enshroud the earlier more detailed, and now less fashionable, facades of the Victorian period" (Francaviglia 1996, 50).

Though much of this sheathing has been removed from buildings in Flagstaff's business district since 1990, some instances of these 1960s facelifts still remain visible to remind the community of its own modern period. Flagstaff's Orpheum Theater is one outstanding example, its modern facing still hiding its original, neoclassical-style façade underneath. Further, numerous modern era buildings constructed during the 1950s and 1960s still exist downtown to represent the progressivist era of development in Flagstaff. The most prominent example is the Bank of America building itself, basically a miniature version of the taller high-rise office buildings known as skyscrapers in larger, more metropolitan downtowns. You will encounter smaller modern-era buildings as you walk along Cherry Avenue and Beaver Street.

The Bank of America building has its roots in the International style of architecture first applied to skyscrapers in the early 1950s. In fact, one of the first International-style office towers, or skyscrapers, appeared very similar to this one, albeit a bit taller (21 floors). Known as the Lever House, this "vertical slab," as architectural historian Leland Roth described it, was constructed in New York City in 1951, ushering in a new era of skyscraper design. Roth's academic description of the Lever House might as well be a description of the Bank of America building seen here; save for their height, both are nearly identical in their form and function:

> At the north end he placed the vertical slab (office tower), sheathed in green glass and vitreous spandrel panels set in narrow metal mullions. The structural columns supporting this curtain wall are entirely hidden so that the wall is a nonsupporting skin. (Roth 1979, 278)

Although other trials with International style preceded it by a few years, the Lever House building became the first of many "anonymous glass boxes" that began to appear in every American city—most of which still exist today. New York's former World Trade Center was one of them, constructed in 1972; the Chicago Sears Tower is yet another. The Bank of America building seen here displays a small-town version, somewhat rare for a place of this size and population.

Before housing a Bank of America branch as it does today, this modernist glass box structure was constructed by Arizona Bank in 1962, according to Steve Vanlandingham (2001). One of three major banks operating in the state at the time (the others being Valley National Bank—now Bank One—and First National Bank), Arizona Bank built this as a branch building and, secondarily, as an investment. The "tower" includes five stories and some 36,000 square feet of office space, designed for leasing out to various companies. For some time, Arizona Bank itself operated on two floors, while the other three floors were rented out (Vanlandingham 2001).

Larger skyscrapers are operated the same way, in that the parent corporation often occupies several floors while renting out the remaining floor space to other businesses. The building was eventually purchased by a local Flagstaff developer, Steve Vanlandingham, who assisted Jim Babbitt with the design and implementation of Heritage Square. In a personal interview, Vanlandingham explained that he purchased the building in 1983 with a partner, given that he alone could not afford to own it outright. In true entrepreneurial spirit, he claimed that "it was strictly an investment. We thought we could operate it better than it had been before" (Vanlandingham 2001).

Asked how the Flagstaff community reacted to the new "glass box" in the downtown, Vanlandingham offered some insightful comments:

> Well, it was a very popular building. You can look around even today, there's nothing like it downtown. It's kind of ugly, it was that period of time in the 1950s and 1960s when architecture was bad, you know, in my opinion…if you had been here 10 years ago, you wouldn't have believed downtown, I mean there were a lot of aluminum facades that have been taken off, because that was the modern thing to do. They covered up some grand building fronts, it was a sin, actually. Anyway, that period of time was terrible, and I was always harassed in the years I was involved with that for having the ugliest building downtown…But I think when it was built

> it was considered to be progressive. Everybody thought that way: Let's get into the twentieth century, let's modernize. That's why they were putting those ugly facades on those great old buildings—that was just the thing to do. (Vanlandingham 2001)

In both form and function, the Bank of America building presents an excellent small-scale case study of larger metropolitan office towers. Whether despised or appreciated by residents and visitors, this structure was indeed progressive for its time, and it represents a distinct historical period of growth and change within Flagstaff's downtown area.

STOP 8
POSTMODERNISM: COUNTY ADMINISTRATION BUILDING

The new county administration building, occupying much of the city block north of Cherry Avenue, represents the latest trend in architectural styles and American aesthetic values (Figure 31). The historic "amnesia" brought on by modernist tendencies proved to be unsustainable in the long term. By the 1970s Americans began to revisit the past like they had not done since before World War I. The optimism for the future that so many Americans—and as a byproduct, their landscapes—embraced for nearly half a century had begun to fade. Some scholars associate this diminishing interest in modernism to a chain of unfortunate events including the Kennedy and King assassinations, an ugly war in Vietnam, and the oil "crisis" of the 1970s. Modernism came to be thought of less as representing a grand, new world and more as an inhumane and sterile way of life (Lowenthal 1985, 381). The past three decades have thus engendered a growing reaction against much of what modernism stands for. America's new efforts to reconnect with its own history are revealed primarily in the cultural worlds of art, literature, and architecture, and are embraced more each year in the field of urban planning. With its newfound resurgence of interest in all things historic, then, America has arguably shifted into a new, postmodern era of thought and ideology. As of this writing we are living in what can be considered an expanding postmodern period of American history, with no obvious signs that it will abate anytime soon.

Figure 31. New county administration building, sporting a distinctly postmodern façade. The architecture is designed to reflect historical styles, but it does not pretend to be a historic building. (Photo: Author's collection)

One symptom of giving up on history for so long, however, is rather amusing—or perhaps not, depending on one's perspective. That is, Americans can't quite seem to decide which histories to pay most attention to, and for what specific purposes. The result has been a seemingly jumbled eclecticism in which we appear to be equally interested in all historic eras, events, and places regardless of how it all fits logically together. Further, there may be very little logic to our historical interests at all. Thus, our focus on the past is, to use Lowenthal's words, "no longer an organized historical corpus but a pot-pourri of everything that ever happened, in which a 1930s cinema attracts the same degree and type of interest as the Parthenon" (Lowenthal 1985, 384).

The consequence for American architecture, and in turn our human landscapes, is a seemingly random adoption of historical styles and architectural features that often make no reasonable sense when integrated together. Postmodern architecture, then, has tended to reflect a general unfamiliarity with the past by the architects who are embracing it. Critics of postmodernism lament that the past is being treated as a "spare-parts warehouse," in that leaders of the architectural profession today appear to be trivializing the past rather than adopting it carefully for purposeful meaning (Lowenthal 1985, 383).

More than representing the latest architectural trends, postmodernism can be described generally as a complex cultural condition. In cities, this condition is often expressed not only within the built environment, but additionally in human patterns of consumption, in various aspects of social life, and in recent developments in philosophy and social theory (Smith 1994, 245). Just as postmodern architecture adopts a plurality of forms, textures, and styles, the notion of postmodernism includes "a collage of local traditions, historic references and vernacular allusion" (Smith 1994, 246). Within any given cityscape, therefore, one may find images, festivals, museums, marketplaces, architecture, and other social and physical spaces that combine haphazardly the cultural characteristics of multiple ethnic groups, social classes, and references to various historical periods. True postmodernism, then, promises to embrace the multiple voices and authors that represent a plurality of cultural and ethnic backgrounds and a wide-ranging variety of human interpretations, perspectives, and approaches to life.

The growth of the historic preservation movement coincided with the rise of postmodernist thinking by the 1970s and 1980s. The race to save everything that could be saved—regardless of its significance or historic appeal—was on. Americans for three decades have been groping around for any history, any connection to the past that they could obtain. Given that solid buildings are the most enduring aspects of a people's heritage, it is primarily buildings themselves that have gained the most attention of historic preservation enthusiasts. Likewise, the commodification of history for the purpose of economic redevelopment has gained prominence and social acceptance, as has the rampant act of theming and image making to tie historical meanings into today's postmodern landscapes.

According to Richard Francaviglia, historic preservationists on America's main streets were facing a dilemma by the 1990s. On the one hand was the resurgence of interest by well-meaning architects in historical building styles. However, those same architects were not necessarily respecting the existing historic fabric of the buildings lining the streets. Newly constructed, "hybrid, pseudo-historic" buildings have thus commonly been constructed adjacent to authentic older structures with the intent of making downtown look more historic (Francaviglia 1996, 53). This trend for architects, designers, and developers to intentionally make new buildings look old has met with much criticism from knowledgeable preservationists. In some cases, the addition of faux historical buildings to existing structures has even led to a building's removal from the National Register of Historic Places.

Consequently, one may find *historical excess* on Main Street today, to use Francaviglia's words. Not only are today's architects commonly designing new buildings to represent historical styles, but they often do so with grossly exaggerated stylistic features uncharacteristic of their more authentic, historical precedents. This practice is common in large city and small town alike. Further, architects have no problem with combining a grab bag of architectural features that represent two, three, or more historical eras that together make little temporal sense. Greek-revival columns can be found on Italianate-inspired buildings with Queen Anne turrets and federal-style entryways, wrapping more than two centuries of architectural history together into one seemingly confused, jumbled mess of a building.

But most important, Americans by and large like it, because it meets the expectations of their contemporary cultural values. Tasteful or not, this is the essence of postmodern architecture today, and historical excess has become a common element of America's postmodern landscapes. Flagstaff's downtown north of the tracks is no exception. The new county administration building seen here embodies well the very ideologies of the postmodernist movement, as does the replication of old city hall at Heritage Square, and the new addition to the county courthouse.

Coinciding with this renewed fascination with the past has been the related trend of theming and image making. In the postmodern metropolis, Americans are witnessing the emergence of what John Hannigan refers to as Fantasy City (Hannigan 1998). Towns and cities across the country have discovered the economic and social rewards of reinventing a tired central business district into a new center for tourism, entertainment, fun, and—above all—conspicuous consumption.

Through some 15 years of privately and publicly funded redevelopment efforts, Flagstaff's downtown has been transformed into a postmodern landscape—at once looking to its past while changing to meet the perceived needs and demands of the future. More than just architecture, entire geographic places can be described as postmodern due to their rampant eclecticism and their multiplicity of images and meanings. This variety of no-rules eclecticism is typically manifested in the landscape through a seemingly disorganized concoction of contrived themes, images, ideas, and symbols that point to a wide variety of historical periods, social processes, and local identities.

Within Flagstaff's new, postmodern downtown, for instance, can be found benches in Heritage Square that combine images and relics associated with the heritage of the railroad and the industrial revolution with those of Arizona's prehistoric Indian tribes. In the summer months the theme of sports reveals itself in banners that announce the arrival of the Arizona Cardinals NFL football team for their annual summer camp, creating an identity with big-city sports entertainment.

In addition to the expanding array of statues, artifacts, buildings, banners, and signage that remind one of the railroad and logging industries in Flagstaff, the imagery of U.S. Route 66 provides yet another important identity. The keen observer may notice that Santa Fe Avenue is no longer "Santa Fe Avenue." The street signs for this thoroughfare have been relabeled "Route 66" to signify its role in the community's collective heritage. Although certainly a part of the fabled cross-country route, locals recall that Santa Fe Avenue had never before been officially designated locally as Route 66.

The postmodern variety that characterizes downtown continues with a host of environmental themes and images, including references to the San Francisco Peaks; this is, after all, the "Mountain Town," according to Flagstaff's Citizen-of-the-Century, the late Platt Cline (1994). Quaint retail business signs sometimes include images of the Peaks, and in Heritage Square one can find a stone monument that represents the entire geologic cross section of the rock strata found within the Colorado Plateau.

Then there are the ethnic and cultural themes, including various American Indian imagery on merchandise and signage. In 2000, one could further experience eating venues that more or less reflected the cultural ways of Australia, Mexico, Germany, Ireland, Italy, China, France, Belgium, and Thailand.

In one sense, the locale of downtown Flagstaff represents yet another intersection of local and global space. Its foods at least pretend to reflect a variety of cultures from around the globe, and the heavily branded merchandise found there is produced in any number of countries outside the United States. The pedestrian-friendly elements of the new streetscape itself—the brick sidewalks, shade trees, benches, information kiosks, and "olde" streetlights—all reflect not a local uniqueness but a standardized, text-book landscape of North American planning that follows the latest philosophies of postmodern urban design. Further, no less than eight new downtown businesses in 2000 focused on global communications related to cell phone, Internet, computer, and Web-based services. Like it or not, this is the trend for America's newly reinvented, reimagined postmodern downtowns. Consequently, a local sense of place will necessarily be found in conjunction with a wide variety of global processes, images, and functions.

Of course, this image making is embedded within the most prominent, omnipresent theme of all, that of "historic old-town." The continuing preservation and revitalization of older structures throughout the downtown area is arguably what provides downtown's local character and sense of place.

Information from city directories can indicate how retail and service businesses adopt particular themes. It is common within tourism business districts for establishments to invoke specific themes or images for use in their names. The business name itself, and thus its associated theme, is usually manifested through the use of the business signage, storefront window displays, and advertisements in local media. I used Flagstaff city directories to determine the extent of theming by local businesses. I created a comprehensive list of all business names that existed in the historic downtown area north of the tracks for each decade starting with 1960. I then counted the number of businesses that had attached some theme to their names, and compiled a list of those general themes (Table 1).

Table 1. Themes in retail business names, downtown Flagstaff

	2000	1990	1980	1970	1960
Heritage Themes:					
Historic or Old Town	3	1	1	1	0
Railroad	1	0	0	0	0
Route 66	0	0	1	0	1
Regional Themes:					
Mountains	10	6	2	2	1
Environment	10	7	0	2	2
Ethnic or Cultural	9	9	9	4	3
Grand Canyon	5	2	2	2	2
New Age	2	3	0	0	0
West or Southwest	1	1	2	2	5
Northern Arizona	0	1	3	5	4
Total Themes	41	30	20	18	18

The beauty of city directories for completing research is found in their format. Unlike typical phone books, these directories are organized by street, so that one can create a rather comprehensive geographical listing of all businesses or residences along a particular thoroughfare. I have accomplished precisely that for the historic district of downtown Flagstaff, bounded by Humphreys and Agassiz Streets on the west and east, and by Santa Fe Avenue (Route 66) and Cherry Avenue on the south and north. Though the information found within city directories is not flawless, it is accurate enough to provide meaningful analysis to indicate how businesses have changed over the years.

Most noticeable is the trend toward increased theme adoption, from 18 themed businesses in 1970 to 41 themed businesses in 2000 (Table 1). Such an increase in business theming is quite typical of emerging tourism business districts, where tourist-oriented businesses are attempting to identify themselves with the dominant attractions of the place. More intriguing is the eclecticism, or wide variety of themes manifested in various business names throughout the historic district. Instead of adopting one dominant theme, the merchants have demonstrated their independent nature by adopting a wide array of images and identities.

Although imagery associated with railroad heritage, U.S. Route 66, and historic preservation appears to dominate the landscape of downtown, business owners have apparently done their own image making, reflecting the free spirit of capitalism and American individuality. Planners and designers of the evolving downtown streetscape may have determined in advance which identities should appear; there is little evidence, however, that the business community has bought into these crafted themes. Instead, they have adopted various *ethnic and cultural*, *mountain-environment*, and to a lesser extent, *Grand Canyon* identities. Only one business in 2000 invoked railroad imagery in its name, the Late for the Train coffee shop. And, not one business identified itself with the railroad in any of the previous decades. Further, those making use of Northland or Northern Arizona in their names have actually disappeared entirely from downtown, though as many as five businesses used this regional identity in 1970.

Instead, the mountain theme was used more than any other for business names, the latest addition being Mountain Sports, across from the old Babbitt Brothers Department Store on San Francisco Street. Also, these businesses most often used generic mountain names, rather than identifying specifically with the San Francisco Peaks. Aside from the distinct mountain theme, numerous businesses used related identities in a catch-all category called *environmental.* This general theme appeared through various references to the physical environment of northern Arizona or the Southwest, including snow, pine, desert, sage, Painted Desert, aspen, creek, monsoons, rain, Mogollon, and plateau. Combined with the mountain theme, these environmental identities constituted the bulk of symbolic images adopted by downtown businesses in 2000.

Explaining the use of these themes presents a greater challenge. More thorough research is necessary to determine why characteristics of the natural environment have been adopted by so many downtown businesses. Most likely, such research will require an extensive survey of business owners themselves to determine how and why particular business names were created.

To hazard an educated guess, however, I imagine that business owners are most likely to associate themselves more closely with the outdoors because Flagstaff's tourism industry is directly related to outdoor activities, reflecting the region's natural amenities. For many visitors and local residents alike, it is Flagstaff's natural environment that provides the community's strong sense of place. Some visitors are explicitly interested in communing with the history of downtown—and others arrive specifically to enjoy some imagined nostalgia of Route 66—but Flagstaff as a distinct place sells itself dominantly as a sort of environmental paradise. It is not surprising, then, that certain businesses would promote the consumption of their products or services by creating symbolic associations between their establishments and the environmental characteristics of northern Arizona.

This explanation for the increasing proliferation of themes in Flagstaff's downtown is supported by sociologist Mark Gottdiener, who has argued that the act of theming is the result of businesses hoping to increase their profit margins. According to Gottdiener, themes are used as direct marketing appeals. "They reduce the product to its image and the consumer experience to its symbolic content" (Gottdiener 1997, 74). The purpose of all commercial businesses and places dependent on consumption of some kind is the *realization of capital*—the selling of goods or services with the primary aim of making a profit. These places cannot afford in many cases, however, to depend entirely on the intrinsic, mundane functions of their products. Instead, "businesses must disguise the instrumental exchange relation of money for a commodity as another relation between commercial place and the consumer" (Gottdiener 1997, 74). In this way, ordinary products are provided with symbolic imagery to create a new and meaningful association between the product and the consumer. The Exxon Corporation's slogan, "Put a tiger in your tank," for instance, attaches a symbolic appeal to otherwise ordinary gasoline. Likewise, the placement of televisions tuned to ESPN and sports memorabilia on the walls of a Ruby Tuesday restaurant create a unique symbolic and entertaining environment in which to eat otherwise mundane American fare. All sorts of themed environments can be found in America today, including restaurants, gas stations, motels, airports, historic business districts, city parks, theme parks, shopping malls, and even temporary local festivals.

What can be viewed downtown, then, are themes and images that perhaps reflect two co-existing values, each materialized somewhat differently in the landscape. On the one hand, the economic-related value of *consumption* commands top priority for local businesses attempting to capitalize on the local tourist trade. On the other hand is the more cultural-based value of local *heritage*, for which images of the railroad, Route 66, and restored historic buildings serve well (Paradis 2002b).

Consequently, two dominant types of theming are exhibited downtown, each predominantly reflecting either economic or cultural values. For those individuals involved with the planning process for downtown redevelopment, aspects of local heritage figured more prominently than did that of consumption. Granted, the creation of various themes associated with Flagstaff's heritage has largely been the work of a vigorous downtown growth coalition—one that is primarily interested in reinvigorating the local downtown economy. Still, the aim of downtown planners was more directly associated with creating dominant images for the district as a whole than for one particular business. When describing the process of designing Heritage Square, for instance, Jim Babbitt explained how he had strongly suggested constructing a building there that directly replicated the architectural style of Flagstaff's old city hall. About the building, Babbitt explained:

> It's almost an exact replica of the first city hall, on a grand, larger scale. The city hall was just down the street on Leroux, where there is now an empty parking lot. It got torn down in the 1970s. It was a small building, but that brick and Romanesque archway and all that detailing [were appealing]. So it's almost an exact copy of the first city hall, an expanded version. Then Main Street picked up on the idea, and everybody liked going back to heritage, and using the heritage theme for the plaza and all that. (Babbitt 2001)

Similarly, city project manager Rick Barrett described the importance of planning for particular themes when the city hired consultant Nore Winter of Boulder, Colorado to craft the downtown streetscape plan. Mentioning the process of theming by name, Barrett recalled:

> In this case we wanted someone to guide our development of the downtown area. We didn't know what we wanted. We didn't know if we needed curb swellings or street trees or benches, the amenities that would be involved in the downtown area. And it's important to establish that at an early point in time. There's a lot of identity associated with this. Theme—you know, we had to

> develop what Flagstaff's theme would be. Some of this stuff sounds silly, but these are the sorts of things for which Main Street and the city of Flagstaff recognized that we needed to have a plan. (Barrett 2001)

In the business of downtown redevelopment, theming is anything but silly. The creation of meaningful identities for a business district on the rebound constitutes nothing less than the reinvention of a traditional commercial space, both its functions and meanings. To recall, this practice mirrors the developments taking place in America's metropolitan settings. The urban economies of these traditional downtown cores are now becoming more rooted in heritage, tourism, sports, culture, and entertainment. Flagstaff's downtown growth coalition has apparently plugged in to this new postmodernist ideology.

The new county administration building is nothing if not eye-catching. Like most postmodern buildings, the façade of this one appears smooth, machined, and sharp—a product of the latest building technologies. Still, its round-arched windows and brickwork, in addition to its multi-colored façade, reflect Victorian era building styles without entirely replicating them. In this way, contemporary architects who design such buildings are embracing the past and the future simultaneously.

It is quite a challenge to find two postmodern buildings that look alike, given that one characteristic of the postmodern style lies specifically in each building's own unique distinctiveness. Consequently, the postmodern style has become a favorite of corporations with their sprawling suburban office parks or metropolitan headquarters. Most often found clustered around suburban freeway interchanges in what Joel Garreau (1988) has termed America's "edge cities," these sparkling, sleek postmodern corporate buildings themselves serve as important signs, or advertisements, for their corporate owners. Each building is distinctive and makes use of an eclectic array of stylistic features, intended to stand out apart from the other buildings surrounding it. Corporations hope not only that passing motorists from the freeway will be impressed with their edifices, but that they will also make instant mental associations between the building and the company housed inside. For Flagstaff's part, the town is slowly accumulating a modest number of postmodern buildings as the community continues to grow. In one sense, a new architectural "layer" is being added to Flagstaff's human landscape.

Notice that the new county administration building is set into the side of a hill, the same hill surmounted by all north-south streets in the downtown. From here, you will see how San Francisco Street gradually becomes steeper as it passes the new county building on its west side. Physical geography is the reason. You are looking at the leading edge of a lava flow that covered the north side of the present-day downtown area about 6 million years ago (Jackson 1999). When molten lava reaches the surface, it cools and hardens into a dark, volcanic rock known as *basalt*. In a more regional context, you are standing on the literal edge of the San Francisco volcanic field, which includes some 600 cinder cones, the elongated dome volcano of Mt. Elden, numerous lava flows, and the impressive stratavolcano known as the San Francisco Peaks.

When the downtown street grid was planned and created by the railroad in the 1880s, little regard was given to this physical feature—the streets were to be oriented to the railroad regardless of what natural features got in their way. This typical disregard for physical terrain reflects a common American ideology that has been with us for generations. That is, humans (Americans) can "conquer geography" with superior technologies and ingenuity. The implication is usually the creation of steep roads, challenging building lots, and expensive hillside construction. The new county building is yet another case in point, with the hillside literally dug out to create the necessary flat lot for construction.

STOP 9
STREETSCAPE: TRANSITION ON CHERRY AVENUE

Scan the sidewalk areas on both sides of Cherry Avenue, and you will notice that the landscapes are different in some ways. For instance, on the left (south) side, part of the sidewalk is brick, whereas there is no brick on the north side. The brick represents one of the recent changes to the downtown, as you are now walking along the northern edge of the downtown historic district. However, just because the city decided to create this artificial boundary does not mean that the landscapes outside of this boundary are any less historic than those inside. What it does mean is that you are witnessing the role of centralized authority. Specific boundaries of the historic district were drawn on a map by local planners and consultants in the early 1990s, and redevelopment efforts have been focused within these boundaries.

The term *district* connotes a geographical space, or a certain area of land. It is most widely used, however, as an administrative convenience, especially for local governments. Basically, a district describes an area subject to various regulations by one or more agencies in a locale. The number of districts nationwide, if we include school districts, has exploded since the early 1970s. Between 1977 and 1987, their numbers grew by 14 percent, and by 39 percent since 1972 (Clay 1996). And their purposes vary widely, as described by Grady Clay (1996, 75):

> There are districts military, magisterial, and judicial; districts metropolitan, suburban, and agricultural. They have been organized to fight fires, to control soil erosion, to occupy foreign territory, and to protect historic areas. They are set up to supply electric power; to manage, and sometimes build, waste and sewage plants, parks, roads, forests, beaches, drainage, irrigation, and other public works...Unknowing, travelers cross hundreds of local districts,

> their borders mostly unmarked, except for the ubiquitous green roadside signs representing 2,994 soil conservation districts.

Some districts, such as historic districts, can be easily detected within the landscape. Most cities and towns since the 1970s have sought to protect their historic resources by officially declaring various chunks of human landscape as "historic," as city leaders have done in Flagstaff. Today's downtown historic district—the northern boundary of which you stand at now—is easily recognized by its unifying landscape features: brick sidewalks, pedestrian *swells* at the intersections, information kiosks, benches, shade trees (fortified with 6-foot iron fences), an army of "olde tyme" pedestrian lampposts (206 of them), and a set of uniform forest-green traffic signals. You have probably noticed many of these features as you walked through the bowels of the historic downtown. The pedestrian lights and brick sidewalks are present along this transect of Cherry Avenue. All of these elements clearly indicate that a certain administrative district is in place here, and that this downtown area has been undergoing a local process of economic redevelopment.

Together, these pedestrian-friendly items constitute an entirely new look for Flagstaff's historic business district, the latest phase of this place's evolution. The trend today throughout America is a combination of historic preservation and downtown redevelopment—that is, an attempt to revitalize the local economies of ailing business districts through the conservation of historic resources, especially older buildings. The new sidewalks, benches, trees, lampposts, and other elements are all part of Flagstaff's new downtown "streetscape," as it is often called, the primary purpose of which is to make the historic district more inviting for pedestrians. If pedestrians are attracted back to downtown, the theory goes, local businesses will benefit as consumption of retail goods and services increases; in turn, investments in downtown properties will increase, along with revenues collected from property and sales taxes. So far, this process has worked well for Flagstaff's own historic business district, having reclaimed itself from the derelict place it was a decade earlier.

The new look of the downtown streetscape as it appeared by the end of 1995 led to much controversy among local residents and city leaders. Aside from losing some 60 on-street parking spaces due to the new sidewalk swells at intersections, the pedestrian lights themselves became an issue. Some locals complained that the lights are inauthentic and standardized, making Flagstaff's downtown look like that of Tucson, Phoenix, or elsewhere. Some people have decried the streetscape as representing the continued trend to "Californicate" Flagstaff. According to these folks, the historic downtown should not merely imitate those of other places, but should reflect Flagstaff's own uniqueness and distinctiveness. On the flip side, others have praised the streetscape with its standardized lights, given its success at unifying the downtown and making it more attractive and appealing to pedestrians once again.

In fact, the streetscape is indeed standardized, just as Main Street business districts have always been. The lights, benches, and other items were ordered from a catalog from which a limited variety of lamppost styles and streetscape features could be chosen. As city engineer Rick Barrett (2001) stated, the streetscape and its elements are "text-book," representing the latest trends in pedestrian-oriented planning for revitalizing older business districts throughout America. The aim is not to represent the historic distinctiveness of a particular community, but to *pedestrianize* a public space, to make it more appealing for walking and—especially—for shopping. That is why downtown business and property owners voted to shell out more than $2 million in extra taxes to pay for it all.

That the standardized lampposts were designed to appear historic is no accident; it has roots in American culture and early twentieth century technological innovations in electric lighting. The single globe atop a post, which describes the style of lamp used for Flagstaff's new streetscape, represents the popular style of lighting used to illuminate downtown city streets throughout the nation during the 1920s (Jakle

2001). In fact, our nation's current love affair with ornamental lampposts represents the second wave of adoption of such lighting, not the first. The first began in 1905 when Los Angeles lit up its Broadway Avenue with lamps directly imitating New York City's own Great White Way.

New York's Broadway was dubbed the "Great White Way" by O. J. Gude, whose company pioneered the street's first electric signs. Thus, Broadway became the first American streetscape to make use of dazzling electric "sky signs" hung on the facades of commercial buildings, supplemented with brilliant, ornamental street lamps to light up the city's most famous and bustling thoroughfare. Glowing first in white light, then with multiple colors in later years, Broadway's "magnificent signs defined the street as an icon representative not only of the city but also of America, comparable to the city's skyline and its most important landmarks, such as the Statue of Liberty," wrote geographer John Jakle (2001, 195).

It was on New York's Broadway that the early electric advertising signs were perfected, and then eventually replicated in other cities. The Great White Way (and its inclusive Times Square) became not only New York's leading tourist attraction prior to the Great Depression but also a new cultural icon for the nation. As such, Broadway inspired "white way" lighting projects in countless other cities and towns desiring to liven up their own downtown business districts with electric brilliance.

Los Angeles was the first city to install replicated white way lighting, in 1905. Some 135 lampposts were each topped with six small glass globes surrounding one larger globe in the middle. "Broadway burst into bloom last evening," reported the *Los Angeles Times*, "with the touch of a magic wand and in a garden of rare color" (Jakle 2001, 227). In a classic case of hierarchical diffusion, other large cities soon followed the lead of Los Angeles, then countless smaller cities and towns did so in turn. St. Louis transformed its downtown in 1908, and Atlanta in 1910. In that city, the *Atlanta Constitution* assured its readers that the new white way lighting on Peachtree Street would be "effective, but not glaring." Further, the lighting would illuminate all buildings "top to bottom," and would "cast over the entire street a radiance which will be soft, brilliant and without casting a single shadow" (Jakle 2001, 228). Indianapolis followed suit in 1912, as did Cleveland and Milwaukee in 1915, to name just a few.

Communities adopting white way lighting treated their new illumination of downtown as another form of consumption, a fact realized early on by business associations and elected city officials. In most cases, business associations themselves promoted and even funded white way lighting, for several economic reasons. With the new lights showcasing street-side businesses and their buildings, merchants hoped to expand business hours and increase sales, property owners hoped to realize higher rents, and city officials certainly viewed their updating efforts in downtown as yet another feather in their caps, perhaps to be reflected in the next local election. Indeed, the introduction of white way lighting to small-town main streets was a sign of progressiveness. From a political economy perspective, then, a small town's choice to create its own miniature Great White Way was hailed as good for business, and excellent overall for the local growth coalition.

Throughout the 1990s America has witnessed a sort of White Way revival, as replicas of the popular lampposts have been reappearing on downtown streets from coast to coast. The goal, once again, is to liven up Main Streets at night, and the lighting is often integrated into a larger package of streetscape features designed by urban planners to entice pedestrians into the redeveloped downtown, both night and day. As you walk along Cherry Avenue and back into the heart of the downtown, imagine how these street scenes must appear differently at night, with the brilliant glare of the lamps complementing the host of colorfully glowing storefront signs. Welcome to Flagstaff's "Little Broadway."

How did the city of Flagstaff pay for its new downtown streetscape? In short, city leaders and planners created a new district, allowed by the state of Arizona through enabling legislation. The sole purpose of the district, known officially in Arizona as a *Special Improvement District*, or SID, is to levy a special tax for property owners within the specified district boundaries. After approval by the city council in a local ordinance, an additional property tax could be collected. Each commercial property owner in the district—anyone who owns commercial buildings, parking lots, and so forth—would be required after 1995 to pay an additional annual tax for a period of 10 years to pay for the streetscape improvements, to the tune of more than $2 million total. The boundaries of the proposed taxing district, or SID, ultimately included the area bounded by Humphreys Street on the west, Elden Street on the east, Cherry Avenue on the north, and Route 66 fronting the tracks.

The process to determine the amount of taxes assessed to property owners for the SID was no walk in the park. First, a uniform formula was devised to determine specific tax assessments for each downtown property. This process alone was contentious, in that numerous factors had to be considered. The formula first included a base rate for the property itself, with an additional rate calculated for the amount of square footage, street frontage, alley frontage, and perimeter frontage. Owning a property on the perimeter of the district actually lowered the rate; presumably, properties that were "landlocked" within the district boundaries would benefit the most from the downtown improvements. Further, several levels of enhancements were planned for different parts of the district, so three base rates were calculated for each of the three enhancement zones.

That various property owners viewed their assessments as unfair was no surprise. One Flagstaff realtor, for instance, owned four downtown properties, the assessments for which he viewed as far too high. The assessment for one property alone was calculated to be $40,000 over 10 years for his 21,300-square-foot parking lot. His other parcels of land along Route 66 would cost him an additional $16,000. "They should have looked at the value of the buildings on the property," he claimed in the *Daily Sun*, because "if you look around, I'm paying the same tax as some of the most expensive buildings downtown, and I just don't have the same income that they have."

After adjusting and reworking the assessment formula so that the greatest number of downtown property owners would approve, the city of Flagstaff councilmembers voted unanimously in favor of "an intent to form a downtown improvement district" in the north downtown area. By this point in the process the area south of the tracks had been eliminated from the plan. "When the north downtown area has been refurbished," explained one *Daily Sun* reporter, "the city and the Main Street Flagstaff Foundation have plans to do the same with the south downtown, creating another special improvement district there." Following the city's vote, letters were sent to all property owners in the new district, explaining that they would be given 15 working days to protest the SID in writing. This process was not to be decided by a simple vote of property owners; instead, a no vote could only be recorded with a letter of protest submitted to the city within 15 working days. Therefore, any property owner not submitting an opposition letter would be counted as a yes vote.

Additionally, the votes did not count equally among the property owners. Those who owned multiple parcels of land were allowed to cast separate votes (of opposition) for each of them. The votes were also weighted proportionally according to a given property's amount of frontage within the district. Given these rules, provided by state enabling legislation, the district would not take effect if more than 49 percent of owners with street-front property opposed it. Stated in another way, if more than half of the district's 14,810 feet of property frontage was assigned a no vote by its collective owners, the district would be defeated. Given the wide range in the amount of property and frontage owned by groups and individuals downtown, it was conceivable that a few large property owners could control much of the decision.

Maury Herman was one such owner who wielded considerable influence. Maury's grandparents had come to Flagstaff in 1898, following what he described as a rather common migration pattern for Jewish families at the time. He explained, "Most Jewish immigration is associated with urban areas, but in fact there's a big rural component too. The typical pattern would be to get a stake and go to a small town and try to make some money and try to move to a bigger city. My family followed that pattern" (Herman 2001). Upon arriving in Flagstaff, his family became established in the downtown area by renting space for a business and eventually constructing their own building. Having made a successful start for themselves, they ultimately moved to Los Angeles, where Maury himself grew up. Still, his grandparents continued to maintain several investments downtown.

In the mid-1980s, he and his wife decided to relocate to Flagstaff, because of what appeared to be his lingering sense of place for the community. "I was really interested in the community, I felt connections here. As with many people who move here, it's sort of an ideal small town. My dad was born here, and my family had kept these buildings. I had come here every year throughout my life and have quite an oral history, and I have a lot of documentation about my family" (Herman 2001). Through one investment at a time, Maury became one of the larger property owners in the downtown area and a key role player in the redevelopment initiatives. When it came time for the downtown property owners to vote on the SID, Maury held approximately 13 percent of the total vote, given that voting would be weighted proportionally to a property owner's frontage. When asked to explain the eventual passage of the SID, Maury commented somewhat humorously, though truthfully that "without too much exaggeration, I could say they had me, and that helped them. I had 13 percent of the vote because of the property I owned. I mean, if you win with 63 percent and somebody has 13 percent of the vote…" (Herman 2001). Maury Herman and other prominent landholders downtown clearly held the key to the successful implementation of the streetscape project.

In an attempt to convince all downtown property owners to support the SID, the city and the Main Street Flagstaff Foundation lobbied heavily for support. Most significant, the city and Main Street together had planned to hold a series of special meetings with property owners during the period between January and March of 1993, leading up to the 15-day protest period. Rather than simply calling one large meeting for all owners, however, those leading the redevelopment effort did something extraordinary in the political sense; every property owner in the proposed district was scheduled to meet individually with five community leaders, namely Jeffe Aronson (director of the Main Street Flagstaff Foundation), Jim Babbitt (president of Main Street's board of directors), Melanie Boone (City Beautification coordinator), Harley Grosvenor (a city engineer), and David Wilcox (city manager). Votes for the district would thus be earned one owner at a time. By meeting with property owners prior to announcing the city council's planned intent to form the SID, Aronson claimed in the *Daily Sun* that the city would "fix the problems before we get to the vote."

The downtown coalition, embodied at this point by the five persons mentioned above, maintained the hefty goal of meeting with no less than 67 property owners in the proposed district. More than one meeting was held with some property owners. The four government organizations owning property downtown were not allowed to vote for the project, though they could choose to participate in the district's funding if they desired. Further, a few residential property owners located within the proposed district were not included in the assessment plan. According to Dave Wilcox, whose office served as the meeting place, the meetings held three basic purposes: (1) to explain to each property owner how their tax assessment was calculated, (2) discuss the plans for changes in the "physical infrastructure" of the area and immediately outside their property, and (3) to solicit questions and concerns of the property owners so that changes could be made if necessary (Wilcox 2001).

In the months leading up to the final vote by property owners, Flagstaff's two primary interest groups competed for community attention and support. In strong support of the SID, of course, was the downtown coalition, with Main Street and its director, Jeffe Aronson, leading the charge. In opposition to the plan were the members of Voters of Flagstaff, who were still attempting to earn a community referendum on the issue. Both community interest groups faced uphill battles, but for different reasons. Although Main Street enjoyed the financial and political backing of the Flagstaff City Hall and other influential business people who owned property downtown, the organization still faced two daunting challenges. First, Main Street and its allies needed to convince enough of the 74 property owners in the proposed district (53 local, 17 outside Flagstaff, and 4 government agencies) to vote in favor of the SID—simply by not submitting letters of protest—by April 20 of 1993. This would be the last day on which dissenting property owners could effectively vote no. At the same time, Main Street struggled to educate the community—and the Voters of Flagstaff—about its true intentions and the presumed benefits of the project. On the other side, the Voters of Flagstaff faced an equally tough battle to win their intended goal of having the community decide on the SID through a referendum, given that the primary economic and political influences were not on their side.

This type of inter-community conflict is common in any town or city faced with major changes in some aspect of its human landscape. Many such issues often become simplified in the media and community discourse so that there appears to be two sides to the issue; the reality is usually much more complex. Rather than a bipolar debate where one side promotes downtown redevelopment and the other side opposes it, however, the distinction between them was not that simple. The complexity of the entire issue surrounding redevelopment was brought further to light through the writing of two guest columnists in the *Daily Sun* approximately 1 month prior to the final vote on SID. In the first article, its author, Jeffe Aronson, expressed as much frustration with trying to understand the motives of Voters of Flagstaff as he did excitement over the proposed downtown plan. "I often wonder," wrote Aronson in the *Daily Sun*, "if what Main Street 'does' is really relevant to most people in the rest of the community…It's difficult for me to determine this objectively, mainly because I've been very directly involved with downtown ever since I moved here ten years ago." He went on to question the motives of the the group: "I believe in this cause and it's potential positive effect in my adopted community. Nevertheless, when groups of people like the so-called 'Voters of Flagstaff' (I hate that name, I mean, *I'm* a voter of Flagstaff, but yet, now, I'm *not*!) attack what I'm doing through Main Street, it makes me wonder."

In a guest column intended to answer Jeffe Aronson, several leaders of Voters of Flagstaff attempted to clarify their intended purpose and goals. In part they maintained that "Mr. Aronson obviously did not read our Initiative Measure to be circulated either. It does not state that we are opposed to the millions of dollars in 'Capital Improvement Projects' to be spent in downtown Flagstaff. It does not state that we are opposed to the $3.2 million in tax dollars to be spent on this 'Special Improvement District'. It does not state that we are opposed to the revitalization of downtown Flagstaff." Instead, the Voters of Flagstaff believed "that the citizens of Flagstaff should be allowed to vote on this matter." They further explained the group's origin about a year earlier "to discuss what we could do to improve our city government, state government, and business conditions both citywide and specifically in east Flagstaff."

Therefore, according to what is found in their guest column, the Voters of Flagstaff were less opposed to the idea of downtown redevelopment and much more concerned with the larger issue of the ability of local government to gain increased powers and to possibly abuse that power.

This issue serves as an excellent case in point—that enabling legislation, whether at the federal or state level, is most often constraining as well as enabling. It works both ways. Perhaps the city, Main Street, and interested local property owners would have taken an entirely different path toward a redevelopment initiative had there been more flexibility at the state level of control. Certainly, other community issues may have surfaced in place of those raised by the Voters of Flagstaff. With the process of redevelopment controlled more or less by the state, it is clear how such enabling legislation—one component of centralized authority—can exert tremendous influence on the processes through which human landscapes are transformed.

Despite a last-minute effort by 17 downtown property owners to protest the SID, the district passed by 63-37 percent. SID supporters were pleased, including the city, which was hoping for at least a 60 percent approval. Following the vote of property owners, the city council was still required to vote one more time to officially implement the SID. Had the vote been closer to 50 percent both ways, there was a chance that the city would have rejected the whole proposal due to insufficient support (Herman 2001). In all, the 37 percent opposition was represented by a total of 28 protests, not a surprise for those monitoring the vote. City project coordinator Melanie Boone stated in the *Daily Sun* that "we're fairly well pleased…It's kind of what we expected." The bulk of protests came from property owners not involved with retail sales. Several comments protested the plan's emphasis on foot traffic, from which professional businesses would benefit little. One opponent commented that "downtown Flagstaff could use a kick start, however it should not come solely in the way of expensive window dressing."

That the SID had passed was certainly no accident. Some geographers and others might attribute the SID's success to strong, local pride for downtown and to individual cultural values that supported a perceived sense of place for downtown. Although these factors were important, it was more the result of a planned and calculated effort by various groups and individuals operating within our political economic system of capitalism. On the political side, the state of Arizona provided through its legislation a decisive advantage for the interests of larger property owners by allowing a vote that was weighted proportionally to the amount of property frontage owned. More than that, the state did not require a community referendum to pass a SID, but instead placed the decision-making power with the property owners themselves. As with larger cities, it is the property and business owners who stand to lose the most on their investments downtown should the central business district (CBD) falter as the traditional commercial hub. It stands to reason that the bulk of membership and leadership within the Main Street Flagstaff Foundation consisted of a mixture of small business owners and large property owners in the downtown area who desperately desired to see an economic rebound. The Main Street program itself became the key agent in coalition building between the economic and political interests of Flagstaff.

The process of voting further provided an advantage for those in favor of downtown redevelopment. Rather than having the state of Arizona allow a simple ballot vote, as in most elections, a no vote required some additional efforts on the part of those opposed; a yes vote consisted merely of inaction on the part of a supporting property owner. A vote of opposition, however, required the writing of an official "letter of protest" (a term with negative connotations) during the protest period. Any owner who did not write a letter and deliver it accordingly was considered to be in favor of the project. Further, not all property owners were interested in the downtown redevelopment efforts. An uncalculated number of institutions and larger businesses downtown, such as the branches of state banks, couldn't have cared less about the SID. These were local issues that the larger corporations may have missed or neglected to study. In any event, apathy or lack of involvement was therefore automatically converted into a yes vote for the SID. When asked to explain the factors leading to the passage of the SID, Maury Herman replied in part, "I think the fact that there were a lot of institutions that didn't take a position, but their votes counted as 'yes'. You know, there's a tactic, there are tactics that are used to build coalitions" (Herman 2001). According to Maury, this process of voting—directed by state law—served as one important tactic in the effort to encourage downtown redevelopment efforts.

What seemed to be the conclusion to this phase of the process came with an editorial in the *Daily Sun* one day after the vote, titled "District serves most interests." While claiming to "respect the concerns of those who voted against the district," the paper provided a strong endorsement to the planned streetscape and to the SID that would partially fund it. The article started with a clear reflection of community sentiments: "Now, with any luck, the debating can end and the improving can begin." Yet, the paper admitted that some property owners would see much more return from their investment than others. Those owning parking lots, for instance, would probably receive the least. Conversely, "those who will benefit from improvements will be getting a bargain." With property owners contributing some $2.3 million to the effort, the city would be responsible for the rest of the tab. In the future, the editorial suggested that the "businesses bear more of project costs. A more even split doesn't seem like too much to ask of businesses that will be the biggest beneficiaries of the improvements involved."

Having been approved by a comfortable majority of downtown business owners, the city council made the SID official with the passage of Resolution No. 1843 on April 26, 1993. The resolution defined once again the specific area of downtown to be included within the district and ordered the improvement of streets and rights-of-way within that district. The resolution specified a wide array of improvements, such as paving, curbs and gutters, landscaping, irrigation, street and pedestrian lighting, traffic signals and new signage, street furniture, water and sewer lines, storm drains, and "appurtenances related thereto." Flagstaff's streetscape plan was off and running. Because all of the improvements in the SID (completed by the end of 1996) ended up costing more than $8 million, the city (and thus its tax-paying citizens) ended up footing the bill for the rest of it, causing no small amount of local controversy.

Given the boundaries of the SID, the south side of Cherry Avenue has been "improved," whereas the north side has changed little. Overall, the pedestrian-oriented streetscape south of Cherry Avenue serves as a friendly and attractive "stage set" through which anyone can enjoy the actual uniqueness and variety of downtown Flagstaff. Although the brick sidewalks, street trees, benches, curb swellings, and new streetlights may indeed be the product of a standardized package of urban planning gimmicks applied relentlessly throughout the nation, there is plenty of evidence that it works. It is probably more appropriate to interpret this updated landscape as a welcoming invitation to experience the local character of downtown than as representing directly some kind of local character in itself. To think of this from another perspective, all of the "historic character" of the downtown area, both north and south of the tracks, was also there in the 1970s and 1980s. Little incentive existed for locals or visitors, however, to experience this history in a safe, clean, and appealing environment given the crumbling sidewalks, boarded-up storefronts, empty streets, and unsafe lighting, and the continual presence of socially unacceptable behaviors. The streetscape and infrastructure improvements have corrected many of these deficiencies, and for all intents and purposes it is working well.

Businesses, people, and numerous public activities have returned to downtown since 1995. Concerts, festivals, memorials, and celebrations are held at Heritage Square and Wheeler Park, and occasional parades still make their way through the downtown as tradition would have it. The downtown's public spaces are sometimes transformed into symbolic places where the community can come together to mourn the loss of local heroes, such as fallen police officer Jeff Moritz in 2000, or to reflect on more global issues such as the infamous September 11, 2001 terrorist attacks. Whether to celebrate, to reflect, to mourn, to socialize, to shop, or to simply have a good time, social activity of all kinds has been on the increase in downtown Flagstaff. On the economic side, consumption has likewise increased, with more people spending more money in a greater selection of shops as reflected by sales tax data. For all of these reasons, there is once again a sense of human vibrancy and activity on the streets, both day and night. That Flagstaff's downtown is alive once again—albeit for more contemporary purposes—is testament to the fact that the community has done right by it. The downtown is once again serving as Flagstaff's central place in the community.

As for Cherry Avenue itself, you are about to walk through one of Flagstaff's first residential neighborhoods developed around the turn of the century, roughly between 1900 and 1920. As the town's population continued to grow, residential neighborhoods began to occupy the hillside (lava flow) north of town, adjacent to the business district. At that time, this was still a *walking city*, as geographers call it, in that the easiest way to get around town was to walk to nearby businesses to obtain goods and services. The friction of distance within all pre-automobile towns and cities was immense. Consequently, for hundreds of years (until the 1890s and electric streetcars), urban landscapes were very compact and densely settled, reflecting the inability to travel quickly through town. The downtown, including this neighborhood, then, was relatively densely populated and highly centralized. The automobile had not yet made a major impact on the community when the homes along Cherry Avenue were built.

Partially as a response to the limitation of space in dense urban areas, *alleys* were commonly included into street plans, consisting of narrow corridors that bisect each city block. You will continue to see these alleys throughout the north downtown and South Side neighborhood, as they were included in the original railroad grid laid out in 1882. Along the alleys, carriage houses and other small garages were built to store and take care of horses and buggies, and small properties were developed along alleys for family relatives and often for rentals for low-income residents. Thus, neighborhoods such as this one often consisted of diverse populations with regard to socio-economic status (income, or economic class), occupation, age, and often ethnicity. The diversity of this neighborhood in its earlier days is evident from the mansion-like Victorian house that Realty Executives now occupies, and the more modest bungalow-style houses on the opposite side of the street.

Cherry Avenue is further a product of the physical geography that underlies it. Many towns and cities across America developed around a river or railroad, both of which tended to divide the town geographically and symbolically along ethnic or income lines. The "wrong side of the tracks," as the saying goes, refers to the low-income and minority neighborhoods that tended to develop on one side of the railroad (or stream) while the middle and upper-class Anglo neighborhoods developed on the other side. If there was a hill on one side of this divide, the wealthier neighborhoods usually occupied it—to enjoy a better view, to escape seasonal flood damage, and because they could afford the higher property values of the hillside. Flagstaff exemplifies this general geographic trait. The grander homes and Anglo-American middle class families of Flagstaff developed on this hillside, north of downtown, whereas Flagstaff's Hispanic, Basque, and African-American populations clustered in their own neighborhoods south of the tracks, in the South Side neighborhood. The railroad has thus served as a sort of cultural divide as well as an economic one.

A reading of the landscape of Cherry Avenue gives a brief lesson about 1920s America. First, perhaps the most dominating feature of this early residential landscape consists of the tidy row of elegant street trees, now close to a century old. Of course, they didn't appear this way 80 years ago when this neighborhood was new.

The idea of placing trees at regular intervals along residential streets is not a Flagstaff original. Rather, Americans began to plant trees in orderly fashion in cities and towns everywhere during the nineteenth century. "Confident of their new status in the world," wrote Craig Whitaker (1996, 247), "Americans burst forth with a desire to beautify the country." One of the most frequent projects of early neighborhood associations and local improvement societies was none other than the planting of trees along their thoroughfares—often before the roads themselves were paved. The American elm became the favorite, due to its impressive, arching canopy which, when fully grown, presented the image of a grand cathedral of trees, instantly declaring the unspoken importance of the street below.

The impression of order and regularity provided by trees lining the street remains a primary concern for urban planners today. When the distances between free-standing houses becomes too great along a residential street, for instance, the street needs to be spatially defined in some other way. In this regard, trees can play a pivotal role. "The trees narrow the space and provide a natural vault that contributes to the pedestrian's sense of enclosure and comfort" (Duany, Plater-Zyberk, and Speck 2000, 79). Further, a tidy row of orderly trees can compensate for an overly wide street space.

Finally, notice on both sides of Cherry Avenue the mixture of land uses as you walk toward Beaver Street. This variety of familiar landscapes includes parking lots, International-style office buildings, and surviving pre-war houses. Combined with occasional business signs adorning the entryways of older homes, these elements indicate that you are walking through a *zone in transition*—in this case, an area in transition from residential to commercial land use (Figure 32). Homes have turned into businesses, a process undoubtedly assisted in recent decades by an official change in zoning along this street, allowing commercial enterprises to exist within a formerly residential area. The commercial functions of the central business district have been, in essence, invading this older residential neighborhood—and the landscapes of the automobile are coming with it.

Figure 32. Cherry Avenue Professional Building. Business signs and parking lots are indicators that a transition to commercial activities is taking place within this former residential neighborhood. (Photo: Author's collection)

From here, finish this first part of the Tour by strolling west along Cherry Avenue to see all of the changes taking place here. Upon reaching Beaver Street, turn south (left) and remain on Beaver Street until you cross the railroad tracks at Route 66. At this point, our tour of the South Side neighborhood will begin, as detailed in Chapter 6.

CHAPTER 6

FLAGSTAFF'S *Melting Pot:* THE SOUTH SIDE NEIGHBORHOOD

STOP 10
MOTEL: THE ORIGINAL U.S. ROUTE 66

Motel Du Beau was Flagstaff's first *motor hotel* (hence the term, *motel*), built at the corner of Beaver Street and Phoenix Avenue in 1929. When Mr. and Mrs. A. E. Dubeau of Los Angeles opened their new *Motel Inn*, the Flagstaff *Daily Sun* described the place as "a hotel with garages designed for the better class of motorists" (Cline 1994, 241). The enclosed, single-car garages came complete with steam heat to warm up pesky engines in the winter (Jackson 1999, 56). The units rented for $2.50 to $5.00, and all had baths, toilets, double beds, carpets, and furniture (Figure 33).

Figure 33. First motel in Flagstaff, built in 1929, at the corner of Phoenix Avenue and Beaver Street. This motel represents the beginning of automobile-oriented commercial development in Flagstaff, a process that continues to this day. (Photo: Author's collection)

Why did Mr. and Mrs. Dubeau choose this unlikely location for Flagstaff's first motel? Between 1926 and 1934 Phoenix Avenue west of Beaver Street served as part of the original alignment for U.S. Route 66. This famous transcontinental highway was completed from Chicago to Los Angeles in 1926, basically paralleling the tracks of the AT&SF along its southwestern route; consequently, this street corner was an excellent location for a motel. According to Art Welsh, a volunteer researcher for the Pioneers Museum, Santa Fe Avenue (now Route 66) served as the original alignment for U.S. Route 66 through downtown coming in from the east. Route 66 then turned left onto Beaver Street to cross the railroad tracks, and then turned right from Beaver Street onto Phoenix Avenue where it proceeded along the alignment of Mike's Pike. Part of the original highway bridge that carried Route 66 over the Rio de Flag just west of Motel Du Beau is still visible today (Wilcox 2002). Thus, Motel Du Beau is actually located on the original route, and the motel further represents the first phase of auto-oriented commercial roadside development in Flagstaff.

It is important to note that the original U.S. Route 66 was not like a freeway that cut its own path across the country. Instead, Route 66 was pieced together with existing old trails through the countryside and existing streets that ran through the downtowns of many communities along its route. Prior to its federal designation of Route 66, it was known as the National Old Trails Highway, and very little of it was paved. Thus, Phoenix Avenue officially remained a part of Route 66 until 1934 when a much-needed underpass was built at Sitgreaves Street a few blocks to the west (Cline 1994), and Route 66 was realigned to the underpass. The railroad company refused to contribute funds to the underpass, so Flagstaff asked for federal assistance. The federal grant of $120,000, funded by Roosevelt's New Deal, made the underpass possible, and it still serves as a vital thoroughfare today. Congestion caused by trains was an issue even in the 1930s, and that is what spawned the necessity for the underpass in the first place.

Understanding the origins of Route 66 and the entire national network of interstate highways that emerged after 1926 requires a look at the country's transportation situation around 1900. The U.S. could brag about having the most advanced and intricate rail network in the world, but it generally had the worst roads. At the time, inventors were still tinkering with self-propelled automobiles ("horseless carriages"). The first real effort to improve lousy road conditions in the United States can be traced to the "good roads" movement that developed before 1900 into a viable and influential organization. By 1900 the idea of good roads had become a central theme for travelers. The movement's beginnings are credited to a Union veteran of the Civil War, Colonel Albert Augustus Pope, who invented the "safety bicycle" in 1878. Bicycles soon became the rage nationwide, and by 1900 more than 300 companies were producing approximately a million bicycles per year (Lewis 1997).

Pope's interest with improving road conditions therefore had little to do with automobiles, but instead with the well being of bicycles and their riders. In a pamphlet titled "Highway Improvement," Pope wrote, "American roads are among the worst in the civilized world, and always have been" (Lewis 1997, 7). He consequently formed an organization called the League of American Wheelmen, and he financed courses at MIT designed to teach road engineering. He even built a short stretch of paved road in Boston to demonstrate the advantages of smooth, hard surfaces. In time, the "good roads" movement swept the country. For its part, the League of American Wheelmen became the first highway lobby group, and it ultimately served as a model for other, more powerful lobbying groups to follow.

On July 16, 1916, President Woodrow Wilson signed America's first federal-aid road act into law. The act provided some $75 million federal dollars over a 5-year period to the newly formed federal Bureau of Public Roads and enabled the federal government to pay half of a state's cost for road building and improvements (Lewis 1997). The timing for the act was particularly bad: When the United States entered World War I in 1917, shortages of all kinds forced a virtual end to roadwork nationally. To make matters worse, the Bureau of Public Roads was steeped in confusion; it had only spent some $500,000 of its allocated $75 million by 1919, and had built to its credit no more than 13 miles of road. Further, the 1916 legislation did not stipulate that roads in one county or state had to connect with those in another. Planned roads, therefore, often consisted of isolated squiggles on maps that would contribute little to a national highway system.

By 1921 the government was correcting these and other problems. In that year Congress passed the next sweeping legislation, the Federal-Aid Highway Act, which funded federal roads at $75 million per year rather than over 5 years. And the money was finally being used for its allocated purpose: By the end of the 1920s the Bureau of Public Roads had spent some $750 million. Further, the 1921 Act was the first to make the idea of a national road system a reality. Each state was responsible for at least 7 percent of its new roads connecting with those of other states. One goal was to link all of the county seats throughout the country with decent roads. Wisely, the bureau worked closely with the states to make sure the interstate road connections actually happened, and an agreement was also reached on standard shapes and designs for highway traffic signs. Route designations were changed from the previous chaotic system of nonstandard road names to a more uniform system of route numbers. With the bureau's leadership, north-to-south routes were designated with odd numbers beginning with 1 on the East Coast and ending with 101 on the West. Likewise, east-to-west routes obtained even numbers, with Route 2 in the north and 70 in the south. Finally, by 1926, the standardized road system was in place, and the now-familiar federal shields began to appear along the new interstate routes emerging throughout the country, including that of the new U.S. Route 66 (Lewis 1997).

The 1921 Act was pivotal in the process of improving America's substandard roads, but it also meant a slow death for passenger rail service. By 1970, nearly 50 years after the Act's passage, virtually all railroad companies had retired their passenger trains, and the federal government was forced to subsidize national passenger rail service in an overhauled skeleton rail network that became known as Amtrak. Somewhat ironically, nineteenth-century railroad companies had supported the good roads movement in order to expedite local road traffic—specifically to get people and goods to and from the train depots. Tom Lewis explained that "with a quarter million miles of railroad track—more than half the rail in the world—they had little to fear from automobiles" (Lewis 1997, 21). By the 1920s, however, the relationship had soured between the railroad industry and emerging automobile interests. For one thing, the railroads argued that truckers should be regulated by the Interstate Commerce Commission, similar to the railroads. By 1929 national track mileage had decreased to a quarter of a million miles, and the number of passengers dropped to

786,000—down from a million riders in 1915. Effectively, Route 66 and the other national roads signified the beginning of the end for the dominance of rail transportation in America. In a sense, the Phoenix Avenue landscape just south of the Santa Fe tracks represents this period of transition from rail to auto-oriented commerce. As indicated by the motels that sprouted along the new Route 66, the free-market economy was quick to adjust to this blossoming mode of transportation.

As you walk east along Phoenix Avenue you will encounter two other early Route 66 motels. None are serving their original purpose; instead they are used now as youth hostels and apartments for NAU students and other temporary residents. Flagstaff's half-century of motel building along Route 66, however, began right here along Phoenix Avenue, representing the beginnings of the motel industry in town. Recall that hotels originally dominated the lodging industry, dependent on their proximity to rail transportation within the downtown business districts. Few of these railroad era hotels ended up being convenient for automobiles (Jakle 1995). Further, hotel design emphasized public space, with features including expansive lobbies, corridors, lounges, coffee shops, banquets, ballrooms, and meeting halls. The evolution of the roadside motel would be decidedly different, however, with few of these features found in such establishments.

As people traveled increasingly by automobile, a variety of auto camps emerged, at first in the western United States to accommodate these travelers. John Jakle has explained that by the 1920s, the auto camp business was in full swing nationally: "The typical camp comprised a central service building and tent sites variously defined by picnic benches and the trodden ground of previous campers. In the 1930s hotel owners attempted to legislate them out of existence under Title One of the National Recovery Act" (Jakle 1995, 174). Increasing numbers of auto camps, hotel owners claimed, were creating unfair competition for their own downtown establishments.

The auto camp concept generally evolved into the development of the "cabin camp." Often considered as America's first motels, cabin camps were generally built in three varieties: the auto camp with cabins added, a cabin camp built from scratch without tents, and the "tourist home" with cabins added. Mostly found in the eastern United States, the tourist home often substituted for an auto camp. The first recorded cabin camp opened in Douglas, Arizona in 1913 (Jakle 1995). By the late 1920s more than 600 cabin camps were scattered along well-traveled routes throughout the country. Cabin camps then evolved into "cottage courts," where the cottages were built of more permanent construction, were more spacious on their interiors, and were winterized for year-round use. "Motor courts" became the next trend, essentially copying the form of cottage courts. This time, however, the cottages were all constructed under a single roofline with shared walls. After World War II, these motor courts came to be called motels, the original term having been coined in 1925 as "Mo-Tel." Motel construction boomed through the 1950s and 1960s, to a peak of over 61,000 establishments nationwide by 1964 (Jakle 1995). This motel boom is reflected well in Flagstaff along the original U.S. Route 66 stretched out to the west and east of town. Today, old Route 66 between downtown and east Flagstaff serves as a virtual clinic on the variations of motel architecture that appeared during the height of roadside commercial development along Route 66 before the 1970s. Of course, the construction of Interstate 40 quickly brought Flagstaff's great motel era along Route 66 to an end.

In 1984 the last part of I-40 was completed around the town of Williams (the last town along Route 66 to be bypassed by I-40). By then, development of roadside services along Route 66 had come to a crashing end as cross-country vehicle traffic shifted to the faster freeway on the edge of town. Locational advantage, of course, dictated that roadside businesses would now orient themselves to I-40 and the town's three freeway interchanges. Milton Avenue then became Flagstaff's primary commercial growth corridor during the 1980s and

1990s. Gas stations, restaurants, new motels, and big-box retail stores have developed southward along Milton Avenue toward the I-40 and I-17 interchange like a thirsty plant's roots growing toward water.

Since the 1970s, roadside motels have essentially come full circle. Today's motels are usually high-rises with luxuries and services that surpass those found in the older downtown hotels of the nineteenth century. Often referred to as "highway hotels," these newer motels tend to be clustered around freeway interchanges on the edge of town, and are well represented at Flagstaff's Milton and Butler interchanges. The entire era of motel building is therefore amply represented in Flagstaff, from the Phoenix Avenue landscape of the 1920s and 1930s to the roadside commercial development along Route 66 after the 1950s, and finally to the freeway interchanges to the south of town by the 1980s. It all started right here at Motel Du Beau.

STOP 11
BOARDING HOUSE: THE TOURIST HOME

Turning south (right) onto San Francisco Street from Phoenix Avenue, I suggest that you pay careful attention to the buildings and businesses along this thoroughfare. This, too, is one of Flagstaff's business districts, but its human landscape contrasts sharply in various ways with that of the north downtown. Try to observe these differences as you walk, and think about the general cultural and economic factors that may have contributed to this distinction.

You are walking through the South Side neighborhood of Flagstaff, where we find a variety of culturally diverse settlements. America itself has been described as a "melting pot," given that ours is truly a nation of immigrants, having come here from all reaches of the globe. In truth, the United States today remains one of the most culturally diverse nations of the world—and Flagstaff's own population reflects a similar type of diversity. Much of this diversity, however, was clustered in the neighborhoods that developed after 1900, south of the tracks, between what is today the Northern Arizona University campus and the BNSF railroad. In short, this expansive South Side neighborhood can be described as Flagstaff's own melting pot, due to the variety of people who have settled here.

Since Flagstaff's founding, the South Side area has become home to Basque people from Spain and France, Mexicans from New Mexico and elsewhere, African-Americans from the southeastern United States, and many others, albeit in smaller numbers and influence.

Representing this diversity well is the *Tourist Home* on the east side of San Francisco Street, having once played a significant social role in Flagstaff's Basque community (Figure 34). The Basques comprise an ethnic group whose homeland exists in the Pyrenees Mountains of northern Spain and southern France. Their language is distinct from that of their Spanish and French neighbors, and they have made a living there as farmers, livestock raisers, fishermen, and whalers. Recently, the Basques have appeared in the news because of their continued goal of gaining more autonomy from the Spanish government.

Figure 34. Basque boarding house on South San Francisco Street. (Photo: Author's collection)

By the late nineteenth century, more than 1,000 Basques worked as sheepherders in California, and by 1900 they had become the most prominent group in California's sheep industry (Woodward Architectural Group 1993). A severe California drought in the 1870s forced a portion of California's Basque sheepherding community to move to the surrounding states of Nevada, Oregon, Utah, Idaho, and Arizona. By the mid-1880s, most of the Basques who relocated to Arizona had decided to settle in or around Flagstaff, already the focus of the region's sheep industry.

Most Basque sheepherders who immigrated to the American West were single men who came to join friends or relatives already established. This is where the Tourist Home comes into the picture. After a small community of Basques would become established in a certain place, they would erect a hotel, or boarding house. Usually, it would be located near the railroad depot to make it easily accessible for non-English speaking Basque people trying to find the boarding house nearby. These boarding houses were among the most important institutions for Basque immigrants in North America, because they served as veritable clearing houses for information about jobs, and as cultural centers for single men who spent most of their working lives alone (Woodward Architectural Group 1993).

The Tourist Home served as Flagstaff's own Basque boarding house after its construction in 1926, and you are standing in the midst of Flagstaff's Basque neighborhood and commercial district. Notice that the boarding house is located on San Francisco Street only a few blocks from the railroad, as was necessary to be easily recognized by Basque immigrants arriving by train.

Another indicator of this place's important social role is the deteriorating structure just to the left (north) of the boarding house, a Basque handball court (*pelota fronton*). In 1926, this pelota court was constructed next to the boarding house, already known as Jesus Garcia's Tourist Home. Although 14 such pelotas are known to exist throughout the American West, this is the only surviving Basque handball court in Arizona.

Just east of the ball court is an area where a cluster of Basque had households developed by the 1920s. Some of these people went into business for themselves, and they became instrumental in developing the South San Francisco Street commercial district here. The various ethnic groups of South Side maintained their own clustered, somewhat segregated neighborhoods, but they all came together here on San Francisco Street to do business and to operate their own establishments. This South Side commercial district served all of them; it thus came to take on the flavor of a multi-cultural, Bohemian-style district—unlike the Anglo-dominated business district north of the tracks (Woodward Architectural Group 1993).

Today, the social character of the South Side business district along San Francisco Street has changed somewhat, as it has become the focus of attention for NAU students and Anglo tourists. Indicative of this transformation since the early 1980s is the variety of antique shops, local restaurants and bars, and other student-oriented or tourist businesses. You will still find some businesses oriented to the local community as well, making this commercial district quite diverse in its retail and service offerings. This also serves as the main corridor for students who walk or bike to businesses and apartments located downtown or further north. The actual campus for Northern Arizona University may not physically extend this far north, but the university's social and economic impact on both South Side and Downtown can be felt and seen in the landscape.

As you walk from the Tourist Home south to Butler Avenue, you will pass on the left a small, one-story building constructed with *Malpais basalt*, very dark, weather-resistant rock. This building is a good example of the numerous basalt houses and buildings constructed throughout the South Side through the 1940s. Although any masonry building material is generally thought to be more expensive than wood, this is not the case here. For many years, Flagstaff residents used local basalt because it was an economical building material (Jackson 1999). They could collect it free of charge and assemble it into walls when time permitted. Thus, a little money and a lot of volunteer labor were sometimes all that were necessary for the working-class families of the South Side. If you walk through more of the South Side residential areas sometime, you will see numerous basalt houses scattered throughout the district—an important aspect of Flagstaff's distinct local geography and its sense of place.

STOP 12
BYPASS: BUTLER AVENUE

While dodging automobiles to cross Butler Avenue, you will sense that this is a major east-west corridor through town. The convenience store and gas station on the southeast corner are other components of this speedy, convenience-oriented auto flume that allows motorists to zoom across Flagstaff from Milton Avenue to the I-40 interchange and to the Country Club residential area of town, 5 miles away (Figure 35).

Figure 35. Looking west on Butler Avenue, at its intersection with San Francisco Street. Formerly Clay Avenue, a quiet South Side neighborhood, this five-lane bypass was built in part to relieve traffic on Route 66. (Photo: Author's collection)

Would you believe, however, that Butler Avenue used to be no wider than any of the other narrow cross streets in South Side? Once known as Clay Avenue, this street was part of the *Brannen addition* grid laid out after the railroad grid was already surveyed. In 1990 Clay Avenue was widened substantially to create today's Butler Avenue. It was built as a bypass route to relieve the increasing traffic congestion along old Route 66, the original auto corridor through town. This indicates how Flagstaff has grown by leaps and bounds since World War II. The other Flagstaff bypass, of course, is I-40. Local roadside businesses have predictably migrated to these newer bypass strips in the typical entrepreneurial spirit of free-market capitalism.

The "S" curve on Butler Avenue just east of this intersection is the result of two clashing street grid patterns (see Figure 21). South Side streets are oriented to the railroad, the Brannen addition is oriented to the National Grid, or Township and Range survey system. The "S" curve was apparently necessary as an adjustment to these two intersecting street grids.

Although I have uncovered little evidence of controversy pertaining to the widening of Butler Avenue, the geographical implications of its widening are clear. This case is consistent with road development projects and their impacts across the country; major cities throughout the United States have lost entire neighborhoods for the purpose of building urban freeways and interchanges and widening existing street corridors. Most often, it was the low-income, minority neighborhoods that suffered the most from highway building during the 1950s through the 1980s. Literally hundreds of thousands of families have been displaced nationwide by highway construction projects and associated urban renewal programs, as will be discussed later.

At the very least, Butler Avenue serves as a physical and symbolic barrier that separates the South Side area into two somewhat isolated communities. Yes, you can still cross the street, but the once cohesive and continuous (and quiet) residential district of South Side has now been sliced through with a major five-lane traffic corridor, probably disrupting previous social connections in this part of South Side. At the same time, Flagstaff's traffic patterns changed instantly after its completion, and now Butler serves as a vital link between the east and west sides of town. If you're in a car and want to avoid old Route 66, Butler Avenue is good news indeed.

STOP 13
TOWN CREEK: THE RIO DE FLAG

Similar to thousands of other towns and cities, much of this town was constructed in the *flood plain* of a stream channel. In this case, Flagstaff's own "town creek" consists of the Rio de Flag (Figure 36). As urbanized Americans, we tend to be brought up with the idea that flooding is bad and controlled streams or rivers are good. However, all streams and rivers naturally flood at times of high rains or snowmelt. Simply, they are supposed to flood occasionally, and streams erode, carry, and deposit the highest amount of sediment during flood events. Like many dry washes in the Southwest, the Rio de Flag flows only occasionally, but when it does it can have serious impacts on businesses and residents located within the natural flood plain.

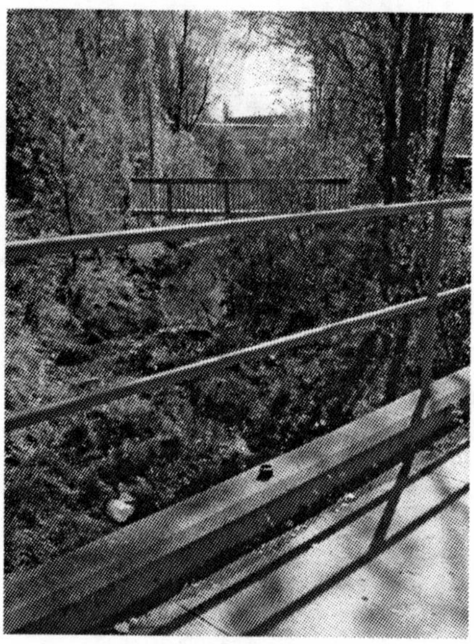

Figure 36. Stream channel for the Rio de Flag, on San Francisco Street just south of the Butler Avenue intersection. (Photo: Author's collection)

The headwaters of the Rio de Flag are found northwest of town, at the base of the San Francisco Peaks. Its occasional flow runs south, roughly parallel to U.S. Route 180, eventually curving its way through the original railroad street grid of downtown and South Side (see Figure 21). From where you stand, its channel continues eastward to the Country Club area, where it turns abruptly north and heads for its confluence with the Little Colorado River, or LCR. The LCR, of course, then joins the Colorado River at the east end of the Grand Canyon, and the Colorado River continues to flow west and south to the Gulf of California. Therefore, Flagstaff and the little Rio de Flag are tied into the Colorado River drainage system that has helped to shape the Grand Canyon.

The implications of the Rio de Flag are numerous. A flood plain consists of the low-lying areas on either side of the stream channel to where floodwaters escape and spread out during a flood event.

Throughout the Tour thus far, you have been walking through the *100-year* or *500-year flood plain.* A 100-year flood plain will flood that area, on *average,* once every 100 years. Nature is unpredictable, however, so it is possible to have two consecutive years of flooding, or 180 years without a flood. The 100-year description is merely an average.

When pavement and buildings are constructed in or around a flood plain, the frequency of major floods *increases*—a trend that is causing havoc throughout the Phoenix metro area as more roads and parking lots are built. As urban areas grow, the frequency and severity of floods also grow. Why? When we build roads and other paved surfaces, we also build drainage ditches, gutters, and sewers that funnel the water to the stream channel very quickly, allowing us to efficiently get rid of the water. Thus, much more water is reaching the stream at a much faster rate, causing a greater risk of flooding and greater flood peaks as well. In contrast, when rain falls on natural ground cover, like forest, much of the water soaks in, and the ground water might not reach the stream for hours or days.

Of course, Flagstaff's north downtown and South Side areas were developed long before zoning codes and federal regulations discouraged people from building in flood plains, so Flagstaff has seen its share of damaging floods from this otherwise benign stream channel. Not only was Flagstaff built in the flood plain, but the Rio de Flag channel itself has been realigned and rechanneled into a narrow trench to provide more room for buildings on the ever-important street grid. The channel located here is not the natural course of the Rio, but instead is the product of a rechanneling effort through this part of South Side. Thus, when water does cruise down the "Rio de Flood," as locals call it, the rising water rapidly overtakes its narrow trench and floods surrounding neighborhoods. The channel you see here can hold only 250 cfs (cubic feet per second) of water, basically enough capacity for a 10-year flood. The natural Rio can potentially carry more than 1,000 cfs during a flood, however, meaning that most of it would be forced to disperse across the flood plain and necessarily into people's homes.

During Flagstaff's early history, floodwater occasionally backed up behind street crossings and culverts in the north downtown, covering much of the area in the 100-year flood plain. Even the basement of the Weatherford Hotel was flooded once. "Streets became gullies, wooden sidewalks floated over submerged streets, and floodwaters destroyed bridges and filled the homes of many residents" (Jackson 1999, 55).

A quick read of the South Side residential landscape may lead to the conclusion that little economic growth and development has taken place here in recent years; many properties and their structures appear dilapidated and ill-maintained. What is seen here, however, reveals only part of South Side's ongoing story of economic and social change. What is unseen is a complex set of federal and local regulations that specifically dictate the types of developments or improvements that may or may not take place within the Rio de Flag's 100-year flood plain. In short, these regulations either effectively prevent new developments from occurring in the South Side area, or at least make the costs prohibitive so that local property owners are disinclined to make improvements.

The influence of centralized authority on South Side exists at multiple levels of governance. Federal regulations, through FEMA (Federal Emergency Management Agency), require that all municipalities generate maps of their local 100-year flood plains. Within these areas, property owners are denied federal flood insurance unless the municipality (city) adopts a minimum set of flood plain regulations in the form of a local ordinance. Flagstaff's own flood plain maps were completed in 1983, and the city's ordinance provides specific requirements for the types of developments allowed within the flood plain. The catch is that regular homeowners insurance does not cover flood damages. The only option to protect property owners from flood damage is the federally backed flood insurance offered through the National Flood Insurance Program. Unless local flood plain regulations are in place that satisfy minimum federal standards, however, federal flood plain insurance is unavailable—a strong disincentive for developing any new property within a designated flood plain. Further, without local regulations in place, a city such as Flagstaff would not be eligible for federal disaster relief in the case of a major flood event, even within an official "disaster area" declared by the U.S. president.

For these reasons, Flagstaff has adopted its own set of local flood plain regulations to maintain its eligibility for federal aid and to allow property owners access to flood insurance. For example, any new development, such as an apartment building, must have its ground floor elevated to at least 1 foot above the level of the 100-year flood plain. In some places, this means that the builder would have to elevate the structure 6 feet or more above the current ground level, making construction costs prohibitive. As for structures already existing within the flood plain—including the vast majority of South Side buildings—the "50 percent rule" applies. That is, when the total value of all improvements and additions over the life of a structure equals greater than 50 percent of the structure's overall market value, then the structure must be brought into conformance with local flood plain regulations. Usually, this would entail nothing less than jacking up the entire structure above the flood plain. Clearly, the cost would be monumental, so the 50 percent rule has acted as a further disincentive for owners to alter or improve their properties. City staff member Kim Gavigan explained that only one structure has actually gone through this process (Gavigan 2002). Also, newer, non-residential structures "can either be elevated or flood-proofed, designed to be impervious to water: flood shields on windows, things like that—basically design it like a submarine. It's not easy to do," explained Gavigan.

The unseen aspects of these federally imposed, local flood plain regulations explain much about the appearance of contemporary South Side. Building restrictions are severe, making new developments improbable and cost-prohibitive. The general appearance of urban blight, therefore, has been induced by a larger process originating at the federal level of control and managed locally through a city ordinance. It is interesting that property values are not declining as might be expected; instead, just the opposite is happening. The small, older houses scattered throughout South Side may not be worth much economically, but the land below them is now worth a small fortune because of a new city project currently in the planning stages that will effectively eliminate the hazards of the Rio de Flag flood plain. After more than a century of threatening the Flagstaff community with potentially devastating floods, the Rio is about to be tamed permanently—or so it is hoped.

Already 8 years in the making, the Rio de Flag flood retention project is currently in phase three of a four-phase process. This project is also federally sponsored, requiring direct approval from the U.S. Congress. The first phase consisted of a 1-year reconnaissance study to demonstrate the need for constructing a major flood retention system for Flagstaff. Following phase one, 3 years were required for phase two—determining the project's feasibility, producing alternative project plans, and completing the federally required environmental impact statement. The project was then authorized by Congress through the Water Resources Development Act. In 2002 the project was in the third phase of design, and the various project alternatives were narrowed down to one specific plan. Numerous public hearings, meetings, and other types of input were necessary to help determine the final alternative. When the necessary federal funds become available, the fourth phase of actual construction will begin (Gavigan 2002).

The funding is a major sticking point. The city is working on the project through the U.S. Army Corps of Engineers. By working with the Corps, the city can obtain an impressive 65 percent federal cost share to complete the project; the city is required to fund the remaining 35 percent. Although the city has already reserved its share of the funding, the federal funds had yet to come through as of this writing. Congress may have authorized the project conceptually, but the city of Flagstaff still must compete with other cities around the nation for its share of funding. According to city staff member and project leader

Kim Gavigan, bids can be sent out for construction after the federal share of funds has been secured—something that may not happen for some time:

> It's just a matter of getting the federal funding in light of recent events. It's competitive, and the current administration is diverting all the money into preparedness and the whole terrorism thing. Potentially, we could get delayed for years on this because of what happened on 9/11. They've always said that the Corps of Engineers is a pork barrel entity, and they want to take funds away from it. So, they're talking about possibly not allowing any new projects to start. (Gavigan 2002)

When the retention project is finally built, it will consist of two principal components. One will include a sizeable retention basin well west of downtown, near the new housing development of Railroad Springs along old Route 66. Although most Flagstaff residents focus on the highly visible Rio de Flag, another equal threat is found in the Clay Avenue Wash, the headwaters of which are well west of town. The purpose of the Clay Avenue Wash retention basin is to hold back floodwater and to meter it out in a controlled manner after the flood. To this day, the wash serves as a tributary to the Rio, joining the Rio near the current intersection of Butler and Milton Avenues just south of the railroad overpass. During a flood event, the combination of Clay Avenue and Rio de Flag will literally flood that major intersection and a large area surrounding it. The water would flow along Butler Avenue to the east, where it would work its way through South Side and into the current Rio de Flag channel. Thus, the Clay Avenue Wash project will prove just as vital for preventing flood events in this area.

The second component of the project will consist of a "true, flood control project," as Gavigan described it, including a system of artificial channel sections, below-ground drainage tunnels, and other necessary infrastructure in the heart of downtown and South Side near the railroad. Although no retention basin is planned, these new modifications will be designed to allow the Rio floodwater to literally wash through—and under—the downtown area toward its natural channel south of town. The Rio de Flag channel has been rerouted several times in the town's history. The hope is that this "final" rerouting will solve the community's flood problems once and for all. Nature will finally be conquered in downtown Flagstaff.

What does this mean for the development of South Side? Plenty. With the threat of floods no longer at issue, the South Side area will be a prime candidate for redevelopment and *gentrification*. Many older downtown neighborhoods in America's cities are being repopulated with middle and upper-middle class Anglo-American residents who prefer to live close to downtown. This process of transforming a relatively low income neighborhood to an upscale residential area filled with well-educated professionals and retirees is known as gentrification. South Side, too, may become gentrified in this way after development is once again permitted; in fact, several local sources have revealed that a quiet "land rush" is taking place now, whereby individuals are purchasing properties in the South Side area with the expectation that property values will rise markedly in the future. To be sure, there will be huge profits for anyone who invests in South Side real estate. From an economic perspective, land is not much different from the stock market, in that the time-honored axiom, "Buy low, sell high" applies to those trying to get rich quick from purchasing run-down properties and selling them at much higher prices. Such entrepreneurial activity is referred to as *speculation*, a practice as old as capitalism itself.

South Side maintains the geographical qualities to which urban professionals (and many others) are attracted, including walking proximity to downtown, existence of a college campus nearby, quaint houses that could be "fixer-uppers," and densely packed neighborhoods that are walkable and friendly. Places like South Side have become trendy, so it is highly likely that the process of gentrification is in this neighborhood's future.

Gentrification often leads to community conflict, however, and it will be interesting to see how the old-time residents of South Side react to such redevelopment. When it does happen, property values—and consequently property taxes—will likely skyrocket, making these little houses very expensive and economically out of reach for the bulk of Flagstaff's working class population. There is evidence that this process is happening already. The social character of this community will change as well, as it comes to resemble more of a professional, suburban population with cell phones and espresso coffee, and less of the rooted, multi-ethnic, working-class culture that still permeates the streets of South Side today. I believe that, for better or worse, this transformation may be right around the corner for South Side.

City staff members observing changes in South Side agree only partially with the above scenario. The continuing demand for student housing since the 1960s has led to the construction of various high-density apartment buildings that have either complied with flood plain restrictions or were constructed prior to their existence. With the flood plain problem eliminated, it is more likely that property owners in South Side will sell their land with huge profit margins to investors who plan to build more apartments. Without any intervention, therefore, city staff members—including Kim Gavigan and Mike Kerski—expect that South Side will convert rapidly into a high-density student housing area. Although Kerski admits that the city really does not have a vision for how they would like to see South Side develop, it is certain that they do not want to see this student-housing scenario play out. Kerski explained how the city and NAU have been working together in an attempt to find a potential solution to the projected growth in South Side: "Our goal is to work with [NAU], so that the area between Phoenix Avenue and the university just doesn't become student housing. If some 5,600 students live on campus, well guess what, all the rest live right around here" (Kerski 2002).

The city holds nothing personal against NAU students, but there is much more interest by those in local government to see the remaining character, or sense of place, of South Side preserved. As Kerski explained, "The staff's vision of South Side is to preserve as much as we can. There's a lot of history there, and [we want to] infill as much as we can with buildings that are sympathetic to that community. There are other people who just want to see the entire area cleared away and have big apartment buildings built there. One of our goals over the next couple years is to do a redevelopment plan from Phoenix Avenue to Butler Avenue that identifies every single property and what the city's role could be" (Kerski 2002). Kim Gavigan agrees, adding that there is already social friction evolving between the old-time, local community in South Side and the increasing number of NAU students moving in. Gavigan provided his own perspective on South Side:

> Basically, it will become the boarding house for NAU students. NAU continues to buy property, and over the years a lot of apartments, duplexes, things geared toward students have gone in, and those people have met the flood plain regulations. The single-family residences and the people who have been there 50 years don't want that to happen. There's always been this disconnect between the NAU students and the local population, whether it comes from all the bars, or students are noisy and don't care. So, the character of the neighborhood, with all these duplexes going up is not the same. (Gavigan 2002)

With speculative real estate exchanges already taking place, combined with the promise of eliminating the flood threat permanently, one cannot be so sure about the future development or character of South Side. Clearly, however, changes will come quickly, and only time will tell whether local centralized authorities—especially those at city hall—can, or should, actually do anything about it. Otherwise, South Side's landscape will allow free-market forces to reign supreme, given the absence of restrictive local and federal regulations.

STOP 14
CHANGING NEIGHBORHOOD: SOCIAL DYNAMICS OF SOUTH SIDE

As you stand in front of Flagstaff's oldest surviving church (walk up the stairs and read the historical plaque on the wall), you are also in the midst of one of Flagstaff's dominantly Hispanic neighborhoods (Figure 37). Flagstaff's early Hispanic community should not be underemphasized; of the 784 families in Flagstaff counted in the 1920 U.S. Census, 245, or 30 percent, were Hispanic.

Figure 37. The "Neighborhood Church," in the Hispanic area of South Side. (Photo: Author's collection)

At this point, I should clarify my use of the term *Hispanic*. Hispanic is an Anglo-American term used to describe people throughout the United States who share common characteristics (language, religion, history, food) that originally diffused from the same source, Spain. The term has no racial, national, or political implication, and is applied to people who share this cultural heritage, whether their ancestors came from Spain, Mexico, New Mexico, Argentina, El Salvador, or other places (Woodward Architectural Group 1993). Ethnic and cultural terminology can be complicated, and ultimately we must speak to individuals themselves to determine their own identities, from *their* perspectives. For geographical and historical purposes, however, it often becomes necessary to generalize so that broad distinctions can be made between cultural groups and the cultural landscapes they inhabit.

The settling of Hispanics in this area predates Flagstaff itself. The first to arrive were Hispanic sheepherders in the 1870s and 1880s. The first substantial employer of Hispanic workers in Flagstaff was the railroad company, beginning during its construction in the early 1880s. Most of the Hispanic railroad laborers were from New Mexico, and after Ayer's Lumber Mill began production in Flagstaff, these people and their families had further reason to stay here as employees of the mill. By 1920, New Mexico—born Hispanics constituted 11 percent of Flagstaff's population. Most of these people lived in Old Town, on the west side of Flagstaff near the tracks.

Another significant group of Hispanics consisted of Mexican nationals who arrived beginning in the 1890s; this is the dominant population that occupied South Side around the turn of the century. They originally migrated seasonally from Mexico in the spring to shear thousands of sheep in Arizona. The most substantial wave of Mexican immigrants in Flagstaff, however, came as a result of the prolonged and bloody Mexican Revolution between 1911 and 1917. Ample employment in local and regional lumber mills provided the incentive for them to come here. By the early 1900s, almost all of the Arizona Lumber and Timber Company's labor force was Hispanic, and most of them were "nationals" from Mexico. By 1910 they were establishing permanent residences here in South Side. By the 1920s and 1930s their American-born children were becoming property owners. This helped to solidify South Side as the city's most substantial Mexican neighborhood (Woodward Architectural Group 1993).

Had Flagstaff's history of development taken a different course, little of this culturally rich area would exist today. The South Side area nearly fell victim to a national redevelopment strategy known somewhat ironically as "urban renewal" in the 1960s. Known mostly for its role in demolishing acres of aging neighborhoods near the downtowns of metropolitan areas, smaller towns and cities were no less immune from urban renewal strategies. There is probably no more appropriate place than here to briefly discuss the history and significance of urban renewal, and the changes that it wrought. Once again, Flagstaff tried to jump on a national bandwagon, this time with respect to downtown revitalization efforts.

According to Bernard Frieden and Lynn Sagalyn (1989, 17), the 1950s and 1960s were an "unprecedented time for downtown planning, with some 700 central business district studies and plans published by 1959." Two federal programs were adopted in an attempt to curb the decline of America's metropolitan downtown business districts: 1) the interstate freeway system and 2) urban renewal. Although neither program was initially designed specifically to assist ailing downtowns, cities used both to their advantage. As for the interstate system, it was not within Eisenhower's original concept to build freeways through urban areas. As first proposed, the interstate system would include some 34,000 miles of freeways across the rural United States, but they would entirely bypass the major cities. The idea of building urban freeways into the national system was frowned upon due to the engineering problems of cutting through wide swaths of urban neighborhoods to reach the downtown core (Frieden and Sagalyn 1989, 20). However, after the Senate and the House rejected major highway bills in 1955, the highway lobby started to look for supporters among big-city mayors and the representatives of downtown business associations. Congress soon became aware of their interest in revitalizing central business districts while at the same time relieving urban traffic congestion. Thus, Alf Johnson, president of the American Association of State Highway Officials, worked to create a broad coalition of pro-highway interests in order to get the national interstate system approved by Congress. To acquire the support of large cities, he persuaded state and federal highway engineers to add more urban freeway routes to the national system already proposed. State agencies were thus invited to propose an additional 2,200 miles of highways (Frieden and Sagalyn 1989, 21). The U.S. Bureau of Public Roads made these additions official in late 1955 with a report showing the new interstate highway plans for 100 American cities. As Bernard Frieden and Lynn Sagalyn have described, the new highway plan closely resembled the freeway patterns found within today's common road atlases of American cities: "For large metropolitan areas, a typical plan showed an inner belt road around downtown, an outer belt highway circling the suburbs, and one or more radial highways connecting the suburbs to the city center. Smaller metropolitan areas had plans for loop roads or spurs connecting downtown to the nearest interstate highway" (Frieden and Sagalyn 1989, 21). Following the passage of the Federal-Aid Highway Act in 1956, President Eisenhower apparently commented that the book of freeway plans for the 100 cities—made available to every member of Congress—had become the main selling point for Congressional members. The growth coalitions of America's cities and downtowns had therefore played a major role in making the interstate system a reality. The final version of the Federal-Aid Highway Act of 1956 included approximately 41,000 miles of interstate freeways, of which 6,100 miles were destined for urban areas.

Urban renewal was the second federal program that downtown coalitions used for their own purposes. Passed as part of the Housing Act of 1949, urban renewal was basically a slum-clearance program promoted by two specific interest groups. First, real estate interests had argued for a federal program that would allow private businesses to convert blighted or run-down neighborhoods into profitable developments. Second, housing advocates sought federal assistance to improve the standards for low-income, inner-city housing. The loopholes embedded within the law provide perhaps a more fascinating story than the law itself. For one, the law provided federal monetary assistance to cities for demolishing slum housing, regardless of what was built in its place. Predictably, downtown interests viewed urban renewal as a method through which blighted, run-down neighborhoods could be turned into flashy new development projects with office towers, downtown shopping malls, and upscale housing projects.

Federal urban renewal funds were meant primarily to improve slum areas described as blighted, deteriorated, or deteriorating, but there was much room for interpretation as to what exactly constituted a blighted area. The consequence was that "city renewal directors were searching for 'the blight that's right'—places just bad enough to clear but good enough to attract developers" (Frieden and Sagalyn 1989, 23). Because the urban renewal program also required that the areas targeted for redevelopment had to be "primarily residential," the program basically served as an incentive for downtown interests to tear down housing near the central business district regardless of its condition. The catch was that there were no specific guidelines for the definition of "blight," so blight was in the eye of the beholder. The impact of this law, therefore, was profound: "If cities wanted federal money for downtown redevelopment, the law prevented them from clearing old factory or commercial areas. Instead they had to find houses—any houses—to demolish. It was tempting to clear whatever houses happened to be on the edge of downtown, and city officials gave in to temptation" (Frieden and Sagalyn 1989, 24). The downtown business coalitions took further action to amend the original law. They convinced Congress to change the law several times to get around the "predominantly residential" requirement. The Housing Act of 1954 allowed only 10 percent of federal grants to be used for nonresidential projects. The nonresidential exception was expanded to 20 percent in 1959, to 30 percent in 1961, and to 35 percent in 1965.

Like the federal highway act, urban renewal had become a powerful tool for downtown redevelopment efforts by the 1960s. Some statistics are revealing: As of 1987, the interstate highway network had cost $105.3 billion to build, $57 billion of which was used to construct the urban routes—54 percent of the total interstate cost. As for urban renewal projects, the federal government had granted funds totaling $13.5 billion by the late 1980s, of which some two thirds went for projects in or near downtown business districts (Frieden and Sagalyn 1989).

Together, the urban renewal program and the new urban freeways conspired to create quite a social mess. Effectively, both constituted massive clearance programs, one for new developments, the other for highways to connect downtown with the suburbs.

Of course, demolishing houses necessarily meant displacing the people who lived in them. As early as the late 1950s, both programs were uprooting families by the thousands in urban areas across America, and a disproportionately large number of those displaced were either low-income or minorities, or—most often the case—both. As of 1967, more than 400,000 families had been forced to move due to urban renewal projects, and 330,000 had been displaced by freeway construction. Generally speaking, highway planners specifically targeted poor and minority neighborhoods because the land was cheaper to acquire, and because they believed that the elimination of slums would benefit the community as a whole. Also, politics played a role in the decision of where to locate freeways, given that wealthier (and whiter) neighborhoods often demonstrated their political clout by successfully protesting a planned freeway project. In Nashville, for example, engineering consultants had recommended a route that would have primarily used old railroad land, in combination with several white-owned businesses. "State and local officials objected and asked for an alternate route through the center of a black community, through the campus of a black college, and through sixteen blocks of commercial property filled with black-owned businesses" (Frieden and Sagalyn 1989, 28).

In turn, research has clearly shown that racism was also a factor in locating freeways. During the formative period of the 1956 highway act, for instance, Alf Johnson had been told by officials from several cities that the freeways would give them a good excuse to eliminate minority neighborhoods. The practice was nationwide, even in places like Minnesota. Very few blacks lived in that state, "but the road builders found them" (Frieden and Sagalyn 1989, 28). In Los Angeles, the highway planners "found the city's main Mexican-American community, Boyle Heights, irresistible. They pushed no fewer than five freeways through this one neighborhood a few miles east of downtown" (Frieden and Sagalyn 1989, 29). On the other side of the country, some 10,000 Baltimore families had their homes torn down for both highway and urban renewal projects. A full 90 percent of them were black. Unfortunately, the answer to displacement for these people was not to be found in the suburbs. Most could not even think of affording a new suburban home, and those who could afford such places were often turned away by hostile neighbors, denied loans by financial institutions for mortgages, or steered away by brokers or real estate agents. Throughout urban America, "black families were trapped between the racism of highway and renewal clearance and the racism of city neighborhoods and real estate institutions" (Frieden and Sagalyn 1989, 30). Adding to this was the fact that the 1956 act did not include any requirement to compensate tenants for their properties, to help those displaced find alternate housing, or to cover moving expenses. Only eight states acted on their own to compensate people with small payments.

Ultimately, the urban blight that downtown authorities and others assumed would simply go away with these federal programs instead shifted to other parts of the city. By most accounts in most cities, urban poverty and the housing crunch was only made worse. Neighborhoods exhibiting previously strong and self-sustaining communities were destroyed, and freeways were built in their place. As a general rule of thumb, you can assume that any urban freeway that today is adjacent to older housing tracts has been built not alongside the neighborhood, but through it. In many cases, houses and their families were once located where the freeway is now.

To add insult to injury, the results of the urban renewal program were less than stellar. In fact, although "hindsight is 20-20," as the famous saying goes, urban renewal is considered today as one of the most disastrous and ill-conceived planning failures in the history of urban America. In part, the failure was due to the federal rules that required a distinct separation between the city renewal agencies and the developers. The city was responsible for acquiring the land and having it cleared. Because most urban renewal lands included numerous houses and commercial buildings, it took several years, and in some cases more than a decade, to acquire the properties so that the bulldozer could tear it all down. Only just before the land was cleared could the city invite proposals for projects from developers, whether it be for office buildings, shopping malls, or new housing. By federal law, developers were not allowed to assist in the initial planning for an urban renewal project, which meant that cities had to take the chance on clearing the land while hoping that some developer from somewhere would be interested in using the cleared site. This was the problem. In many cases, neighborhoods were displaced and land was cleared only to find that no developer was interested in building there. The result was large tracts of vacant land near downtown where people had previously lived their lives. "St. Louis had its *Hiroshima Flats* and St. Paul its *Superhole.* Vacant lots littered with junked cars, piles of garbage, and rat nests were the most visible results of thirteen years of work on the ambitious Ellicott project in Buffalo" (Frieden and Sagalyn 1989, 44). By 1971 more than half of the urban renewal projects begun between 1960 and 1964 had not attracted a developer to build something new.

It is no surprise that as Americans learned more about the failures of urban renewal in their cities, they became more critical of the program. The formation of renewal opposition groups became commonplace by the 1960s and 70s, and by 1974 the urban renewal program as America knew it was over. Urban renewal funds were merged with other funding programs that cities could use more flexibly for almost any type of development. Known as CDBGs, or community development block grants, this new system provided federal funding to cities, but the downtown coalitions could no longer acquire those funds designated in advance for their own specific projects. Instead they were now required to compete annually with other cities and neighborhoods for a share of federal money allocated for the CDBGs.

Although urban renewal projects were associated most closely with America's metropolitan areas, small towns and cities like Flagstaff were not immune from urban renewal planning. Indeed, much of the South Side area nearly became part of the program. For many small towns the dominant philosophy for dealing with declining downtown areas came to be symbolized by the bulldozer. Abandoned storefronts were torn down instead of saved, and obsolete commercial building blocks were turned into parking lots, for lack of any better idea of what to do with them. In Bellefonte, Pennsylvania, for instance, the community's 12,000 residents had no answer during the 1960s for the town's continued loss of retail stores, jobs, and people to the nearby town of State College, the newest booming regional hub. Like many small towns at that time, Bellefonte's modest business district was experiencing severe decline. According to Peirce Lewis, who studied Bellefonte in the early 1970s, the dominant causes for decline "were initiated by events far away and largely beyond the control and even the comprehension of local people" (Lewis 1972, 332). The community's reaction was to tear down the abandoned buildings, whereby "bulldozers have been busily engaged in the wrecking operations that Americans continue to call 'urban renewal,' with no touch of irony" (Lewis 1972, 347). The construction of new highways had taken its toll on the town as well, having inflicted serious damage to several previously pleasant, tree-lined residential streets so that automobiles could move more efficiently.

Even smaller towns such as Galena, Illinois (pop. 3,600) could be influenced by urban renewal. With its own Main Street business district falling into decline, the city submitted an application in 1966 to the Department of Housing and Urban Development (HUD) to finance a downtown survey in which 160 buildings would be studied for potential redevelopment through urban renewal. The ensuing study resulted in the consultant's recommendation to develop a new shopping complex in the heart of the historic business district. The consultant's philosophy was "Build new to preserve the old." If the new shopping center was not located downtown, it was believed that the competitive merchants would move to a more accessible and spacious site on the periphery of town. This issue virtually polarized the community that had, by 1970, been informed about the failures of urban renewal projects elsewhere. In the end, the required referendum squelched the 4-year debate over urban renewal in Galena. The question posed to voters, "Shall the City of Galena preserve and restore downtown Galena by undertaking with State and Federal assistance, an urban renewal program?" failed by a vote of 1,361 to 340. It was considered to be "one of the heaviest elections here in recent years" (Paradis 2000, 73). At least one small town had thus saved its historic commercial buildings from the bulldozer, revealing the potential power of local individuals and interest groups to oppose urban renewal development projects. The town has subsequently become one of the most popular tourist attractions in Illinois, due in large part to its impressive collection of historic architecture (see Figure 6).

Another significant community battle against urban renewal occurred right here in Flagstaff's South Side neighborhood during the late 1950s. At the height of the federal clearance program in 1958, the Flagstaff city council investigated the potential for local urban renewal projects. Predictably, the targeted area for a major renewal zone consisted of 10 blocks of South Side, where "there were houses that might be rated sub-standard—but not, as it turned out, by the people living in them," recounted local historian Platt Cline (1994, 423). Apparently, the city planned to sell the land to a developer, who would bulldoze all of the older houses and replace them with new ones. The owners would make monthly payments on long-term loans. What the city did not predict, presumably, was the strong attachment that local South Side residents felt for their dwellings and for the neighborhood as a whole. Many residents and their families had built these houses room by room, often from locally quarried basalt extracted from lava flows north of town. The use values of these homes were far more precious to these folks than the potential exchange values of redeveloping the land. Not surprisingly, the public opposition to the proposed project was intense, and even hostile. The city council's housing director, if not others, received threats, and many longtime residents were deeply offended that their cherished neighborhood was being referred to as a "slum."

To garner more political clout, residents formed a local interest group known as the South Side Property Owners Association, supported in turn by a young attorney named Joseph R. Babbitt Jr. (Cline 1994). Eventually the city was forced to back down, and the entire urban renewal proposal was dropped. Clearly, in Flagstaff as elsewhere, local—and federal—proponents of the urban renewal program failed to consider the strong emotional and sentimental feelings of neighborhood residents for their homes and communities. Urban renewal represented a direct affront on the community's sense of place. Some neighborhoods, such as those in Galena, Illinois, and Flagstaff, Arizona, successfully defeated such projects, but many others did not.

At the intersection of Dupont Avenue and Beaver Street you will find one of the "gateways" to the NAU campus, signifying a transition from residential to institutional land use. Thus far we have discussed several examples of gateways: the gateway to the Pacific Rim (San Francisco or Los Angeles), the gateway to the Grand Canyon (Williams or Flagstaff), and the pre-auto gateway to the *metropolitan corridor*, Flagstaff's train depot. The city of St. Louis, Missouri, even built a grand archway, the famous Gateway Arch, to claim its status as the "Gateway to the West"—notwithstanding the geographical fact that it was Chicago—not St. Louis—that ultimately became the true gateway to the West after the Civil War. Chicago became the hub from which numerous transcontinental rail lines fanned out into the West, completely bypassing St. Louis.

In any case, gateways can be interpreted at practically any geographic scale, and here we see a small-scale example of one gateway to the campus of Northern Arizona University. The central authority of NAU has determined which gateway entrances to promote heavily, and the institution has marked them accordingly, with standardized "Northern Arizona University" signs placed strategically at ground level. These signs, or *markers*, serve to inform the observer that a change in purpose is taking place, as one moves from one side of the marker to the other. They confirm the territory that is under control of a given entity or institution, displaying its significance through expensive, stylish signage at their gateways of choice. That much money and design work was required to create signage such as this indicates that you are about to enter a rather important place. It follows that the look of the landscape will change as well, when you have moved past the gateway. In this case, the ad hoc, sporadic development that describes the South Side area is now giving way to the more disciplined, controlled landscape of a major academic institution.

STOP 15
FRONT: EXPANSION OF NORTHERN ARIZONA UNIVERSITY

As you walk south along Beaver Street, you will notice indicators suggesting that fundamental changes are taking place here. Parking lots now separate small, rundown houses, and standardized, blue signs adorn the lawns of small cottages (Figure 38). East of Beaver Street, other cottages can be seen with overgrown landscaping and trash spewed around nearby vacant lots. To the west is a contrasting geography of "newness," representing the centralized, institutional control of Northern Arizona University and its massive, sleek brick buildings constructed not long ago. How can we effectively read this landscape and the processes that are currently shaping it?

Figure 38. University buildings and parking lots surround these older South Side homes as Northern Arizona University continues to expand its domain. (Photo: Author's collection)

From one perspective, you have reached a geographical *front.* A front is a place where "the energies of the city and the country mix, merge, and compete; where the number of cross-grain commuters exceeds the number going into and out of the old Center; where struggles for control and political wars between places are yet to be resolved" (Clay 1996, 96). Not unlike a weather front, where one air mass is attempting to overtake another, so too is one landscape—and the population that controls it—slowly closing in on another as it expands outward. The front is where use values and exchange values compete, or to put it another way, where the struggle between "developers" and "sustainers" plays out.

Often, the type of front described above applies to the expanding urban fringe, where parking lots are overtaking farmland—the ubiquitous process referred to as urban sprawl. New land uses overtake older ones, usually based on economic contrasts that involve differing land values. Although your current location on the edge of campus is not exactly the urban fringe, the dynamics taking place here are quite similar. Keep in mind that these so-called fronts are not so much distinct boundaries as they are transition zones, or dynamic swaths of land that are undergoing change while under intense pressure to do so.

In this case, the contest involves two basic entities: an expanding NAU campus and a surviving South Side residential neighborhood. From where you stand looking south, the front is slowly moving from west to east, from the center of campus outward into formerly residential territory.

You can bet that this parking lot (labeled antiseptically as "P2" on a university map) is occupying space where a house or houses once stood. A similar fate may be in store for its next-door neighbors. Across the street from P2 is another cottage, still surviving but with new colors—labeled with a standard NAU sign as "19A, Employee Assistance and Wellness Office." What is unseen is the amount of property already purchased by NAU along this front that has not yet been altered. One would need to visit the county administration building to uncover recent property transactions in this neighborhood to gain a better understanding of NAU's expansion into the South Side. With these things in mind, it is clear that just because the new campus buildings "end" at Beaver Street, the influence and financial power of this grand institution does not.

In this case, you are walking through a zone in transition—in this case from residential to institutional land use. The power of investment, growth, and institutional energy is gradually taking its collective toll on a once-vibrant residential neighborhood. Beyond the immediate geography of the front are the peripheral implications of this transition. Numerous properties along nearby streets in close proximity to NAU have been changed from owner-occupied to rental housing, primarily as cheap housing for students. The periphery of NAU, then, is becoming more of a "student zone" than it once was, although our fellow student residents are currently mixed in quite well with more old-time South Side residents who have yet to sell their properties. With the front, then, comes a new social dynamic, the implications of which have yet to be studied. Make no mistake, however: The growth machine that envisions a larger, bigger NAU has not finished its job on this particular front. The university cannot easily expand in any other direction. To the south is Interstate 40; to the west and east are various cemeteries and private properties. One of the only options is for NAU to expand northward.

Having experienced the front, it is time to venture onto the campus itself, to witness a highly structured landscape produced in nearly every way through centralized authority. It is not surprising that such a place looks and functions quite differently from the other less disciplined landscapes already encountered.

Chapter 7

Flagstaff's *New Urbanism:* Northern Arizona University

STOP 16
Campus: A Century of Growth at NAU

Surrounding you at this spot are buildings that represent every major era of expansion at NAU. As you walk underneath the skywalk and face west, in front of you is Hanley Hall, constructed of Arizona Red and representing the physical edge of the World War II era campus. To the north (right) is the newest addition to campus, a sleek-looking, postmodern biochemistry building (Figure 39). To the south you will see structures from the modern era representing the 1960s—namely, the International-style physical sciences and chemistry buildings. You are thus standing at the intersection of three different phases of expansion at NAU.

Figure 39. The postmodern architecture of NAU's new Biochemistry building (right) contrasts sharply with Campbell Hall (left) representing the edge of the World War II-era campus. (Photo: Author's collection)

After experiencing the free-market world of downtown business districts and working-class residential neighborhoods, the sudden transition to a university landscape can be startling. With every shrub, building, sidewalk, and light post controlled aggressively by the highest levels of university administration, an American campus like that of NAU provides a rather unique example of a geographical space manipulated almost entirely by a centralized authority. The American college campus is a distinct landscape type, where the typical rules of culture, economics, and politics do not always apply as they do elsewhere across the American scene.

As you wander through the rather pastoral campus landscape of NAU, the notion that the university has developed as a community unto itself will become plainly evident. In this regard, NAU is little different from most other American universities and colleges. The planning concepts for American campus landscapes and architecture have since colonial times followed an ideal rooted in medieval English universities. In England, the idea of being "collegiate" included the notion that students and teachers would live and study together in "small, tightly regulated colleges" (Turner 1984, 3). This English ideal of college life contrasted sharply with that of continental Europe, where universities paid little attention to students' extracurricular activities outside of academics. Thus, the American university campus has followed the English precedent to a large degree. Even Thomas Jefferson, who designed the campus of the University of Virginia in 1817, described his goal as creating an "academical village" (Turner 1984, 3). American campus landscapes, then, have developed as inward-focused and relatively self-sufficient communities that include not only classrooms and laboratories, but recreational facilities, dining halls, student housing, sports arenas, social venues, and numerous other functions.

At the 1986 dedication of the Northern Arizona Normal School Historic District, NAU's vice president, Frank Besnette, spoke proudly of the community-oriented role played by our own campus:

> Today, NAU spans over 700 acres and includes some four million gross square feet of building space. Along the way to this point our traditions have followed. Of 88 primary campus buildings or complexes, 24 are residential quarters for some 6,000 occupants. This NAU characteristic has strongly reinforced an early aspiration that this institution be an academic community. Furthermore, I believe at last count, 30 campus buildings or complexes, including some of the oldest and most recent, are named after associates and supporters of the institution over the past 87 years.

Although the "college as community" ideal was initially derived from England, the American campus has developed some of its own distinct characteristics, so that "the physical forms of American colleges and universities—their buildings, grounds, and spaces—are different from anything elsewhere" (Turner 1984, 3). A variety of distinctly American characteristics can be seen on the NAU campus. Whereas English campuses have generally developed within urbanized areas of large cities, Americans began early on to place college campuses in remote and rural locales. Reflecting what still exists today as a characteristically American anti-urban sentiment, the ideal of a "college in nature" prevailed, with the notion that learning should take place in settings "removed from the corrupting forces of the city" (Turner 1984, 4). Of course, the colleges themselves were required to become miniature cities in their own right if they were to succeed at becoming their own self-sustaining, academic communities.

A related trait of American college campuses is found in their low-density openness and expansive qualities—largely rejecting the English tradition of a compact, clustered urban campus. In the United States, campuses with widely separated buildings and manicured carpets of lawn have become the norm. The word "campus" itself reflects this idea of "college as countryside." At first, the term campus was used in its strict Latin meaning for "a field," describing the green, expansive grounds of Princeton and other American universities already developed by the late eighteenth century. Eventually, the term assumed a wider significance, as a college campus came to represent the entire college property, including the buildings as well. Together, these distinctly American ideals of college as community and college as open space practically define the experience of NAU today.

Consequently, the NAU campus and many of its counterparts elsewhere can be perceived of as experiments in urbanism. The American university campus represents a rather successful attempt at bringing many of the positive social attributes of the city into the countryside. Of course, like all social experiments throughout history, none are ever completely successful. Still, NAU can be viewed here as a local model of urban development that has occurred outside of the typical city setting, and through processes other than those provided by typical free-market forces. As Flagstaff and other rapidly growing communities struggle to hang on to some of their rural, small-town traits, the experience of NAU and its campus can be instructive.

The geographical development of NAU compares very closely to most major universities throughout the United States. As with commercial and residential architecture, the institutional buildings of a college campus serve as excellent clues to how, and when, the college campus grew or remained stagnant. Many mid-sized to large universities were originally *teachers colleges*, where the primary goal of the college was to prepare future teachers of America; NAU is no exception. Even today, the education programs at NAU are among the largest of the university, a product to some degree of NAU's traditional reason for being.

Even more important, the pattern of NAU's development throughout the past century strongly reflects geographical trends and major historical events at the national level. For instance, NAU grew slowly from 1899 through 1925, when a grand total of eight buildings were clustered around Old Main on North Campus. Like most colleges in America, NAU saw very little building construction during the 1930s because of the Great Depression, when approximately a quarter of all American workers were unemployed. Building construction had stopped throughout the country for some 15 years, from 1930 to 1945. This was true for houses and commercial buildings as well.

There were a few exceptions. One of them was the movie theater. These places provided some much-needed, inexpensive entertainment for a country suffering from economic depression. Another exception was American roadside commercial development. Throughout the Great Depression, few new automobiles were purchased, but many used cars were still being driven, and their life spans were prolonged. Thus, Americans continued to travel, especially along the major U.S. routes that had been authorized a few years earlier. So, motor courts and cabins, early motels, gas stations, and roadside diners fared relatively well during the Depression (Liebs 1995).

A third exception to the lack of growth during this time consisted of the larger college campuses, such as the Big Ten or Pac Ten schools and their equivalents. These schools were financially well endowed and thus had building projects funded well in advance. These large schools tended to keep building right through the Depression using the wealth acquired during the Roaring Twenties. Accordingly, these colleges kept hiring faculty and staff; these people needed places to live, so it was not uncommon to see new housing tracts pop up in the adjacent college town during the 1930s. Due to NAU's modest size at that time (then known as Northern Arizona State Teachers College), not much growth and expansion took place on campus or in Flagstaff.

The pattern of growth at NAU since World War II is indicative of national trends. Mirroring the population explosion of the "baby boom" years following the War, college campuses were forced to expand to meet a rapid increase in enrollment. First, World War II veterans took advantage of the G.I. bill for education, a federal monetary incentive that encouraged soldiers to go back to school following the war. In succeeding years, colleges also saw ever-greater numbers of students knocking on their doors as the baby boom generation came of college age during the 1960s (Turner 1984). Further, higher education was becoming accessible to a greater proportion of Americans. Between 1951 and 1961, the proportion of the population that went to college increased from 24 to 37 percent. Paul Turner, author of *Campus: An American Planning Tradition* (1984, 249), explained, "The words 'desperate,' 'unprecedented,' and 'terrifying' were commonly used to describe this 'educational explosion,' and projections of future enrollments became a major preoccupation of educators and college planners." Northern Arizona University was clearly riding the wave of this expansion.

NAU benefited greatly from this national boom in college expansion, during the late 1950s and throughout the 1960s. Growth continued slowly but steadily through the 1970s and 1980s, and many more buildings and academic programs were added during that time. A second, minor boom occurred during the 1980s and into the 1990s. Between 1987 and 1993, for example, NAU saw the construction of several new dormitories (including Mountain View), the new Cline Library, the University Union building, and the NAU Recreation Center, which cost 4 million dollars in 1989. These are all considered vital facilities to today's campus. Students and faculty (including myself) take these facilities for granted today, but try to imagine an NAU campus without them, as recently as 1988!

The student population boomed during this period as well, with amazing enrollment increases of 11.5 percent during 1988 and 8 percent in 1989. In July of 1990, an enrollment cap was placed on the campus to prevent any more students from enrolling that year; this was NAU's first enrollment cap ever. At that time, university officials were predicting a student population size of 17,000 by the mid-1990s, and this expectation has been nearly fulfilled. Since then, enrollment has stabilized, and NAU is currently experiencing slow growth in terms of additional campus facilities and infrastructure. By 2001 NAU was being challenged by minor budget cuts and a slow decline in enrollment, which continued to challenge the school's leaders through 2002.

More than a half-century after World War II, many universities including NAU have come to resemble full-scale cities in themselves. Of course, the typical challenges associated with rapid economic growth have accompanied the national expansion of universities. NAU and its counterparts have had to face very real, urban problems since the 1950s, such as higher population densities, conflicting land uses both within and around campus, increasing traffic congestion on campus streets, and opposing interests of a highly diverse population of students, faculty, and staff. NAU's own experiment with urbanism in the countryside has indeed led to perhaps a more realistic urban environment than some would have hoped for.

One dominant reason for NAU's overall growth during the past two decades is found 140 miles south of campus—the Phoenix metropolitan area. NAU depends heavily not just on in-state students, but more specifically on students from Maricopa County, the home of Phoenix and its suburbs. Arizona has been one of America's fastest growing states, and by the year 2000 it was the second fastest growing state with only Nevada surpassing it. Arizona State University and the University of Arizona have also seen enrollment growth during these decades. We can conclude generally that the growth of Arizona's three primary universities is a reflection of continued population growth in Arizona.

The growth in Arizona is one part of a larger, national trend that geographers refer to as the migration shift from the *Snow Belt* to the *Sun Belt*. What is probably the most significant movement of population during the last few decades is the continued migration of people, jobs, and industry from the industrial Northeast and Midwest (Snow Belt) to the warmer climates of the southern United States. Although there is no official definition of the Sun Belt, in most people's minds it generally consists of those regions from the Carolinas and Florida to southern California. Arizona has clearly been on the receiving end of this continued migration trend. NAU's growth since the 1960s, therefore, is indirectly a product of this national population shift.

From where you stand near the skywalk, continue to walk south into the central part of campus, along the brick pedestrian path. If you are fortunate enough to be walking here during the change of class periods during fall or spring semester, you will quickly realize that the automobile is not the dominant mode of transportation. Perhaps more than anywhere else in America, the typical university campus is one of the few landscape scenes that still behaves like the traditional *walking city*, where foot and bike traffic persist as the most convenient transportation modes.

STOP 17
BREAK: NAU'S PEDESTRIAN CORRIDOR

Just as major roads and freeways are designed to enhance efficiency and speed by minimizing "obstructions" (especially pedestrians, cross-traffic, and residential neighborhoods), NAU has created its own corridor for students, who are often expected to move north or south in a hurry on their way to class (Figure 40). Consequently, NAU's rush hour takes place for 15 minutes or so every hour when classes are in session during the day.

Figure 40. Looking north along NAU's pedestrian-bike corridor near the University Union. This is a geographical break in the landscape, where the buildings in the background are oriented to the railroad street grid, and the pedestrian path in the foreground is oriented to the Township and Range survey system, lined up directly north-south. (Photo: Author's collection)

The idea of such a corridor, if we apply more geographical logic to it, is to decrease the friction of distance between north and south campus. Instead of making students weave around buildings in all sorts of directions and trajectories, why not provide a corridor dedicated to the speedy movement of north-south traffic on campus? That is exactly what has been done. So if we stretch the imagination a bit (a common exercise of geographers), NAU has reduced the *effective* time and space between north and south campus.

Of course, the necessity for such a bike-pedestrian corridor is due to the campus's geographical situation. The general shape of NAU's campus is an elongated rectangle oriented north-south, and it is quite spread out over a large area which represents the typical American pastoral ideal. These spatial factors made it necessary to link the north and south parts of campus for four different modes of on-campus transportation: foot, bike, car, and transit bus. Many students and employees have already experienced society's over-reliance on the automobile on campus, as our main campus roads (especially Knoles and San Francisco) are often extremely congested—consisting at times of one long string of cars from south to north campus between classes. More students, faculty, and staff now recognize that it takes just as much time to drive through campus as it does to walk or bike. Even if walking takes longer in some cases, many people find out that it is less stressful, good exercise, and downright enjoyable. Certainly, a walk through campus today gives us some idea of what it was like to walk through pre-automobile America, when we took more time to travel and to experience the details in the places that we encounter along the way.

Just north of the University Union building you will notice a kink, or bend in the landscape of the pedestrian corridor and actually the entire central part of campus. As indicated by the bend in the corridor itself, the northern part of campus is skewed slightly to the northeast, somewhat out of alignment with the southern part of campus (Figure 40). You are standing at what geographers refer to as a *break in the landscape*, or just simply a *break*. In this context, a break is defined as an abrupt and visible transition, or switch, in the design of the streets and the landscape features existing within those streets (Clay 1980). Breaks are most often found where one grid of streets seemingly clashes with another street plan oriented in a different direction. The break itself, or the intersection between two opposing street plans, is often characterized by a series of bizarre, irregular intersections and sometimes strangely shaped buildings that attempt to adapt to the configuration. Often, the break separates landscapes based on their specific periods of development, given that one street plan or area of development has often preceded an adjoining one by a decade or more. Thus, the break can become the visible division line between different architectural styles, land uses, and street patterns.

You are familiar with numerous breaks already, and you have certainly encountered several along the Tour thus far. The transition from South Side to the campus of NAU was one type of break, as was the "edge" of the original campus we inspected at the skywalk. The break at which you stand now consists of a very common one found on the periphery of railroad-town street grids, whereby the original street grid laid out by the railroad company makes a sudden transition to newer developments aligned with the Township and Range survey system. Streets, sidewalks, and buildings to the north of where you stand (basically north of the University Union) are oriented to the railroad, whereas the campus landscape to the south is oriented to the cardinal directions of the Township and Range survey system. You are thus standing on the physical edge of the original railroad town grid.

A closer inspection of this spot reveals something more. You will notice a garage door just to the north with a "no parking" sign on the east side of the building, curiously with a grass lawn growing in front of it. Another clue is based on what isn't there: no structures in any direction north, south, east, or west of this little pedestrian plaza north of the Union. To the east and west are narrow streets that apparently continue on both sides of the walkway. Why is this? These indicators in the landscape suggest that this bike-pedestrian thoroughfare was once a street and intersection for cars and delivery trucks. In fact, the pedestrian path on which you have been walking consisted of an extension of Humphreys Street from the South Side (see Figure 21). More recently, NAU has been developing a more pedestrian-friendly environment, and the University Master Plan, still under revision, promises to make many more changes toward this end.

Just south of this transformed intersection is one of the most important places on campus—the University Union. The term "University Union" says something about its geographical significance. Just as a city's Union Station once gathered passenger trains of various railroads into one central urban hub, the University Union here gathers numerous centralized activities of great importance to a student body. This is basically a university's version of a community center. Here is yet another hub, or symbol of centrality, constructed near the geographical center of campus. One student's hypothetical suggestion to "meet at the Union," is immediately understood by another, one convenience of a central feature or *landmark* commonly known to everyone.

As you continue along this corridor past the Union, you will notice a variety of landscape features that indicate the presence of larger American cultural values and contemporary trends. For instance, our interest in environmental conservation is displayed through the occasional appearance of blue recycling bins, both inside and outside buildings, and along this very path. Our need for safe and secure public spaces—given an overall perception that America is not as safe as it once was (even prior to September 11, 2001)—is witnessed through the existence of posts with emergency telephones attached to them and a distinct lack of tall, dense shrubbery that might hide potential criminals. Likewise, we reveal our strong community pride in the variety of social activities available here on campus, including places to sit and talk, throw the frisbee, play volleyball and basketball, and eat outside. Further, our desire as Americans to control nature, or to conquer geography, as Peirce Lewis put it, is seen with the immaculately planned and maintained vegetation (in this context, landscaping) that is so nicely ordered and neatly trimmed. All of these aspects of American culture can therefore be read in the very landscape through which you are walking.

There is a growing movement across America to replicate the types of pedestrian-oriented and people-centered landscapes that you have been walking through on campus. Since the early 1990s, a growing reaction to the auto-dominated world of suburbia has emerged, where, many claim, community interaction has diminished to almost nothing. The United States is the most suburbanized country in the world, and the most dependent on the automobile. This is not to say that the automobile is entirely bad for our society. However, it is important to understand how the automobile has transformed our nation's spatial structure and human landscapes like no other technology in the history of this country (though the railroad came close). America's love affair with the automobile is not diminishing either, and perhaps it shouldn't. The auto symbolizes increased mobility and, for someone who can afford it, more freedom to live where one chooses, away from the workplace. The hope, of course, is that automobiles will become much kinder to our natural environment than they are currently. The advent of hybrid cars and other gas-less wonders offer hope that improved air quality is on the way.

The goal of this new movement, then, is not to eliminate the automobile or to curse it as evil. Instead, the idea is to de-emphasize the role of the automobile in our local communities while promoting residential developments that emphasize people. This growing movement that is working to put people first and the automobile second is called the *new urbanism.*

The concepts of new urbanism specifically involve spatial, or geographical relationships between houses, businesses, streets, and public spaces. Just some of the major design features of "new urbanist" communities include the following: (1) Garages are being placed in the rear of the properties, not attached dominantly to the fronts of houses. (2) Small public park areas are encouraging neighborhood interaction. (3) Houses, townhouses, and apartments are clustered relatively densely, even if they have their own separate lots. (4) In *mixed-use development*, retail businesses are allowed to coexist with housing so that residents can walk or bike to the local store. Today, local zoning laws often prevent mixed uses, and we tend to live far from commercial businesses and work places. We need a car to get anywhere, even to do our grocery shopping. Combining commercial and residential land uses in appropriate ways can eliminate countless trips in the car. (5) Houses are located close to the street rather than in the back of the lot. (6) Incorporation of alleys helps to eliminate driveways. (7) A wide variety of building designs and architectural styles promote some individualism among residents.

These are only some of the new urbanist concepts increasingly being applied to new housing subdivisions and planned communities, but they are vital if we are to de-emphasize the automobile and encourage community livability. You might recognize some of these ideas from neighborhoods you have already seen on this Tour—indeed, many of these new urbanist concepts are not new at all, but have been tried and tested for over a century in older American neighborhoods and throughout European villages and towns. Architects, planners, and even developers have begun to realize that there is an increasing demand for such neighborhoods, and the new urbanism movement will likely continue and expand uninterrupted for quite some time.

The new urbanism is conceived of as a market-driven process—it is not communism or socialism as some critics may naively think. Instead, architects have been on the leading edge of new urbanism concepts, and they have enlightened developers who have in turn become interested in incorporating these concepts into their developments. Now that more than a few developers have taken a chance to try it, even more are coming on board. As much as America likes to view developers (and lawyers, of course) as evil, they are now responsible for planning and building the bulk of our housing stock in America. It therefore makes sense that they would play a leading role in creating people-friendly communities and building these new urbanist ideas into the landscape. Basically, if the demand is there, they will build it for the profits—the American way. One can only hope that the result will be more livable communities. In a sense, then, you have been experiencing the ideas of new urbanism throughout the Tour, and now on the relatively pedestrian-centric and student-oriented NAU campus. Indeed, from campus, things will change. We will be moving shortly into a realm where the automobile is King, and where landscape features revolve around the needs of the car.

From here, either walk through the Union building to its west entrance, or walk around the Union toward Cline Library. A brief stroll through the Union will reveal many of its central functions, from student bulletin boards with club and organization announcements, to various eateries and services. If the Union happens to be closed for some reason, simply walk around the pathway to the Union parking lot on the west side, eventually meeting Knoles Drive.

STOP 18
URBAN INFILL: CLINE LIBRARY

From a geographical perspective, Cline Library represents nothing less than NAU's gateway to the world of information and resources—both printed and electronic. Thomas Jefferson was actually the first prominent American to view the university library as the main feature of a campus, and it was he who introduced research as a significant university function. The primary function of the library itself is to "obtain, catalogue, and shelve printed matter, and—through architecture, among other means—to suggest the importance of the printed word" (Gaines 1991, 14). Although their interiors are usually designed to appear grand and impressive, the library buildings themselves are designed to be functional. Each library always requires a huge quantity of space for the meticulously organized stacks of books, and it requires specific spaces designed for specialized purposes, such as circulation, references, periodicals, reading rooms, computer rooms, archives, card files, music listening rooms, micro-film viewing, and all of the behind the scenes control centers of the library itself. With all of these functions aimed specifically at providing access to information, the campus library serves as a focal point for any university. Here we have another veritable intersection between local and global spaces, essentially a gateway—information wise—to the rest of the world.

Cline Library today maintains all of these functions and more, but this was not always the case. In the midst of NAU's booming growth period, the university in 1989 undertook by far the most expensive project in NAU's history, and arguably the most vital. This new addition to Cline Library cost $17 million and added 120,000 square feet of space to the original 83,000 square feet—a 150 percent expansion (Figure 41). Essentially, it gave NAU a new, state-of-the-art library that satisfied the criticisms of student leaders and university officials that the former library was inadequate. The library now stands as a prominent, postmodern feature within NAU's campus landscape, and it serves as a good example of how local projects such as this are often made possible by external, or non-local factors.

Figure 41. Cline Library addition, with the San Francisco Peaks in the background. An infill project completed in 1991, the library's striking postmodern architecture contrasts greatly with the 1960s-era International-style surrounding it on central campus. (Photo: Author's collection)

In this case, the library's expansion was enabled by the Arizona State Legislature's approval of a bill that added about $264 million to the bonding capacity of the state's three universities. NAU received a share of that allocation, and that funding was used to pay for Cline Library's expansion and the $5.1 million renovation of Old Main and Ashurst. In this case, the state of Arizona had to approve the money that could be used for bonds by the three state universities, who could then decide how to use their bond allocations. Wisely, NAU's administration decided to update a sadly lacking library to what it is today—a big step in the right direction as NAU competes nationally for students and recognition.

An article in the *Daily Sun* documented the groundbreaking ceremony that took place on May 10, 1990 for the new library expansion. Flagstaff's own "Citizen of the Century," Platt Cline (who died in October of 2001 at the age of 90), for whom the library is named, attended the ceremony, saying, "This is a historic event; one of the most important in this university's 90 years." Platt Cline paid special tribute to NAU students, including student-government leaders, for their impressive lobbying for the library expansion. A *Daily Sun* article recorded the event, quoting Cline as saying: "The students know that the library is the heartbeat of the campus, and we all know that the students are the heart of the university."

Platt Cline was for many years the editor of the *Daily Sun*, and after that he wrote several monumental books on the history of NAU and Flagstaff. He and his wife, Barbara, had lived in Flagstaff since 1938, and Platt earned the Arizona Newspaper Association's Master Editor-Publisher and Golden Service Awards. At one point, he was also named Flagstaff's Citizen of the Year, and later, Citizen of the Century. If you walk inside the library's main entrance, you can see a photo of Platt and Barbara Cline on the south wall of the lobby.

If you have been paying attention to the buildings that surround Cline Library, you may have observed that the new library doesn't quite fit in somehow. And you'd be right, from an architectural standpoint. You are now standing in the midst of the 1960s era campus, where a hoard of plain and boxy International-style buildings reflect the university's most rapid periods of growth. The Blome, Gammage, and North Union buildings suggest a campus moving gradually north from Old Main prior to the 1950s. However, the rapid expansion of the 1960s saw the campus reorient itself to the south. You are now standing in the midst of that expansive period, and consequently it is the rather drab, unappealing architecture of the modern era that dominates this landscape.

There are certain exceptions to the rule, however, and it is the geographer's job not only to notice such exceptions, or intrusions, in a particular landscape, but also to attempt an explanation. In this case, Cline Library represents a new intrusion into a previously settled campus landscape—what planners would call *urban infill.* Generally, urban infill projects have become a rather recent trend in the discipline of urban planning, a concerted effort to diminish the negative impacts of urban sprawl (Duany, Plater-Zyberk, and Speck 2000). Instead of continuing to develop widely scattered pieces of territory on a city's periphery, the philosophy of urban infill dictates that new developments be constructed in the existing urban area. The idea is to focus growth inward rather than outward. Some cities have succeeded with urban infill projects more than others, and certain cities have even legislated the need for infill development through the use of *urban growth boundaries.* Portland, Oregon often serves as the classic example of a major city that has literally made development outside of its "growth boundary" illegal. Other cities, including Flagstaff, are just beginning to learn the costs and benefits of infill development.

Currently, infill projects are being promoted in Flagstaff as concerns about rapid growth and environmental decay become more elevated in people's minds. Recent examples of infill projects in town include the construction of Walgreen Drugs and Barnes & Noble, both along Milton Avenue not far from the downtown. Some people have expressed concern, however, that such infill development will only lead to increased traffic nightmares on major thoroughfares. Others applaud the philosophy, given the notion that for every new building constructed within town, one more tract of land has been saved from development on the periphery. Flagstaff's city leaders have recently established our own urban growth boundary; it is too early to determine its implications for the community.

On campus, Cline Library serves as an excellent example of infill, whereby a new building (really a massive addition to the old one) has appeared in the previously developed landscape of central campus. Also in the early 1990s, NAU witnessed several other infill projects, including the University Union building. Given the geographical restrictions that all but prevent expansion in the future, it is likely that these will not be the last infill projects to be seen on this part of campus.

From Cline Library, walk north along the curving Knoles Drive to the front side of Old Main.

STOP 19
HISTORIC DISTRICT: NAU'S NORTH CAMPUS

This is where NAU began, right here in Old Main just over a century ago (Figure 42). This is NAU's first and only true Victorian era structure, representing the Romanesque Revival style similar to that of the Courthouse. Construction on Old Main required 5 years, from 1894 to 1899, for reasons that will be discussed shortly. The 1890s were the last years during which Victorian styles remained popular throughout the United States. Consequently, unlike other college campuses in the East and Midwest that developed during or prior to the Victorian period, NAU was a late bloomer—reflecting the later settlement of the American West. Romanesque features on Old Main consist of rough-faced and thick masonry walls, a large, round-arched entryway, two prominent towers with conical roofs, parapeted dormers, and numerous round-arched windows.

Figure 42. Old Main, the first structure built on the campus of present-day NAU, completed in 1899. In 1986 it became one of numerous buildings on north campus listed on the National Register of Historic Places. (Photo: Author's collection)

If you notice a resemblance to other buildings already seen along the Tour—including the County Courthouse, the old train depot, and the Weatherford Hotel—you'd be right. Old Main was constructed with Moenkopi Sandstone, or Arizona Red, quarried locally as discussed earlier. Further, according to the National Register of Historic Places nomination form, Old Main is the best-preserved and largest example of the Romanesque Revival style in northern Arizona.

Although Old Main is thought of as NAU's first building, the structure was not originally intended to serve as the beginning of an eventual 15,000-student campus. Instead, the project began at a Flagstaff town meeting on May 21, 1894—the same meeting where the decision was made to construct the new county courthouse. At the meeting, citizens approved the construction of two new educational buildings: a territorial reform school building, and a new public school building for Flagstaff. It is important to remember that Arizona was a territory, not a state, prior to 1912. The territorial government in 1893 had approved a tax levy to raise $30,000 to construct a reform school building in Flagstaff. However, the start of construction was postponed because of insufficient funding, namely $300 to pay for the 130 acres of railroad subsidy land on which Old Main stands. Thus, at the 1894 town meeting, the hat was passed, and $400 was raised instantly through donations. The walls and roof were soon constructed, but the building stood unfinished for some time, almost 4 years, lacking its windows and interior woodwork.

This construction delay was precisely what the Flagstaff community hoped for, amazingly enough. Its immediate completion would have allowed fulfillment of the structure's originally intended purpose—a reform school, housing "vicious youths of both sexes," as the newspaper put it at the time. The town wanted a territorial building so that their new community would gain prominence, but they were not particularly thrilled about the reform school; instead, the community had other ideas for its use (Cline 1994). A political battle was waged between the community, the territorial legislature in Phoenix, and the U.S. Department of the Interior, pertaining to the building's eventual use. Initially, it was territorial governor Murphy who wished to have the planned structure used as a reform school in 1894. His successor, however, Louis Hughes, proposed that the Department of the Interior approve and fund the use of the building as a summer school for science, supporting the community's interest in using the building for educational purposes. This proposal received additional support from a well-known newcomer to town, astronomer Percival Lowell. In 1893, Flagstaff became the new home of an astronomical observatory established by Lowell himself. He and other community leaders hoped that the establishment of the observatory would lend credibility to the idea of using the new campus structure as a school of science. In short, the Department of the Interior declined Hughes's recommendation. The school of science idea received another setback when Hughes was succeeded by Governor Benjamin J. Franklin, a descendant of the famed colonial forefather, who had little interest in the idea. Local leaders were not discouraged, however, and continued to lobby at the capitol in Phoenix.

By 1897, the incomplete building had become an embarrassment and a huge controversy within the territory. At the same time, the territorial government was struggling to secure funding for a new capitol building in Phoenix, further draining funding possibilities. In 1897, funds were finally available to finish the new structure in Flagstaff, but this time as a branch of the hospital for the insane. Apparently, however, few were convinced that its use as an asylum would actually become reality. The struggle finally ended on the side of community interests in 1899 when Governor Murphy announced that the building should either be sold or transformed into a normal school in Flagstaff. To the satisfaction of local community interests, Murphy signed House Bill No. 41 establishing the Northern Arizona Normal School on March 11, 1899. The official future of NAU had just begun.

By 1899, more than 300 normal schools had been established throughout the United States. The normal school at Tempe eventually became Arizona State University. Like the others, the new northern Arizona institution offered 4 years of high school and additional training that would lead students primarily into a life of teaching, through the issuance of official teaching certificates. The school began with an initial enrollment of 23 students in 1899, and awarded only four high school diplomas in the 1900–01 school year, indicating the school's meager beginnings. Proposals in the territorial legislature to discontinue funding placed the normal school's future in a position of uncertainty during its first few years. To keep the school and to encourage its growth, local citizens had to fight hard, including George Babbitt, who lobbied for new residence halls. As a result, the school's next two buildings—Taylor Hall and Bury Hall—were constructed in 1905 and 1908, respectively.

Lowell Observatory, and Percival Lowell himself, played a further role in the school's eventual success. An advertised attraction of the new school included instructional access for students to the observatory's 24-inch telescope. Dr. Lowell also lectured occasionally to the students about matters of astronomy and the research being conducted at the observatory, located west of downtown on Mars Hill. An early Lowell associate, Andrew Douglass, was also listed as the school's "resident astronomer" in the 1901 catalog. Thus, although Lowell Observatory is most often promoted today through its association with Flagstaff's heritage and development, the observatory played an equally significant role in the early development of the future of Northern Arizona University.

There are some important geographical lessons in the story above. First, projects like this usually require some form of state or federal funding because cities and towns often cannot support such extensive projects on their own. Thus, Flagstaff wisely took advantage of Arizona Territory's funding for a reform school, though they desired to eventually use the new building for other purposes. Human landscapes, then, are often the product of some combination of local, state, or national political decisions and funding sources. The free-market economy, as cherished as it is in this country, still plays only a part (albeit a large one) in the building and shaping of our human landscapes.

A second lesson has to do with geographic proximity. It is common in America today, as well as in the past, for citizens to oppose projects that may detract from their quality of life or private property values. A contemporary example is the recent opposition to a Super Wal-Mart store in Chandler (a suburb of Phoenix). The proposed store would have been placed very close to an upper-middle class neighborhood, and consequently local residents rebelled and protested passionately against the store. Still, they were not necessarily against Wal-Mart itself; more accurately, they did not want to see Wal-Mart built at that location. They feared, probably correctly, that the store would lead to increased traffic congestion, crime, and a diminished local environmental quality. This type of reaction to any development project is known as *NIMBY*, or *Not In My Back Yard*. Look for it in a community near you! The development of Old Main here was also a product of NIMBY, given that the local community wanted the prestige of acquiring a territorial building that they could not afford. However, they did not want to see a reform school built in their "back yard," a use that they felt would detract from the positive qualities of the community.

A third geographical lesson involves Flagstaff's burning desire for a territorial building of any kind, even if it was planned initially as a reform school. The period of American history roughly between 1840 and 1900 represented America's primary town-building era. During that time, new town sites often developed along a transportation corridor, at an opportunistic physical location to capture the trade of its hinterland, or at a location where natural resources could be developed. Regardless, all new towns desired economic and population growth, and many hoped to become the next regional metropolis if at all possible. Of course, the vast majority of these small towns did not succeed, otherwise we would have too many large cities for our economic system to handle. But a few, all of which began as small villages or towns, did make it to the big time: Phoenix, Los Angeles, Chicago, Charlotte (N.C.), St. Louis, and so forth. The point here is that all communities wanted to grow, and their town "boosters," such as their chambers of commerce, widely advertised their towns to prospective businesses, merchants, and settlers. This situation has not changed to this day, as towns and cities continue to compete for regional—and now global—business interests and new links to the developing global economy. Thus, the drive for growth is not a new idea, but quite an American ideal rooted in our drive for "progress." During the age of town-building in America, progress generally referred to continued economic growth and efficient production of natural resources for human use and consumption. The Flagstaff community was no exception. After being founded as a railroad town in 1882, its new citizens immediately began the process of growth and development. Old Main, as we know it now, became one part of that process.

The early development of NAU's north campus landscape provides a fascinating story. Old Main, of course, was the first building completed on campus in 1899. Its sandstone construction served as the model for numerous other buildings on campus, right through the 1940s. For 9 years following the start of construction, Old Main was the only building on campus. Therefore, it housed all necessary activities and functions of the early school, which consisted of an assembly room, library, classrooms, recitation rooms, offices, and cloak room, according to the National Register nomination form. As new buildings were added around it during the ensuing four decades, many of these primary functions were decentralized into their own dedicated structures, one building at a time.

The second and third buildings on campus were the aforementioned Taylor (1905) and Bury (1908) residence halls, constructed to house the increasing student population. Taylor Hall was named after the Normal School's first president, Almon Nicholas Taylor, who presided over the school from 1899 to 1909. A separate dining facility—later named Hanley Hall—was added in 1912. Affectionately referred to as "Mother Hanley," Margaret Hanley was the first dining room superintendent and long-time school employee. Two years later, a third dormitory was constructed, Morton Hall. Bury, Hanley, and Morton Halls were all constructed with the locally quarried Arizona Red sandstone in an effort to project a unified campus appearance in accordance with Old Main. By this time, the use of this rock had become a central theme for the developing campus.

The growth of campus picked up its pace just prior to the 1920s. Campbell Hall, the fourth dormitory, was constructed in 1916 directly east of Morton Hall and was the only structure to actually face away from the central campus. In 1920 the center of campus activity came to focus on the new Ashurst Auditorium, built on the west side of Old Main. Prior to its construction, the school made use of the Orpheum Theater downtown for large gatherings such as dances and graduation ceremonies. Indicating the continuing link between Lowell Observatory and the school, the observatory's director, Dr. C. O. Lampland, formally announced the discovery of Planet Pluto in Ashurst Auditorium in 1930. Although not a physical part of Old Main itself, the red sandstone construction of Ashurst Auditorium provided, for Old Main, a more symmetrical appearance. Old Main was planned initially to be symmetrical, complete with east and west wings. Only the east wing was ultimately completed, however, and the west wing idea was scrapped due to funding limitations.

The reputation of the school was further enhanced with the construction of what later became known as the Blome building, also in 1920. It was constructed specifically for use as a training school for elementary teachers. It was under the leadership of the school's second president after 1909, Rudolph Blome, that the normal school gained a reputation as an excellent teachers' school. Blome successfully placed the school on a more secure financial base, and he presided over the normal school throughout World War I. He was eventually asked to resign, however, due to his previous German education. The training school, later named to honor President Blome, served primarily as an on-campus elementary school where elementary education majors could practice their student teaching.

A 1904 Victorian-style cottage had to be moved to make way for the Blome building. In 1920, Lynn Banks McMullen became the next president of the normal school, and it was McMullen who had the cottage moved to its new location directly south of Ashurst Auditorium in 1921. Initially, the state had allocated $9,500 for a new building to be used as an on-campus residence. McMullen saved the state (and thus the taxpayers) this money, however, when he decided to renovate the relocated 1904 cottage into the residence of the president. McMullen used his designing skills to remodel the Victorian cottage into a bungalow. Between 1921 and 1959, every school president used the bungalow as his residence, which was officially named Herrington House after its original owner.

President McMullen, for whom McMullen Circle is named, was also responsible for initiating a variety of campus beautification projects during the 1920s and 30s. Prior to 1921 the entire campus remained treeless and grassless; in 1921 a student community landscaping project took care of the problem. The first phase of environmental improvements came when McMullen and a small army of students hauled in topsoil and planted a wide variety of trees in the central campus area in front of Old Main. Their inventory of trees included ponderosa pine, Colorado blue spruce, Douglas fir, elms, and poplars. Throughout the years many of these trees have matured to provide for the park-like campus area that you see here today. Further, concrete sidewalks and curbs were added, light fixtures were placed along the roads, and flowerbeds were constructed, along with a fountain. Also in that year, a tennis court that had been in front of Old Main was moved north to make way for the new east-west campus street, today's McMullen Circle. By the time the institution was designated Northern Arizona State Teachers College in 1925, nearly the full complement of buildings and landscaping were in place on north campus. Except for the vegetation that has matured over the years, the scene here on north campus today has changed very little since its 1921 makeover.

Today's north campus continued to grow sporadically between 1920 and World War II. Located just south of Old Main, the Physical Education building was completed in 1926, with the first indoor swimming pool in northern Arizona. Four years later, just after the beginning of the Great Depression, Gammage Library was completed under the direction of then-president Grady Gammage. After the library was completed, students assisted with moving books from the old library in Old Main to the new facility. Grady Gammage assumed the presidency in 1926 and is remembered for his efforts to have the institution's name changed yet again in 1929, to the Arizona State Teachers College at Flagstaff. As expected, the Depression brought campus expansion to a near standstill. The exception was the construction of North Hall in 1935, made possible through the financial assistance of Roosevelt's New Deal and the Public Works Administration. Serving both as a dormitory and campus dining facility, North Hall completed the collection of red sandstone dormitories that had begun 21 years earlier with Morton Hall. North Hall was also the last building constructed on campus during the historic period, the development of today's North Campus. No permanent campus buildings were constructed for 14 years following the completion of North Hall.

In the latest fashion of historic preservation interests, most of the original north campus was officially designated as a historic district on the National Register of Historic Places in November of 1986. The original boundaries of the official NAU district are seen in Figure 43. This is the only official National Register district that you will encounter on this Tour. To better understand the origin and significance of this particular historic district, we should review the basic history of the government's role in the preservation movement itself; the origins of the National Register itself are historically complex.

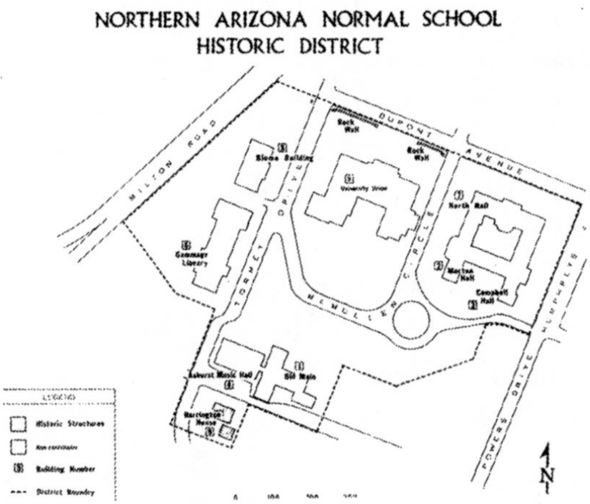

Figure 43. Map of the Northern Arizona Normal School Historic District, accepted to the National Register of Historic Places in 1986. (Map courtesy of National Register nomination form)

One important contributing factor to the rise of heritage and historic preservation is the increasing role of government, at both local and federal levels. It is important to note that early leadership in the emerging preservation movement was characterized by its reliance on private citizens, not government (Murtagh 1988). During the nineteenth century, a certain set of assumptions was established regarding how preservation efforts were to be undertaken. These assumptions included "the idea that private citizens, not government, were the proper advocates for preservation; that only buildings and sites associated with military and political figures were worthy of preservation; that such sites must be treated as shrines or icons; and that women would assume a dominant role in the acquisition and management of such properties" (Murtagh 1988, 30). The latter assumption was most heavily influenced by Ann Pamela Cunningham's efforts to save Mount Vernon, the Virginia plantation home of George Washington and his descendants. When developers sought to purchase the house and transform it into a hotel, a public outcry ensued, with the hope that either the state of Virginia or the federal government would purchase the estate instead. Neither government body was interested, so Ann Cunningham organized a patriotic group of women in 1853 that sought donations from throughout the South and ultimately from the entire country for its purchase. "Their gentility belied by their determination, this Mount Vernon Ladies' Association of the Union accepted no answer but 'yes'. In five years, Mount Vernon was theirs—and remains so today, despite subsequent offers by the government to relieve the ladies of their trust" (Murtagh 1988, 28).

Substantial federal government involvement in preservation can be dated to the early twentieth century. Prior to the 1930s and the Great Depression, the government took two important actions that set the stage for the modern preservation movement. The first was the passage of the Antiquities Act, passed by Congress in 1906, designed in response to increasing pressure from educational and scientific groups including anthropologists to better protect the prehistoric ruins in the

Southwest (Murtagh 1988). Most important, the Act provided for the creation of national monuments, many of which would eventually be upgraded to the status of national parks. It is interesting to note that the original purpose of designating particular lands as national monuments was to protect specific cultural, historical, and scientific aspects of concern within a designated area (Sellars 1997, 13). Further, such monuments were to be no larger than necessary to protect the particular human artifacts in question. The main idea was to protect these places from unregulated intrusion and destruction before appropriate scientific research could be conducted.

Not just incidentally, the Act provided the president of the United States with sole authority to proclaim new monuments without congressional approval. During President Theodore Roosevelt's administration, the Act promptly encouraged the creation of numerous monuments: Devils Tower (1906), Chaco Canyon (1907), Muir Woods (1908), Mount Olympus (1908), and the Grand Canyon (1908). The Act came to be used early on, not just for the preservation of historic sites as originally intended, but also for federal protection of scenic lands, including the Grand Canyon and Mount Olympus (Sellars 1997). As recently as the 2000 presidential election, the issue of establishing new national monuments by presidential decree remained a contentious issue, especially in the Southwest, where then-President Clinton had established no less than eight new—and quite expansive—national monuments during his administration. He was not the first president to invoke the Antiquities Act, however, and assuming the legislation does not change substantially, he will certainly not be the last. In this way, the federal government became involved in early preservation efforts more than perhaps it ever had before. The trend of increasing government involvement would continue to expand from there as the twentieth century progressed.

Subsequently, the federal government established the National Park Service in 1916 to "promote and regulate the use of the federal areas known as national parks, monuments, and reservations" (Murtagh

1988, 53). A variety of national parks were already in existence and regulated by the government at the time the Park Service was created. The world's first national park—Yellowstone—had been established by Congress on March 1, 1872, followed in the next decades by the establishment of Yosemite, Mount Rainier, Sequoia, and others (Sellars 1997). The Act of 1916, according to Richard Sellars (1997, 29), "established a fundamental dogma for the Park Service—the chief basis for its philosophy, policies, and decision making." The Park Service's principle mandate was that the parks be left "unimpaired for the enjoyment of future generations". Since the Act's creation, critics have bemoaned the continual drive toward tourism development in the parks because this behavior does not promote the preservation of natural conditions. However, the legislative history of the National Park Service Act "provides no evidence that either Congress or those who lobbied for the act sought a mandate for an exacting preservation of natural conditions" (Sellars 1997, 29).

Indeed, the major western railroad companies, including the AT&SF, Northern Pacific, and Great Northern, were the most significant promoters of the early national parks. In fact, the establishment of parks such as Sequoia, Yosemite, and Glacier was largely the product of intense political pressure exerted by the railroad companies. In short, the railroads recognized the immense potential for the parks to attract tourists from the East, and in turn, to ride their respective trains to access the parks. That tourism was to become prominent in the West's developing economy was made quite clear with the 1872 Yellowstone legislation. The Northern Pacific Railroad believed that as it continued building its transcontinental railroad to the West, it could monopolize tourist traffic into the area where Yellowstone was to be created. Thus, a kind of resort-style model of development became the tradition as national parks were created over time. The AT&SF played a significant role in monopolizing the developments and services offered at the south rim of the Grand Canyon, as did the Northern Pacific Railroad with regard to tourism developments at Yellowstone. "Making a business out of scenery" reflected the utilitarian drive to establish the national parks, and in turn, the National Park Service (Sellars 1997). Proponents viewed the parks first and foremost as scenic recreation areas that should be vigorously developed for the use and enjoyment of visitors.

Even so, the development and expansion of the National Park Service and the earlier Antiquities Act played a vital role in the future growth of the preservation movement, and served as precedents for government's expanding role in preservation as well. The case for preservation progressed further with the passage of the Historic Sites Act in 1935, which gave the secretary of the interior great latitude to act in three ways: "first, to establish an information base for preservation by conducting surveys and engaging in research; second, to implement preservation by acquiring, restoring, maintaining, and operating historic properties and by entering into cooperative agreements with like-minded private organizations; and third, to interpret the heritage thus identified with historic markers or by other educational means" (Murtagh 1988, 58). By 1936, a staff of historians, architects, and archaeologists was working for the federal government, particularly within the Park Service, which proved to be one of the few resources available to a growing number of local preservation groups seeking assistance. Thus, the Park Service proved to be instrumental to the growth of the preservation movement in America. Its employees would end up playing a part in the eventual creation of the National Trust for Historic Preservation in 1949 and the seminal National Historic Preservation Act of 1966.

The National Trust today remains the largest single national organization representing local preservation groups and individual citizens with regard to preservation issues; indeed, the Park Service was directly involved in the formation of the National Trust. Among the trust's earliest promoters was the former National Park Service director, Horace Albright. In light of "the changing nature of postwar technological America" and the associated economic growth and development associated with it, the pressure to create a national organization to promote historic preservation was deemed all the more urgent (Murtagh 1988). The trust's size and influence grew significantly through ensuing decades, reflected in part from its growth in individual memberships. Barely reaching 20,000 before 1966, the trust's membership grew to well over 100,000 within only a few years of the passage of the National Historic Preservation Act. In addition to its traditional stewardship of various historic properties around the nation, the organization has six regional offices and one field office designed to assist local preservation problems and projects with professional skills, and to bring its expertise closer to the grassroots level. Significantly, the National Historic Preservation Act of 1966 called for the establishment of grants to support the expanding activities of the National Trust (Murtagh 1988). Further, it was the Act of 1966 that broadened the federal government's role in preservation, taking it beyond its traditional, narrow interest in properties of national historic significance. The government now recognized the role of historic preservation at the state and local level, with regard to architectural significance and local heritage. By Title I of the legislation, the secretary of the interior was directed to create a national listing of sites and properties worth preserving, whether they were significant at national, state, or local levels. This list is more formally referred to as the National Register of Historic Places.

Further, it was through the Act of 1966 and the creation of the National Register that the concept of "historic district" became prominent. When concerned individuals and organizations increasingly spoke about entire neighborhoods and their potential for preservation, Congress adopted the word "district" in the formal goals of the new National Register. The register was to include "sites, buildings, objects, districts, and structures significant in American history, architecture, archaeology, and culture" (Murtagh 1988, 66).

Despite what many believe, it is not the federal government or its National Register that places heavy restrictions on property alterations within an official National Register district such as that of NAU. The register simply provides for a review of historic resources that may be threatened by federally funded projects. Rather, it is *local* government authorities who can pass regulated preservation ordinances providing the most controls and restrictions for property owners. Such historic preservation ordinances may or may not coincide with a National Register district. Flagstaff's downtown business district north of the tracks is regulated by a local *historic preservation ordinance* that provides guidelines to property owners about what types of alterations and maintenance are suitable for that area. The downtown is not included within a National Register district, however. Conversely, NAU's north campus district (officially the Northern Arizona Normal School Historic District) is listed on the National Register of Historic Places, but there are no additional local controls. This partly explains why it was so easy to raze the historic Herrington House, once located just south of Ashurst Auditorium. When north campus officially became a historic district in 1986, Herrington House was in need of much maintenance, so it is no surprise that it was torn down entirely rather than renovated. The demise of Herrington House reinforces the fact that the National Register provides little assurance that listed buildings will not be torn down for various reasons; instead, stricter local controls, usually in the form of a local historic preservation ordinance, are required to prevent the demolition of historic structures.

From Old Main, continue walking north on Knoles Drive to the Blome building, located in the extreme northwest corner of campus.

STOP 20
GREEK REVIVAL: BLOME BUILDING

The architectural style of the Blome building has an impressive history. It began with Thomas Jefferson, who—aside from becoming a U.S. president—enjoyed studying architecture in his spare time. Jefferson had managed to travel to France, where he learned about the various styles of Greek and Roman architecture still dotting the landscape. To make a long story short, Jefferson came home from Europe energized and ready to start nothing less than a new trend in national architecture. Jefferson brought back to our new country in the 1790s an architectural style that would come to be referred to as *Greek* (or Classical) *Revival.* He argued that such a style, with its impressive temple front and Greek columns, was more representative of our new democratic republic. In turn, old English building traditions, such as the still-popular Georgian style, had to go.

Jefferson experimented with the new Greek Revival style with his first architectural masterpiece, the Virginia State Capitol building, completed in 1789. Essentially, it was a spitting image of the famous Greek Parthenon. After that he designed the entire central campus of the University of Virginia, in similar fashion, with little Greek temples and classical Greek columns. From there, the style diffused quickly throughout the northeastern United States, and eventually throughout the South. Although Pennsylvanians were not so enthused with the Greek Revival style, continuing instead to build Georgian row houses up through the Civil War, Jefferson's new symbol of democracy spread like wildfire through much of the early nation. The style remained popular between roughly 1800 and 1850.

This history of architectural diffusion is important for understanding the appearance of the Blome building. What this building represents is actually a revival of the Greek Revival style. One of the period styles that became popular by the 1920s was *Neoclassical*—basically another name for the newer version of Greek Revival style. With its temple-like porch and thick, Greek columns, Blome represents well the Neoclassical period style (Figure 44). Due to the style's stately appearance, Neoclassical remained an immensely popular building style for American campuses right up through World War II.

Figure 44. Blome Building, on NAU's north campus. The neoclassical style of period architecture is prominent on Blome's façade, unmistakable with its thick Greek columns and temple-front entrance. (Photo: Author's collection)

It was this architecture of the Greek Revival combined with Arizona Red that surrounded the students and faculty of Arizona State College (ASC) during the 1940s and into the 1950s. None of the current campus south of Old Main existed at that time, so all social and academic activities on campus were focused in this area. This was the entire campus in 1950—not all that long ago. As of this writing, plenty of former students, faculty, and administrators could still easily recall what campus life was like around a half-century ago.

One such individual was Dr. J. Lawrence Walkup, who served between 1957 and 1979 as president of ASC/NAU and oversaw the college's transition to full university status in 1966. His full list of accomplishments is too great to mention here, but it was under his skillful leadership that NAU's booming era of growth took place after World War II—from "a small teachers' college of just over 1,000 students and 18 buildings to one of the nation's major multipurpose universities of more than 12,000 students and 80 buildings on its expanded campus" (Walkup 1984, 695). Walkup first came to ASC in the summer of 1948, however, as a new assistant professor of education and psychology, having just received his Ph.D. degree from the University of Missouri. Revealing a more informal approach to academics at that time, it is interesting to note that ASC's president in 1948, Dr. Lacey Eastburn, personally interviewed Walkup at Union Station in Kansas City, Missouri, on his way to a meeting in Chicago. Little did Eastburn know at the time that Walkup would successfully preside over one of the most troubling times for ASC, as well as one of its most rapid periods of growth. Appropriately, the unique 15,300-seat NAU Walkup Skydome, completed in 1977, was named after him to honor his accomplishments here.

I mention Dr. Walkup not only for his numerous accomplishments but also because of the impressive volume of memoirs that he wrote, *Pride, Promise, Progress: The Development of Northern Arizona University*, published in 1984. I highly recommend this book for anyone who is further interested in learning about the life and times of ASC and NAU following World War II. The book includes not only his own personal memoirs and accomplishments, but also the commentaries and recollections of former students and faculty whom he interviewed in detail. Here, I offer a few items of interest from his text that help to illustrate what life was like at ASC in the decades following the war, and during the troubling period for ASC that directly preceded the building boom of the 1960s.

Walkup's first impression of the ASC campus upon his arrival in 1948 was less than complimentary. For him, the maintenance and appearance of the campus and facilities was sadly lacking and in much need of attention. The confusion of World War II and an extreme lack of funding for maintenance had clearly taken its toll on campus, with its large tracts of dry, brown lawn and buildings that showed the results of many years of neglect. Their eaves had rusted through, and water regularly ran down their sides. Wood surfaces and trim were deeply cracked, and the interior of Old Main itself was in critical need of renovation. Further, heating and water pipes broke frequently, requiring temporary repairs that always kept some parts of the campus landscape torn up.

These concerns paled in comparison to a much larger problem in the late 1940s, however. During Walkup's first year on campus, the North Central Association denied accreditation of the school's graduate program and directed that ASC terminate its entire graduate curriculum. In fact, Dr. Eastburn was enroute to his meeting with North Central in Chicago to rectify this problem when he stopped in Kansas City's Union Station to interview Dr. Walkup. In any case, the termination of the graduate program dealt a serious blow to ASC—more so than one today might expect. At that time, the graduate program was of primary significance to the entire college, because a master's degree was required to teach high school. The college had already gained an excellent reputation for training public school teachers and administrators, so the loss of the graduate program represented a serious crisis for the fledgling institution (Walkup 1984).

During this time, other serious problems only compounded the situation. After talking with faculty and students for some time after his arrival, Walkup observed that "all of these problems seemed to stem from the fact that the Flagstaff college, for many years, had been considered the step-child of the state's higher education system, as it were, as far as financial support from the legislature was concerned" (Walkup 1984, 9). The remote geographical location of ASC provided the college with little political clout—a situation that is improved though still problematic for NAU in current times. In contrast, the University of Arizona at Tucson maintained strong support from Arizona's rural counties because of its position as a land grant institution; consequently, the U of A enjoyed the lion's share of state funding.

In 1946 there were serious rumors and concerns among the faculty that ASC would close permanently. This sentiment was exacerbated when ultimate control of the college shifted from a local, three-man board to the Arizona Board of Regents, which held authority over all three of the state's main college campuses. Many believed that the Board's presumed biases against the remote and struggling ASC in Flagstaff would be the kiss of death. Enrollments steadily declined at

ASC throughout World War II and into the 1950s, and reports were published acknowledging that the state could have sent all of ASC's students to Harvard for less money than what it was costing the state to send them to Flagstaff (Walkup 1984). Given all of these concerns, along with the accreditation problem, it is not unrealistic to imagine that the Blome building might have ultimately marked the campus's furthest extent. This gloomy scenario did not come to pass, of course, due to a very committed faculty and some very competent and visionary leaders—including Dr. Walkup himself.

Dr. Walkup attributed ASC's turnaround in the 1950s to the dedicated efforts of the faculty who decided to remain at Flagstaff and forge onward through the challenges. He stated that "it is very clear to me that it was the faculty who, individually and collectively, provided the binding force that kept the college going, that these fine men and women kept alive the goals and ideals of the institution" (Walkup 1984, 19).

More than anything else, it was the strong community attachment between students and faculty at ASC that provided a unique learning environment. Recall, it is a characteristic trait of American colleges and universities to view their campuses as full-fledged communities rather than simply as locales for academic training. There was perhaps no better example of this than what existed at ASC in the 1950s and 60s. The faculty at ASC played numerous roles, including that of counselors, confidants, philosophers, friends, and even servants, cooks, and waiters. In fact, student life itself on campus was under the direct supervision of the faculty, and for some time the faculty lived in the very same dormitories as the students, right here on today's north campus. Faculty members who planned trips to Phoenix would occasionally offer rides to students, and faculty participated regularly at student dinners, picnics, and other social events. It was not uncommon, either, for faculty members to invite students into their homes for evening meals.

Dr. Walkup interviewed Dr. Richard Lloyd, a former student and later a professor of education at NAU, about his recollections of student-faculty interaction on campus. In Walkup's words, Lloyd recalled that the faculty "accepted any kind of challenge, always on a volunteer basis. They didn't volunteer because they were expected to or because of whom it might impress. They did it because of their concern for the students, their fellow faculty members and for the institution...Homecoming cookouts were always marked by the spirit of a family reunion. One might find faculty members cooking, serving, cleaning up or doing a myriad of other chores and not because they had to, but because they wanted to" (Walkup 1984, 21).

This commitment among the faculty toward the student body was transferred to academic adventures outside the traditional classroom. From his first days on campus, Dr. Walkup had perceived one of ASC's greatest educational advantages, that of its location amidst an amazing diversity of geographical and cultural landscapes and environments. The faculty took full advantage of their remarkable setting in northern Arizona, as did the students. Botonist Chester Deaver, for instance, recalled the beginnings of what eventually became the Deaver Herbarium, a unique research collection of botanical specimens of plants and grasses from around the state. He later started courses in field biology and conservation education that enabled both students and faculty members to undertake field studies of vegetation in areas off campus.

Perhaps the most popular field experiences of the time were those led by Dr. Agnes Allen. Allen was the head of the science department on campus, and her two academic fields of expertise consisted of geography and geology. During student-faculty picnics to Oak Creek Canyon, Dr. Allen often took the opportunity to provide on-the-spot lectures about the surrounding physical environment. For many years, she led an immensely popular field course that included nothing less than an annual hike through the Grand Canyon to the Colorado River. Dr. Walkup recalled, "It was by far the most popular class at ASC during these years, with many non-science students eagerly participating" (Walkup 1984, 32). Also credited with initiating the

Department of Geography on campus, Dr. Allen firmly believed that "there was no better place in the world to teach these subjects than here at ASC," to use her own words (Walkup 1984, 33). To be sure, the sentiments regarding NAU's surrounding environment today are no less passionate among the many faculty members who teach geography, geology, forestry, environmental sciences, and numerous other related fields of study. Today, the Department of Geography and Public Planning, for example, continues Dr. Allen's tradition of field-based experiences in the form of an intensive 3-week field class for geography majors each May, during which students and faculty partake of a variety of multi-day adventures and lessons throughout the Southwest (Figure 45).

Figure 45. NAU geography students enrolled in their "capstone" field course, posing here at Boulder City, NV, for a group photo. Courses like this one have kept the tradition of field-based experiences alive and well at NAU. (Photo: Author's collection)

A statement by Dr. Allen further reveals the strong sense of place that both students and faculty felt for ASC during those years:

> There was a spirit which bound the people working for the institution together. What greater satisfaction can come to a teacher than to feel that in some way one has really traveled the lives of others?

> ...No matter what internal squabble might have taken place, there was still a deep-rooted respect for the accomplishments of each and everyone on the faculty. We were Lumberjacks, whether the football team won or not. We each knew that they had given the best that was in them. This was true whether it was on the athletic field, in the campus theater or music hall, or in the classroom. (Walkup 1984, 31)

It was this strong spirit and sentimental attachment for ASC that was shared among students and faculty. Some people lament the loss of this close-knit community atmosphere of the 1950s and 60s, but given the tremendous growth of the institution since then, the truth is that one of NAU's most cherished characteristics today remains the faculty's overall interest in the students and their commitment to undergraduate education. Granted, in the year 2002 it was very possible for students to feel like a "number" as they do at other large universities. Still, compared with larger, research-oriented institutions, NAU clearly succeeds with its long-standing tradition of faculty attention toward students. The fact that students regularly transfer to NAU's Department of Geography and Public Planning from ASU and the University of Arizona is indicative of NAU's strength in this regard. These students often transfer specifically because of the greater sense of community and faculty attention they believe exists at NAU. I have heard new transfer students in our department speak of how impressed they were to have faculty members show them around the building or sit down with them on a one-to-one basis.

Just as student-faculty interaction was critical to the continued success of ASC a half-century ago, it is this same unique sense of community that continues to separate NAU from all the rest. Whether we are students, faculty, or staff, we cannot afford to ignore this strength.

Chapter 8

Flagstaff's *Miracle Mile:* Milton Avenue

STOP 21

Approach Strip: Milton Avenue Corridor

There is probably no better place along this Tour to experience the dynamism and diversity of Flagstaff than here on this unceremonious sidewalk behind the Blome building. This is one of those unsuspecting places that most people overlook and simply bypass on their way to somewhere else. By now, however, you should be accustomed to finding significance and meaning in rather ordinary places. As far as interesting landscape scenes go, this one is a gem. Looking between the trees, you have at least a partial view of all four human landscapes experienced along the Tour: Downtown and Old Town to the north, the commercial corridor of Milton Avenue safely below you to the west, the bulk of NAU's north campus to the east, and a portion of South Side just to the north of Butler Avenue. Occasionally snaking through this jumble of landscapes but out of sight are the trains of BNSF's Transcon, with the westbound trains struggling to climb Mars Hill. On top of Mars Hill is Lowell Observatory, one reason for locals wanting to keep the lights low at night around town. In the background to the north is the mountain from which Flagstaff gains its dominant identity, the commanding volcano known as San Francisco Mountain, or more simply, the Peaks (Figure 46).

Figure 46. Milton Avenue, part of old U.S. Route 66, looking north to the San Francisco Peaks. This is Flagstaff's most recent *approach strip*, connecting downtown Flagstaff with Interstate 17. Predictably, this busy corridor continues to attract a wide diversity of commercial roadside development, oriented primarily to the necessities of the automobile. A Route 66-era motel is visible on the left. (Photo: Author's collection)

Here is where the Flagstaff railroad grid, the NAU campus, and the auto-dominated commercial strip of Milton Avenue collide in one confusing though fascinating intersection of contrasting landscapes. This is the "mother" of geographic breaks in the landscape. Most people are used to being located within various landscapes, but not necessarily between them.

Depending on what direction you look in, each landscape reveals distinctive patterns that appear to clash when one landscape intersects with another. Further, each elicits different emotions and sentiments, perhaps interpreted by specific senses of place. Your own thoughts, then, will most likely change with a simple twist of your head, as you gaze in various directions.

If you allow yourself to sense these changes, even for a moment, it may be easier to appreciate the widely varying processes and histories that have prevailed in the creation of each landscape scene. This simple exercise should be evidence enough that, even within the same small town, one landscape can contrast widely with another. For instance, the nearly military-like centralized authority that dominates the pedestrian-oriented patterns of NAU form a stark contrast to the bustling entrepreneurial energy of free-market capitalism at work along Milton Avenue. To the northwest is the original settlement area of Flagstaff, representing the first Anglo-American sequence of occupancy in this western railroad town. What you are looking at is a veritable layer cake of growth and settlement that encompasses more than a century of history—a century of humans changing and altering their physical surroundings in their own cultural ways.

Perhaps the most dynamic and confusing landscape scene consists of Milton Avenue itself and its surrounding commercial activity (Figure 46). From this spot on the sidewalk, you can view the dynamism of Milton Avenue without having to concern yourself with safety. This type of fast-paced, auto-dominated development is not entirely a recent trend as some might think. As early as the 1920s, central business districts nationwide were becoming congested with automobiles—a continuing dilemma for many urban centers today. In 1926, for instance, a report distributed by the New York—based Beeler Organization concluded that "growing traffic congestion in cities is making it increasingly difficult for the suburban customers of city stores to reach these stores and shop in leisure and comfort. Surveys show that these people are reducing the number of their shopping trips to the stores in the congested centers" (Liebs 1995, 29). The solution, it seemed, was to bring shopping to the suburban residential areas already beginning to develop on the peripheries of major cities. This realization eventually led to the development of the *shopping center.* The primary functions of Main Street, thus, were preparing little by little to move out to the periphery.

In the 1920s speculators created small shopping plazas that were, for the first time, set back from the street itself to make room for off-street parking. By the 1930s, this idea was expanded upon, as expansive lots were purchased on the edge of town along developing auto corridors. Here, developers increased the setbacks to provide more parking, and they began to add to the formula other services including supermarkets, gas stations, and even small department or five-and-dime stores (Liebs 1995). In this way, the neighborhood shopping center was born, the first-ever master-planned retail areas adapted specifically to the needs of the automobile. The typical formula for these shopping centers evolved early on, characterized by their L-shaped layout, with a string of attached storefronts facing a central parking lot set back from the street.

Local shopping centers encouraged more businesses throughout World War II to relocate to these evolving commercial strips. It was the eventual development of regional shopping centers and malls, however, that completed the move of Main Street to the periphery of town. By the 1950s developers were taking the shopping center idea one step further with the creation of climate-controlled, indoor shopping malls—basically transplanting Main Street to an indoor setting, but this time on the edge of town. One of the first such complexes was Southdale, in Minneapolis, constructed in 1956. Chester Liebs described this new phase of shopping center development this way: "In this complex, the central common, or mall, was roofed over, creating an 'air-conditioned outdoors,' indoors. Free of vehicles, protected from the weather, with a department store instead of a church or courthouse as central focus, Main Street had been successfully condensed, repackaged, and transported to the Miracle Mile" (Liebs 1995, 31).

For a nation conditioned to years of economic depression and, later, World War II, the relatively rapid transformation of a previously rural stretch of highway at the edge of town into a bustling shopping corridor was nothing short of miraculous. The original *Miracle Mile*, as it was called, consisted of the now-famous stretch of Wilshire Boulevard in Los Angeles—referred to as such for the way it boomed with auto-oriented commercial development following the war (Liebs 1995). The "miracle" of Wilshire Boulevard may not have been so much its new, innovative orientation to the automobile and accessibility, but more the fact that the place developed at all (Longstreth 1997). At the time, potential investors considered this site too remote from downtown Los Angeles, and municipal codes prevented commercial development along Wilshire. Initially, property owners in the area had envisioned Wilshire Boulevard as becoming a grand residential avenue of houses and apartments, stretching out from downtown LA westward to the coast. Thus, when the city of Los Angeles annexed this area along Wilshire in 1925, it was zoned for residential purposes only.

Not to be denied his dream, however, a little-known real estate agent named A. W. Ross envisioned a new kind of retail center, far removed from the traffic congestion of the traditional downtown. The name of this new development, the "Miracle Mile," was suggested to Ross by a client during the time the area was successfully starting to develop (Longstreth 1997, 127). Soon, Miracle Mile became a household term around the LA region, and after World War II the term came to be used nationally "to denote a form of commercial development in outlying areas that challenged the hegemony of downtown in a way seldom known before" (Longstreth 1997, 127). Due to the residential zoning, Ross was forced to seek a high-risk development strategy: that of obtaining zoning variances for commercial buildings on a case-by-case basis. Although this strategy proved successful in the long term, the effort was more time consuming than Ross had originally anticipated. The benefit of this process, however, was that he enjoyed more control over specific commercial developments along the boulevard. Not only did Ross play a large role in determining the choice of businesses, but he also exerted much influence on the size, placement, and character of the buildings. Many investors were initially skeptical of Ross's unconventional development plan for Wilshire, its proximity to a large urban market and its general lack of traffic congestion encouraged more investors over time. Eventually, Ross began to aggressively promote the Miracle Mile as the new downtown for the western two thirds of the city (Longstreth 1997, 131).

Although the evolving Miracle Mile was not a fully integrated business district, it did include attributes similar to more traditional downtowns. Richard Longstreth described the character of this first Miracle Mile:

> The Miracle Mile codified and intensified those characteristics that made Wilshire so important to Los Angeles: a linear structure, punctuated by freestanding towers that rose amid low-density development, the whole anchored to a broad street where traffic flowed unimpeded—a place that was easy to reach, that always seemed busy but never crowded, a place permeated with natural light and air, a place that fused the best qualities of Main Street and metropolis, evoking memories of both but unlike either one. (Longstreth 1997, 133)

Just as new and exciting ideas tend to diffuse from place to place, so too did the idea of the Miracle Mile. Speculators, developers, and city leaders across the nation were quick to celebrate their own local examples of roadside commercial development. Soon, the term Miracle Mile was adapted by numerous localities to describe almost any evolving commercial corridor from Long Island, New York, to Phoenix, Arizona.

Welcome to Flagstaff's own Miracle Mile, still developing and evolving today. Times have changed, however, and it seems that fewer and fewer people are willing to think of this type of auto-dominated landscape as the "miracle" that it once was. In overlooking Milton Avenue, you have reached the "Geography of Nowhere," or "Anytown USA." These are only some of the terms used to describe the look-alike commercial strips that extend outward along busy auto corridors in towns and cities across the country. These places are at once criticized and celebrated, depending on the perspective. These strips are criticized for their sameness—their lack of distinctiveness from one place to another, and even for their role in the national degradation of community. They represent perhaps a negative side to globalization, given that multi-national and national corporations have come to dominate commercial strips across the country with the same fast food joints, gas stations, and motel chains. These strips represent the homogenization of America, where one roadside strip looks pretty much like all the rest. The creativity and local entrepreneurial experimentation that characterized emerging commercial strips during the early half of the twentieth century have been mostly replaced by the standardized, replicated stores of national chains.

Conversely, these strips are at the same time celebrated by many as uniquely American, a product of America's fast-paced culture, hunger for mobility, and creative entrepreneurial spirit. To be sure, the commercial roadside landscapes that dominate the edges of our cities and are clustered around freeway interchanges today can be found in no other country in the world. Here in the United States, free enterprise is just that—relatively free to roam the country and occupy the edges of our cities anywhere profits might be made. The past 70 years of commercial strip development have given us a unique collective blend of architecture devoted specifically to the American roadside, and you can now find scholarly books about the development of America's commercial strips and the architecture that lines them (e.g. Liebs 1995; Longstreth 1997). You can also find books whose authors have lamented the unabated rise of the commercial strip and the ways in which it promotes the degeneration of American society and community values (e.g. Kunstler 1993). In any case, these strips are part of our human landscapes now, and geographers are inherently interested in understanding how and why such places have materialized as they have, as well as their implications for America as a whole.

Milton Avenue is a classic example of an *approach strip* (Liebs 1995). As retail commerce gradually moved over the past several decades from

Flagstaff's traditional downtown location to more auto-accessible land on the edge of town, it was the main traffic corridors already in place that received the bulk of roadside development. U.S. Route 66 had become Flagstaff's first true approach strip prior to the era of interstate freeways. Before the federal government passed the Interstate Highway Act of 1956, which initiated the building of a national network of limited-access freeways, auto traffic coming into any town in America did so from its original roads and streets, radiating outward from the center. If the town or city had one or more U.S. routes coming through (the 1920s federal highway system that preceded the interstates), that is where the approach strips—and their accompanying roadside commercial development—would be. Such was the case along Flagstaff's own Route 66, oriented east-west through town. Thus, roadside commercial development in Flagstaff, with its first motels, fast food restaurants, and gas stations, extended outward along Flagstaff's approach strip of the 1950s and 1960s—Route 66. You are looking out over the original Route 66 from this vantage point, today consumed by its more recent co-designation as Milton Avenue and U.S. Route 89.

Milton Avenue represents a much newer approach strip, made possible only by the construction of Interstate 40 and, even more important, I-17. Aside from some older World War II era motels dating back to Route 66 days, today's Milton Avenue thrives due to its direct connection with I-17 a couple of miles south of here. The completion of I-17 years ago instantly reduced the friction of distance between Flagstaff and its very important regional neighbor, the Phoenix metropolitan area. With I-17 came increased day-trippers from Phoenix for the purpose of either escaping the heat or going skiing, and now I-17 is the lifeline for Flagstaff's growing number of second-home owners whose first homes are found in the Phoenix area.

This trend represents a national one, given that the smaller towns and cities most likely to grow are those in close proximity to a large metropolitan area. Now that Flagstaff is 2 hours away, it has *effectively* become closer and much more accessible to the expanding Phoenix population. Flagstaff has become a haven for those seeking amenity values, including clean air, an attractive four-season climate, recreation in forests and lakes, perceived small-town quality of life, relative lack of crime, and escape from urban pressures and congestion. As long as Phoenix continues to grow, Flagstaff will likely grow as well, because the geographical links between them are so tight. Therefore, it is important for geographers to understand how urban patterns affect rural and small town growth. The same trend—Phoenix moving north—is taking place in the Payson area, the Prescott and Cottonwood area, and the White Mountains. One Arizona historian has dubbed the process as the "urbanization of the rural" (Sheridan 1995). Rural America is becoming resort-ified, as these attractive places are increasingly becoming tourist havens for America's urban middle and upper class populations that can afford to get away.

The Milton Avenue approach strip, therefore, has gained prominence as a commercial growth corridor during the 1980s and 1990s, taking over the previous role of U.S. Route 66. Thus, it makes logical sense that commercial businesses are going to align themselves to Milton Avenue and its connecting roads to capture potential customers from this heavy traffic flow into and out of town. Rather than being oriented to the east and west as it had been prior to the 1980s, Flagstaff now looks primarily to the south for its continued economic prosperity. Rather than looking at extractive industries such as logging and ranching for its continued growth, Flagstaff now looks to the tourism industry. Indeed, Flagstaff is following a national trend, whereby cities and towns throughout America have shifted their local economies from traditional, place-based extractive industries, such as mining, ranching, farming, and logging, to the very mobile industry of tourism and related services. This transformation in the rural (and urban) economic structure has taken place largely between the 1970s and 1990s as America continues to transition into a newer, postindustrial economic era.

Returning to the local scene, it is interesting to note the historical geography of Milton Avenue. Before Milton Avenue became an approach strip, it was for many years the right-of-way for the *Central Arizona Railroad*, essentially a branch line that enabled logging companies to extract timber from the forests south of Flagstaff. It occupied today's Milton Avenue from downtown to the lumber mill, which was located just west of where the intersection of Route 66 and Milton Avenue is today (the last stop on the Tour). From its connections with the lumber mill, the railroad ran pretty much down the route of today's Milton Avenue, and the steam locomotive that you saw downtown ran regularly on this route. The railroad continued south, along today's "urban trail" through Fort Tuthill and the County Fairgrounds (immediately adjacent to the Commercial Building there), continuing south to Lake Mary and beyond.

Therefore, prior to this becoming a commercial strip, it was once a railroad corridor, supplying lumber for Flagstaff's primary economic activity of the past. Incidentally, the name Milton is derived from "Mill Town," the residential area that surrounded the lumber mill on the west side of town for the first half of the century. The history of Milton Avenue is a long one, and it has only served as Flagstaff's approach strip to I-17 for some three decades.

Another interesting aspect of today's standardized roadside business chains involves their most visible feature: their signs. Since the 1950s, corporate chains have learned that Americans prefer predictable, standardized service from one place to another. As a result, these chains have invented relatively simple and very recognizable logos, or icons, that travelers can easily recognize with a quick glance down the road. The logo specifically symbolizes a predictable, comfortable, and familiar setting. When we see the famous "Golden Arches," for instance, we probably think of Big Macs, extra value meals, Egg McMuffins, electric hand dryers in the bathrooms, happy meals, and now McDonald's "playlands."

This strategy of using familiar logos is used primarily by fast food chains, motels, gas stations, and—more recently—the large retailers known both colloquially and academically as *big-box* discount stores for their simplistic, windowless, box-like design (especially in the cases of Wal-Mart, Target, and Kmart). Every so often a well-known logo will be updated by its parent corporation, but the alterations are usually very minor. For instance, Burger King has recently added another color (blue) to its "burger bun" logo. This strategy of *difference in sameness*—the altering of a company's logo but only in subtle ways—is used to reduce confusion among the company's loyal customers while at the same time updating it to contemporary times and trends (Jakle 1994).

Here is one more reason that explains why the Milton Avenue approach strip appears as it does: Along most commercial strips, you might expect the business signs to be much larger overall than they are here. Flagstaff's *sign ordinance* is the reason (the same one that regulates downtown signs). For many years, no signs in Flagstaff could be taller than 8 feet. In 2001 the city council amended the sign ordinance so that signs could be as large as 12 feet (there are other regulations beyond this, but the size is the most visible aspect). This was a very controversial change, as many residents favored the stricter ordinance of the past.

This roadside landscape can be partially explained by the free-market economy with its wide range of private, roadside businesses all competing for visitor traffic along a busy auto corridor, but this is also a landscape of *centralized authority*. The corridor is regulated by city zoning codes and the aforementioned sign ordinance. These and the other factors mentioned above help to explain why this particular landscape scene appears and functions as it does.

It is time to experience the commercial strip more intimately, with a simple walk along Milton Avenue, a landscape dominated by the needs of the automobile rather than the pedestrian. Continue south along the sidewalk behind the Blome building that slopes down to meet Milton Avenue. The Tour officially ends at the prominent intersection of

Route 66 and Milton Avenue, where Route 66 veers off to the west and Milton continues south to Interstates 17 and 40.

STOP 22
BIG BOX: BARNES & NOBLE BOOK STORE

In the popular 1998 film, *You've Got Mail*, starring Tom Hanks and Meg Ryan, the storyline revolves around the inability of a small neighborhood bookstore to compete with a national bookstore chain. With Hanks as its corporate representative, the large discount bookstore chain is portrayed as the evil corporate giant that moves into neighborhoods and communities at its own accord and unceremoniously forces smaller retailers out of business. Of course, being the romantic comedy that it is, Hanks and Ryan eventually put aside their own business interests in favor of a relationship that will presumably last happily ever after.

Minus the romantic comedy component, a similar scenario has been playing out in Flagstaff with the recent arrival of bookstore giant, Barnes & Noble (Figure 47). However, any actual impacts of the store's arrival, whether for better or worse, are far from black and white. For some time the business community waited skeptically to see which local book retailer would be the first casualty of Flagstaff's newest national big-box discount store. Nearly 2 years had passed with little indication of any significantly negative impact on smaller bookstores in town, until one of Flagstaff's most cherished independent bookstores suddenly called it quits on August 19, 2001.

Figure 47. Barnes & Noble store, one of the latest big-box retailers to enter Flagstaff. The structure was built several feet above street level to comply with floodplain regulations. (Photo: Author's collection)

A fixture in the heart of Flagstaff's downtown for 50 years at the corner of San Francisco Street and Aspen Avenue, McGaugh's Newsstand held a clearance sale and promptly closed with little warning. As of this writing the store's closure remains somewhat of a mystery, though many have been quick to blame competition from Barnes & Noble. Still, the only official information provided by McGaugh's manager suggests other reasons. The full text of the press release reads as follows:

> After being a mainstay in downtown Flagstaff for more than 30 years, McGaugh's Newsstand will be closing their doors on Sept. 1, 2001. There is no sensational story about being run out of business by the 'Big Box' stores. Quite simply, due to one of our major vendors pulling out of the area, increases in overhead, and our lease expiring Oct. 1, it seemed an appropriate time to make a change. And after 23+years, all of us who are involved in McGaugh's are ready for some new adventures. We will all very much miss being a part of the downtown community. It has been our privilege and honor to serve all our loyal customers and our great community. (Frazier 2001)

The store's closing probably represented the most significant symbolic blow to the historic district since the loss of Babbitts' Department Store in 1987. On the first day of McGaugh's announced closing, the corner of San Francisco Street and Aspen Avenue became a sort of instant shrine where people came to take their last photographs of the storefront and to purchase discounted books. As I arrived Monday afternoon for my own personal photo shoot, I noticed others taking pictures of the nostalgic sign that presumably would soon be coming down (in fact, it hasn't come down as of this writing). Also on the corner was a photographer from the *Daily Sun* doing the same thing, indicating the importance of the event. Other passersby were stopping to read the giant "Going out of Business—Everything must go" signs placed in the windows, and the activity of individuals going in and out was brisk. "For magazine lovers, those who love books about Flagstaff and the Southwest, and even for cigar and popcorn lovers, the loss was huge," exclaimed an article in Flagstaff's newest newspaper, the *Flagstaff Tea Party* (Frazier 2001).

With the closing of McGaugh's came an intensified community debate surrounding the perceived and real impact of big box stores on other, more established local businesses. The front-page headline of the *Flagstaff Tea Party* article cited above, for instance, revealed its own skepticism by asking, "What really happened to McGaugh's?" Underneath, the subtitle read, "If Barnes & Noble didn't kill McGaugh's Newsstand, what did?" (Frazier 2001). Revived here was a community debate, like many ongoing across the nation, regarding the various implications of big-box discount stores for their host communities. Barnes & Noble may have been the most recent big box to enter Flagstaff, but it certainly was not the first.

History shows that the downtown department store was the king of retail centers until roughly the 1950s. By then, World War II had ended and decentralization was beginning to take place at a more rapid pace. Retail stores began to move away from their traditional downtown locations to cheaper land in the evolving commercial strips on the edge of town. As mentioned above, various one-story L and U-shaped shopping plazas were the result; there are numerous shopping plazas of this variety still located along Route 66 east of town, intermingled with motels.

By the 1960s and 1970s, another retailing trend was sweeping the country—the indoor shopping mall. Flagstaff's own shopping mall is a good example, constructed on the east side of town in 1978. During the 1960s and 1970s developers couldn't build shopping malls fast enough, and for more than two decades there was so much land and space out by the freeway interchanges that developers devised their own formulas for building and replicating malls all over the country. By the middle 1980s, however, shopping malls had generally saturated the available land around America's freeway interchanges and other prime, auto-centric locations so that the fast pace of mall construction slowed dramatically. In the 1990s, new mall construction was the exception rather than the rule, and only in rapidly growing areas (including Arizona and southern California) were new malls being built with some regularity.

By the 1980s and 1990s, scholars had noticed a new trend in retail shopping—namely, the big box discount store (and its cousin, the *outlet store*). Although shopping malls remain popular, they are not what they used to be. We are now in an era of minor decline for shopping malls, and the past 10 years have seen some malls disappear altogether—something unheard of 20 years ago. Other malls have undergone massive makeovers to enhance their image and attractiveness to middle-class American shoppers. The owners of the Flagstaff mall have recently done just that, with its grand stone fireplaces and sitting areas, and new color schemes and entryways.

The existence and proliferation of big-box stores has been partially enabled by *economies of scale*. Basically, economies of scale are made possible when a certain type of economic activity (such as retailing) becomes more profitable as the operation becomes larger. You have experienced the effects of economies of scale if you have purchased an item singularly at a higher price than if you had purchased that item in bulk.

The same is true at the production end—if the company can purchase its merchandise from the wholesalers in bulk rather than a little at a time, overall costs go down, and profits go up. This is one fundamental reason why big-box retailers have been dominated by national and international chains such as Wal-Mart, Kmart, Target, and Home Depot. The more stores they add to their chain, the more profits are generated. Thus, big box chains must continue to grow if they are to realize increased profit margins.

Fast-food restaurant corporations operate similarly. For instance, McDonalds was, for some time, opening a new restaurant somewhere in the world every hour on average. This global corporation has hit relatively rough times, however, since it has saturated the American market and may have few places left to build. The company has thus expanded overseas and added a new development phase to their existing restaurants, the "playland" mini-theme parks that can be found attached to many McDonalds today—another scheme to attract more customers in the guise of entertainment. As evidenced around Flagstaff and elsewhere, other fast-food chains are following suit.

Wal-Mart, too, has saturated rural America since the early 1990s, and is now trying to compete in metropolitan realms with other big-box giants including Kmart and Target. We can't forget, however, the factors that make big-box retailing—and thus economies of scale—possible today: the dominance of the automobile in American society (all big-box stores require oceans of parking), reduced friction of distance for the transport and distribution of merchandise to all of a company's stores, and plenty of open space on the edges of our towns and cities on which to build cheaply (on land that was often used at one time for agricultural production).

Another important factor that enables these giant stores to be built is the role of local and county governments. These governing bodies actively promote and encourage big-box stores and other developments to be built on the edge of town. More stores mean more sales and property taxes for local government budgets, so American towns and cities are still hooked on growth and want to see growth happen. Finally, the demand for big-box stores is there as well. Certainly, if America as a whole flat-out rejected the big box as a bad way to shop, then these large retail chains wouldn't be so successful in the first place. Instead, Americans like the big-box store concept because of its wide selection of merchandise at relatively inexpensive prices, and its convenience for one-stop shopping. Indeed, it is nigh impossible to experience Flagstaff's own Wal-Mart store without the challenge of navigating through hoards of people looking for the best bargains. It has not been without controversy, however, and Flagstaff is a fine example of the debates that continue to center around big-box retailing.

The big-box era of retailing in Flagstaff began with a new Kmart store in the Sunnyside neighborhood in 1972. Kmart lasted two decades at that location with little competition from other big boxes, and it became a neighborhood fixture in the Sunnyside (Fourth Street) area. Other local businesses viewed it as a sort of anchor establishment on the east side of Flagstaff. Then in 1987 Wal-Mart made its debut appearance in Flagstaff. The initial negative reaction from the community involved the amount of forest that would be removed for the new store. Letters to the editor poured in to the *Daily Sun* lamenting not only the loss of ponderosa pine trees but also the poor location for the store. Wal-Mart's plan was to build its store on the northwest corner of the I-17 and U.S. Route 89 intersection on the south end of town. Being the perceived gateway to Flagstaff, this area was instead cherished as a "green belt." The very perception of Flagstaff's image to the outside world was at stake. The last thing that store opponents wanted to see was a Wal-Mart at the entrance to town. Unfortunate for these folks, that is precisely what they got.

In the months prior to the store's grand opening, others voiced concern about Wal-Mart's potential economic impacts. Small, locally owned businesses would be most at risk, claimed Wal-Mart opponents. In a *Daily Sun* article, Karen Bullock noted that "many little pharmacies, sporting good shops and hardware stores in towns where the retail giant has made its mark are seeing customers disappear, revenues shrink and well-stocked shelves collect dust." Mountains of academic research reports and papers confirm this trend nationwide. Although numerous discount retailers were becoming prominent by the 1970s—Kmart and Wal-Mart both opened their first stores in the same year, 1962—Wal-Mart has taken the brunt of opposition from smaller towns and communities.

There is good reason for this. As Thomas Graff (1998) has pointed out, Wal-Mart and Kmart have pursued quite opposite growth and marketing strategies. Both firms opened their first stores in 1962. Since then, however, Kmart and other discount retailers have expanded their markets by adding stores in largely metropolitan regions, whereas Wal-Mart proceeded to compete primarily within rural areas. The highest concentration of Wal-Mart stores is within small towns of the mid-South, primarily centered on Rogers, Arkansas, home to the firm's first discount store. Having more or less saturated rural America by the 1990s, Wal-Mart was forced to compete in more urban settings. Further, in the 1980s, both Wal-Mart and Kmart started to experiment with a combined grocery and discount store format that had already been introduced in Europe, the *hypermart* (Graff 1998). Through these experiments evolved the now-familiar *supercenter*, the first one opened by Wal-Mart in 1988 and Kmart in 1991. By the mid-1990s the supercenter format had become the focus of expansion for both firms. By the end of 1996, Wal-Mart had opened 332 supercenters, about half of which (177 of the 332) are found in nonmetropolitan, or largely rural, counties. Many of these supercenters have replaced older, smaller discount stores already in existence.

Small towns, rather than large cities, therefore became the primary stomping ground for Wal-Mart. In Illinois, for instance, the average population size of Wal-Mart communities in 1990 was only 18,721

(Gruidl and Kline 1992). Consequently, it is this discount retailer that is most associated with impacting small-town economies. Local businesses on America's main streets have felt the competition from this discount chain more than from any other. Given this strategy of capturing America's rural market first, it may not be surprising that Flagstaff was chosen as the site for the state of Arizona's first Wal-Mart store—not Phoenix or Tucson.

By the mid-1990s, the damage to small-town business districts was nearly complete, and their respective communities had learned more or less how to deal with their new, big-box neighbors on the edge of town. Numerous "how to survive the discount retailer" articles appeared in both academic journals and magazines oriented to local businesses and other laypersons. In *What Happens When a Large Discount Store Comes to Town*, for instance, John Gruidl and Steven Kline (1992) offered advice to businesses facing new competition from the edge of town. Their advice became common wisdom in small towns nationwide and, in short, included the following tips: Be prepared to make changes and assess how changes can be made; take proactive action, anticipating a period of declining sales followed by a rebound; identify unfilled market niches or segments that other merchants have overlooked; improve your level of customer service; carefully evaluate your ability to compete on price. The consensus among numerous small-town merchants was that attempting to compete directly with the discount retail store was not a wise move (Gruidl and Kline 1992). Given these words of wisdom for small businesses, it is clear that smaller communities stood to face rapid and significant changes in their local retail economies during the 1970s and 1980s. Downtown businesses adapted either by altering their product lines or by moving out to the new Wal-Mart plaza themselves. Otherwise, they simply went out of business. No doubt, the rise of big-box retailing in America has only encouraged the transformation of downtown business districts from traditional trade centers to places focusing instead on entertainment and tourist-oriented specialty functions.

The opening of Wal-Mart in 1988 may have signaled a new era for big-box retailing in Flagstaff, but the store's direct effect on downtown businesses was most likely marginal. Given Wal-Mart's expansion strategy of moving outward from its original Arkansas hub, this retailing giant was a latecomer to the Arizona scene. In Flagstaff, the march of businesses to the periphery of town had begun years earlier with the loss of three major downtown department stores, the growth of outdoor shopping centers along Flagstaff's commercial strips, and especially the opening of the Flagstaff Mall in 1978. In fact, Wal-Mart's arrival in Flagstaff coincided closely with the appearance of the Main Street Flagstaff Foundation, signaling that plans were already well underway for the revival of downtown. Still, many cautioned that Wal-Mart would only add to the competition with a downtown area already in decline.

This is not to say that big-box retailers as a whole have had little impact in Flagstaff, whether positive or negative. They have clearly changed the retailing patterns of the community. Aside from Kmart's early arrival on the east side of town, Wal-Mart became the first arrival in a full series of new discount retailers scattered around west Flagstaff. Four years later in 1992, Kmart made a very controversial move from its original Sunnyside store to a plot of land directly north of Wal-Mart; not only would more trees be destroyed on the south end of town, many complained of the move, but Kmart planned to close its east-side store entirely, leaving numerous local businesses very nervous about their future in Sunnyside. During this time, the warehouse version of Wal-Mart, called Sam's Club (for Wal-Mart's founder, Sam Walton), arrived on the scene, and in 1994 Target opened its own store along Flagstaff's booming commercial strip, Milton Avenue. A pair of big-box specialty stores, Home Depot and Barnes & Noble, arrived 5 years later in 1999. The construction of these two stores sparked not only community debate surrounding the costs and benefits of big-box retailers, but several on-street community protests as well. It is no wonder, then, that the announced closing of McGaugh's in 2001 aroused the immediate suspicion that competition from Barnes & Noble was the culprit.

The economic and environmental issues surrounding the development of big-box stores were serious enough in Flagstaff to warrant a community panel and forum on this topic. As one event in its Building for Community series at Northern Arizona University, the Master of Liberal Studies program organized and hosted a "Big Box Luncheon" at the Little America Hotel on April 18, 2001, in conjunction with the Friends of Flagstaff's Future (affectionately referred to locally as "F-cubed"). In attendance was a full room of community members including representatives from numerous interest groups and organizations in Flagstaff. The luncheon was designed to provide an open arena for the exchange of ideas and concerns about the pros and cons of big-box development in town. The first part of the luncheon consisted of five panelists who presented their own perspectives on issues of retailing. Representing the full gamut of viewpoints, the panelists were Al Madle, chair of the Northern Arizona Restaurant and Hospitality Association; Stacy Mitchell, researcher with the Institute for Local Self Reliance; David Mauer, head of the Flagstaff Chamber of Commerce; Pete Wolf, a small-business owner in Flagstaff, and Constance Beaumont, a representative of the National Trust for Historic Preservation. Fortunately, I was able to attend and record the panelists' speeches during this luncheon to determine more precisely the dominant arguments pertaining to Flagstaff's new era of big-box retailing.

That the issue of discount retailing weighed heavily on the community's collective mind was perhaps underscored by David Mauer's initial comments. While preparing his talk at the podium, he deposited a cardboard box on the table next to him and extracted a pair of boxing gloves, putting them on. Clearly prepared for battle, he continued the joke by stating, "I'm the only one who brought a big box, in case there was any question of where I'd be coming from." Following the ensuing laughter from the audience, he continued, "When I told my wife that the MLS program had invited me to this big-box luncheon she said, 'I think you misunderstood—they want to *have* you for lunch.'" Mauer's good humor revealed his understanding that various segments of the community maintained serious concerns about the future of retailing in Flagstaff, and that he would clearly face an uphill battle at this luncheon to promote the continued growth of big-box retailing in town.

The panel was fairly well balanced with regard to perspectives, with Mauer and Madle advocating the benefits of big-box stores for Flagstaff, and Mitchell and Wolf generally supporting the opposition. Constance Beaumont attempted to find a middle ground to the argument. Mauer and Madle faced an uphill battle with the audience, however, as Mauer had accurately predicted. The bulk of questions and comments in the period following the presentations were less than sympathetic to the big-box advocates.

On the positive side, Mauer and Madle together attempted to separate fact from myth. Big-box stores are not new to the community, argued Mauer, claiming that Babbitt's Department Store served as Flagstaff's first big box for nearly a century. This is true. The advent of large-scale department stores in the nineteenth century turned traditional small retailers on their heads, trying to adapt to the new department-style establishment. Further, Mauer continued, the newer, discount-store variety had existed in Flagstaff for nearly three decades without having caused economic harm. Collectively, these stores have provided sales tax revenues to the city that may not have been provided otherwise. Coming prepared with statistics, Mauer found that nearly 18 percent of Flagstaff's sales tax revenues come from the town's eight big box stores alone. He added that the growth of other businesses has been relatively steady, dispelling the myth that big boxes have caused a loss in sales tax revenues from other sectors of the community. He added that small businesses fail not only from competition from larger retailers, but also from poor management practices and business decisions. On the whole, his primary message involved the importance of networking among "big boxes and small boxes."

Conversely, the dominant negative perceptions and aspects of big boxes are many. The following issues sum up the principal arguments presented by the panelists: (1) Small, locally owned businesses that have served the community for a long time will not be able to compete with the low prices and convenience provided by a big box. (2) The development of big boxes promotes and contributes to urban sprawl, where large tracts of undeveloped land turn instantly into seas of parking with their associated big-box buildings. Further, more acres of trees or farmland are consumed, detracting from a community's natural amenities and quality of life. For nearly every big box that has fought its way into Flagstaff, the loss of more trees has been one of the primary issues here in Flagstaff—most recently concerning the new Home Depot store (or "bomb crater," as some called its construction site). (3) Big-box chains have little interest in supporting the local community in the short or long term, and they are not expected to hang around a long time. If this location fails to be profitable in a few years, the store will close and a new one will be built elsewhere. The vacant big-box store is practically useless for alternative purposes; in contrast, historic downtown buildings have changed hands and been modified many times over the course of a century. (4) Each new big box serves as a new *central place* that attracts thousands of people per day. If the store is located near a residential neighborhood, residents nearby will tend to be concerned with potential increases in traffic congestion. Such streets, they argue, were not designed to handle big-box traffic, and these stores are often associated with increased crime, noise, and localized air pollution from delivery trucks and thousands of automobiles coming to "their" neighborhood. Thus, NIMBY-ism can be a prominent issue depending on where the big box is located. (5) Numerous studies have revealed that big stores can destroy as many jobs and as much tax revenue as they create. This is possible given the assumption (not always accurate) that retail spending in any given market is a relatively "fixed pie." It will grow incrementally as population grows, but for the most part there are only so many dollars to go around. It is thought that adding a substantial amount of new development all at one time can lead to a failure to promote existing businesses, some of which will be forced to scale back their operations or to close altogether.

All of these major concerns will vary in their importance from one place to another, but they are generally universal. These issues have clearly played center stage with the recent wave of big-box store development in town, but Flagstaff is not unique. Local communities across the country are struggling to adapt to this new way of retailing. Wal-Mart has received the bulk of negative attention over the past two decades primarily because of its marketing and growth strategies. Thus, small-town main streets and their associated local retail businesses have on many occasions been forced out of business, been forced to relocate to a more favorable location near Wal-Mart, or been forced to specialize in products (usually tourist oriented) that don't compete with Wal-Mart product lines. As of the 1990s, however, most small towns had learned to adjust to the "Wal-Martization of America" as they see it, and now downtowns are once again serving their own specialized market niches. This is Flagstaff's story as well, and you have seen this reflected in the downtown landscape.

From one perspective, then, the transformation of small-town central business districts into specialty and tourist districts has been necessitated by the global process of big-box discount stores spreading across the American landscape. Whatever one thinks of big boxes, though, one thing is sure: they are here to stay (at least for the time being), and they constitute a significant feature in our daily lives and in our human landscapes.

Epilogue

This relatively short walking excursion has taken you through more than a century of development and its resulting human landscapes. As Chester Liebs (1995) titled his book, you have effectively experienced the transition from *Main Street to Miracle Mile.* This tour focused specifically on geographical aspects unique to Flagstaff's local landscapes, from the north downtown and South Side areas to the NAU campus and Milton Avenue. Certainly, a similar tour could just as easily occur in nearly any small town or city throughout the nation. Very similar local, regional, and global processes have been at work to create these landscapes, and by now it should be evident how much can be learned about America as a whole through a brief walk through a specific community's own landscape scenes.

To learn something about our own human landscapes is to learn much about ourselves, and the culture in which we operate. Rather than taking it all for granted and letting it all pass by unnoticed, the landscapes that we create as a society hold the ability to bring it all alive for us as we continually attempt to make sense of the world in which we live. One lesson that comes to mind particularly from this Tour is how interrelated and connected everything is within our built environment. On this tour we encountered four distinct landscape scenes—a historic downtown business district, an ethnic working-class neighborhood, a university campus, and a pretty typical commercial strip. None of these places is isolated from larger processes and events, however. For instance, we learned how the economy of the north downtown has been affected one way or another by places outside of that arena: business competition from the periphery of town, the downtown's increasing popularity for NAU students and visitors, and the challenges presented by a very busy transcontinental railroad line. The way in which downtown continues to develop and change, therefore, will be in part a product of its relationships with trends that originate outside the immediate downtown area.

South Side, too, has been impacted substantially by circumstances from outside: NAU's nondescript invasion from the south, and pressures of downtown redevelopment efforts from the north. A major auto thoroughfare originating at Milton Avenue has been constructed through the heart of South Side, and investors lick their chops at the thought of a flood-free Rio de Flag. In these ways and many more, our four distinct landscape scenes are not isolated, but integrated into a larger geographic locale that is, in turn, linked into regional and global-scale processes. Although many of these external trends affecting Flagstaff and its neighborhoods may be out of this community's immediate realm of control, we have also seen how local community members and their various interest groups and organizations can work together to make the best of Flagstaff's ever-changing geographical relationships.

Happily, at the local level individuals do enjoy a certain ability to transform and improve their own environments. Local decisions are made, and landscapes are altered through countless numbers of individual decisions and actions—hopefully in the name of improving the quality of life for one or more people. The various regulating influences of local and state government enable cities such as Flagstaff to make their own decisions that will affect their own futures in various, often unpredictable ways. The political economic system of capitalism and democracy thus mandates a certain level of freedom for individuals and groups to make choices about how to live and improve the places in which they live and work. Many of these choices and decisions are made within the context of deeply rooted cultural values and ideals, and if we know what to look for we can see the marks of our cultural roots within the landscape itself.

Through a complex interaction of local decision making, global influence, cultural ideals, economic goals, and centralized control, places like Flagstaff gain their own unique sense of place while fitting into a larger geographical, or spatial system. As we have seen here, we can make sense of our landscapes and at least begin to understand why places like NAU and Milton Avenue look and behave the way they do. In the future, the interactions of places and people are only going to become more complex. An understanding of these geographic processes will be even more vital for our society's understanding of how our world is changing, and what the implications will be. Perhaps a brief walk through a place called Flagstaff will play a small role in encouraging such an understanding.

Finally, within what type of built environments do we wish to live in the future? The four distinct landscape scenes experienced here provide a sample of the geographic spaces common throughout America. Since the 1970s there has been an emerging reaction to the automobile-dominated landscapes associated with places like Milton Avenue and the suburbs on the edge of town. The new urbanism movement is strengthening nationwide in an effort to at least partially counter some of the negative impacts of our car culture and the landscapes it has created. Which of the four landscape types experienced along this Tour might represent the best model for future American development to support the mutual goals of community and family rather than merely that of increased mobility? Perhaps all four landscapes, from Main Street to Miracle Mile hold the answers in part with respect to how Americans would prefer to live in future decades.

Downtown Flagstaff is almost a model landscape for a city center making use of the principles of new urbanism. With its pedestrian-friendly streetscape, narrow streets, back alleys, and especially its mixed-use development (combination of residential, commercial, and institutional land use), downtown districts like this one now serve as virtual clinics on how to create entirely new "new urbanist" town centers that have previously lost their former sense of place. Likewise, the South Side neighborhood illustrates what may seem to be a radical alternative to today's sprawling residential suburbs and housing tracts. Far from radical, however, this is how the bulk of urban Americans lived prior to the 1960s. South Side's combination of a rectilinear street network, small residential blocks, back alleys, neighborhood friendliness, and human scale all emphasize community rather than the automobile. Here the car has become South Side's "second-class citizen," so to speak, not entirely eradicated as some might have it, but relegated to garages in alleys behind the homes, allowing the houses themselves to front the street. American architects and planners are realizing that spaces like these represent the types of developments that we should be building in the future. In a sense, new urbanism isn't new at all, but makes use of a variety of historical urban patterns already in use around the world for centuries. As the famous saying goes, "what goes around comes around."

Currently, the comfortable spaces found in the north downtown, in the South Side, and on the NAU campus are gaining more recognition right here in the community. Flagstaff's city leaders have become aware of the national trend toward creating more livable spaces. Flagstaff planners and other city leaders have also been promoting new design guidelines for auto-centric places like Milton Avenue. In future developments along Flagstaff's commercial strips, distinct changes in street and building layout may become reality, including big-box retail stores lined up close to the street with their oceans of parking placed in the back. It is interesting that this was the pattern of the original Miracle Mile in Los Angeles discussed earlier, which allowed the auto thoroughfare to maintain an active pedestrian street life. Lately, everything from street plans and building designs to bike and pedestrian access has been valid for serious consideration, now that more Flagstaff residents realize that the landscapes of Milton Avenue may not represent the way we wish to live in the future.

An associated concern in Flagstaff reflects another national trend—that of trying not to lose the small-town feel, or sense of place, that has made Flagstaff and other towns like it special. Currently, the "urbanization of the rural" is taking place in small towns in relatively close proximity to large metropolitan areas. Many residents are concerned about rapid changes taking place that signify this transition from small town to small city, as evidenced by the popular local bumper stickers seen around Flagstaff that plead, "Don't PHX FLG"—short for "Don't turn Flagstaff into another sprawling Phoenix." The shorter version of this is found on bumper stickers that simply read "FLG," indicating in three letters the strong sense of place that many residents feel for the town.

In our capitalist economy, it is unreasonable to expect that growth and development are simply going to stop at some point, to be replaced by some sort of utopian community model. Economic growth (or decline) will continue to occur as investors come and go from one place to another. This should be clear given the former discussion about why economic growth takes place, and the major role players who promote it. Perhaps a wiser, more reasonable goal would be to channel, or direct this economic growth into different situations that encourage more community-oriented design while maintaining its general economic benefits. To this aim, the emerging new urbanism movement is promising. Whether "old" or "new," places like downtown, South Side, and NAU can teach us excellent lessons about how we might want to improve our living environments in the future—if we are only willing to pay attention. Fortunately, it appears more of us are beginning to learn, and this Tour may represent a decent first step for some.

Please see the author's Web site at **http://jan.ucc.nau.edu/~twp/americatour** for additional current and historic photos of the Tour. This site also includes a link to the author's *Architectural Styles of America* Web site as well as other useful links.

Bibliography

Agnew, J. 1993. Representing space: Space, scale, and culture in social science. In *Place/Culture/Representation*, edited by James Duncan and David Ley. London: Routledge.

Babbitt, J. 2001. Interview by author. Tape recording. Flagstaff, AZ. 08 May.

Babbitt, P. 2000. Interview by author. Tape recording. Flagstaff, AZ. 08 September.

Barber, B. 2000. Jihad vs. McWorld. In *The globalization reader*, edited by Frank Lechner and John Boli. Malden, MA: Blackwell.

Barrett, R. 2001. Interview by author. Tape recording. Flagstaff, AZ. 14 August.

Blair, G. 2001. Interview by author. Tape recording. Flagstaff, AZ. 21 August.

Booth, D. 1999. Spatial patterns in the economic development of the mountain West. *Growth and Change* 30(3): 384–406.

Brass, J. (Ed.). 1994. Community tourism assessment handbook. Corvallis, OR: Western Rural Development Center, Oregon State University.

Bryant, K. 1974. *History of the Atchison, Topeka and Santa Fe Railway.* Lincoln: University of Nebraska Press.

Burgess, P. 1996. Of swimming pools and "slums." In *Planning the twentieth-century American city*, edited by Mary Sies and Christopher Silver. Baltimore: Johns Hopkins University Press.

Clay, G. 1980. *Close-up: How to read the American city.* Chicago: University of Chicago Press.

Clay, G. 1996. *Real places: An unconventional guide to America's generic landscape.* Chicago: University of Chicago Press.

Cline, P. 1994. *Mountain town.* Flagstaff, AZ: Northland.

Cohen, P. 1998. Geography redux: Where you live is what you are. *The New York Times* (21 March).

Conzen, M. 1990. The progress of American urbanism, 1860–1930. In *North America: The historical geography of a changing continent*, edited by Robert Mitchell and Paul Groves. Savage, MD: Rowman and Littlefield.

Dilworth, L. 1996. *Imagining Indians in the Southwest.* Washington, DC: Smithsonian Institution Press.

Duany, A., E. Plater-Zyberk, and J. Speck. 2000. *Suburban nation: The rise of sprawl and the decline of the American dream.* New York: North Point Press.

Engler, M. 1994. Theme towns: The pitfalls and alternatives of image making. *Small Town* (January-February): 14–23.

Francaviglia, R. 1996. *Main Street revisited.* Iowa City: University of Iowa Press.

Francaviglia, R. 1998. Landscape and cultural continuity: The case of the Southwest. *Journal of the West* 37(3): 9–21.

Frazier, D. 2001. What really happened to McGaugh's? *Flagstaff Tea Party* 2(9), September.

Frailey, F. 2001. The empire of BNSF. *Trains* 61(6): 30–41.

Frailey, F. 2002. Who's got the vision? *Trains* 62(2): 34–37.

Frieden, B., and Sagalyn, L. 1989. *Downtown Inc.* Cambridge, MA: MIT Press.

Gaines, T. 1991. *The campus as a work of art.* Westport, CT.: Praeger.

Garreau, J. 1988. *Edge city: Life on the new frontier.* New York: Doubleday.

Gavigan, K. 2002. Interview by author. Tape recording. Flagstaff, AZ. 19 February.

Getis, A., J. Getis, and I. Quastler. 2001. *The United States and Canada: The land and the people.* New York: McGraw-Hill.

Getz, D. 1993. Planning for tourism business districts. *Annals of Tourism Research* 20: 583–600.

Goldberger, P. 1981. *The skyscraper.* New York: Knopf.

Gottdiener, M. 1997. *The theming of America.* Boulder: Westview Press.

Graff, T. 1998. The locations of Wal-Mart and Kmart supercenters: Contrasting corporate strategies. *The Professional Geographer* 50(1): 46–57.

Groth, P. 1997. Frameworks for cultural landscape study. In *Understanding ordinary landscapes*, edited by Paul Groth and Todd Bressi. New Haven: Yale University Press.

Gruidl, J., and S. Kline. 1992. What happens when a large discount store comes to town? *Small Town* (March-April): 20–25.

Hannigan, J. 1998. *Fantasy City*. London: Routledge.

Hayden, D. 1997. Urban landscape history: The sense of place and the politics of space. In *Understanding ordinary landscapes*, edited by Paul Groth and Todd Bressi. New Haven: Yale University Press.

Hemphill, M. 2002. Map of the month: Traffic over the Divide. *Trains* 62(4): 62–63.

Herman, M. 2001. Interview by author. Tape recording. Flagstaff, AZ. 11 May.

Holdsworth, D. 1997. Landscape and archives as texts. In *Understanding ordinary landscapes*, edited by Paul Groth and Todd Bressi. New Haven: Yale University Press.

Hornbeck, D. 1990a. The far West, 1840–1920. In *North America: The historical geography of a changing continent*, edited by Robert Mitchell and Paul Groves. Savage, MD: Rowman and Littlefield.

Hornbeck, D. 1990b. Spanish legacy in the borderlands. In *The making of the American landscape*, edited by Michael Conzen. London: HarperCollins.

Howard, K., and D. Pardue. 1996. *Inventing the Southwest*. Flagstaff: Northland.

Hudson, J. 1990. Settlement of the American grassland. In *The making of the American landscape*, edited by Michael Conzen. London: HarperCollins.

Jackson, J. 1994. *A sense of place, a sense of time*. New Haven: Yale University Press.

Jackson, M. 1999. *Stone landmarks: Flagstaff's geology and historic building stones*. Piedra Azul Press.

Jakle, J. 1990. Landscapes redesigned for the automobile. In *The making of the American landscape*, edited by Michael Conzen. London: HarperCollins.

Jakle, J., and K. Sculle. 1994. *The gas station in America*. Baltimore: Johns Hopkins University Press.

Jakle, J. 1995. Motel by the roadside: America's room for the night. In *Fast Food, Stock Cars, and Rock and Roll*, edited by George Carney. Rowman and Littlefield.

Jakle, J. 1999. America's small town/big city dialectic. *Journal of Cultural Geography* 18(2): 1–28.

Jakle, J. 2001. *City lights: Illuminating the American night*. Baltimore: Johns Hopkins University Press.

Johnson, H. 1990. Toward a national landscape. In *The making of the American landscape*, edited by Michael Conzen. London: HarperCollins.

Kerski, M. 2002. Interview by author. Tape recording. Flagstaff, AZ. 14 February.

Knox, P., and S. Marston. 1998. *Human geography: Places and regions in global context*. Prentice-Hall, Inc.

Kunstler, J. 1993. *The geography of nowhere*. New York: Simon & Schuster.

Lai, D. 1997. The visual character of Chinatowns. In *Understanding ordinary landscapes*, edited by Paul Groth and Todd Bressi. New Haven: Yale University Press.

Lechner, F., and J. Boli, 2000. *The globalization reader*. Blackwell.

Lemon, J. 1990. Colonial America in the eighteenth century. In *North America: The historical geography of a changing continent*, edited by Robert Mitchell and Paul Groves. Savage, MD: Rowman and Littlefield.

Lew, A. 1989. Authenticity and sense of place in the tourism development experience of older retail districts. *Journal of Travel Research* (Spring): 15–22.

Lewis, P. 1972. Small town in Pennsylvania. *Annals of the Association of American Geographers* 62(2): 323–351.

Lewis, P. 1979. Axioms for reading the landscape. In *The interpretation of ordinary landscapes*, edited by Donald Meinig. New York: Oxford University Press.

Lewis, P. 1987. Taking down the velvet rope: Cultural geography and the human landscape. In *Past meets present: Essays about historic interpretation and public audiences*, edited by Jo Blatti. Washington, DC: Smithsonian Institution Press.

Lewis, P. 1990. The Northeast and the making of American geographical habits. In *The making of the American landscape*, edited by Michael Conzen. London: HarperCollins.

Lewis, T. 1997. *Divided highways*. New York: Penguin Books.

Liebs, C. 1995. *Main Street to Miracle Mile*. Johns Hopkins University Press.

Logan, J., and H. Molotch. 1987. *Urban fortunes: The political economy of place.* Berkeley: University of California Press.

Longstreth, R. 1997. *City center to regional mall.* Cambridge: MIT Press.

Lowenthal, D. 1985. *The past is a foreign country.* Cambridge: Cambridge University Press.

Mangum, R., and S. Mangum. 1993. *Flagstaff historic walk.* Flagstaff, AZ: Northland.

McAlester, V., and L. McAlester. 1997. *A field guide to American houses.* New York: Alfred A. Knopf.

McCallister, M. 2001. Interview by author. Tape recording. Flagstaff, AZ. 31 August.

Meinig, D. 1979. Symbolic landscapes. In *The interpretation of ordinary landscapes*, edited by Donald Meinig. Oxford University Press.

Meinig, D. 1993. *The shaping of America: Continental America, 1800–1867.* New Haven: Yale University Press.

Meinig, D. 2001. The Southwest: A definition. In *The multicultural Southwest: A reader*, edited by A. Gabriel Melendez, M. Jane Young, et al. Tucson: University of Arizona Press.

Murtagh, W. 1988. *Keeping time: The history and theory of preservation in America.* New York: Sterling.

Paradis, T. 2000. Conceptualizing small towns as urban places: Downtown redevelopment in Galena, Illinois. *Urban Geography* 21(1): 61–82.

Paradis, T. 2002a. The political economy of theme development in small urban places: The case of Roswell, New Mexico. *Tourism Geographies* 4(1): 22–43.

Paradis, T. 2002b. Flagstaff's downtown 'theme park.' *Flagstaff Tea Party* 2(12), December.

Patton, P. 1986. *Open road: A celebration of the American highway*. New York: Simon and Schuster.

Plezia, M. 2002. *History and Development of the Port of Long Beach*. Public presentation, field trip, Association of American Geographers National Meetings. March.

Poling-Kempes, L. 1989. *The Harvey Girls: Women who opened the West*. New York: Paragon House.

Pooley, E. 1997. The great escape. *Time*. December 8, 52–65.

Port of Long Beach. 2000. *Annual report*. Long Beach, CA: Author.

Port of Long Beach. 2001. Founders show foresight and tenacity. *Re-port: A newsletter for the community*. Fall.

Pulsipher, L. 2000. *World regional geography*. New York: W. H. Freeman and Company.

Richmond, A. 1995. *Cowboys, miners, presidents and kings: The Story of the Grand Canyon Railway*. Grand Canyon Railway.

Riley, R. 1985. Square to the road, hogs to the east. *Illinois Issues* 11(7): 22–26.

Roth, L. 1979. *A concise history of American architecture*. New York: Harper & Row.

Robins, K. 1999. Tradition and translation: National culture in its global context. In *Representing the nation: A reader*, edited by David Boswell and Jessica Evans. New York: Routledge.

Rowntree, L., M. Lewis, M. Price, and W. Wyckoff. 2000. *Diversity amid globalization*. Prentice-Hall.

Rubenstein, J. 1989. *The cultural landscape*. Merrill.

Schein, R. 1997. The place of landscape: A conceptual framework for interpreting an American scene. *Annals of the Association of American Geographers* 87: 660–680.

Sellars, R. 1997. *Preserving nature in the national parks*. New Haven: Yale University Press.

Sheridan, T. 1995. *Arizona: A history*. Tucson: University of Arizona Press.

Smith, S. 1994. Urban geography in a changing world. In *Human geography*, edited by Derek Gregory, Ron Martin, and Graham Smith. Minneapolis: University of Minnesota Press.

Stilgoe, J. 1983. *Metropolitan corridor: Railroads and the American scene*. New Haven: Yale University Press.

Stutz F., and A. de Souza. 1998. *The world economy*. Prentice Hall.

Tayler, A. 1996. Illustrated history of North American railroads. Edison, NJ: Chartwell Books.

Taylor, H. 2000. Interview by author. Flagstaff, AZ. 26 September.

Turner, P. 1984. *Campus: An American planning tradition*. Cambridge: MIT Press.

Upton, D. 1997. Seen, unseen, and scene. In *Understanding ordinary landscapes*, edited by Paul Groth and Todd Bressi. New Haven: Yale University Press.

Vanlandingham, S. 2001. Interview by author. Tape recording. Flagstaff, AZ. 24 July.

Walkup, J. 1984. *Pride, promise, and progress: The development of Northern Arizona University*. Flagstaff: Universal Publishing.

Watkins, H. 2001. Interview by author. Tape recording. Flagstaff, AZ. 07 May.

Whitaker, C. 1996. *Architecture and the American dream*. Three Rivers Press.

Wilcox, D. 2001. Interview by author. Tape recording. Flagstaff, AZ.

Wilcox, S. 2002. Interview by author. Flagstaff, AZ. October.

Wishart, D. 1990. Settling the Great Plains. In *North America: The historical geography of a changing continent*, edited by Robert Mitchell and Paul Groves. Savage, MD: Rowman and Littlefield.

Woodward Architectural Group. 1993. *City of Flagstaff: South Side/Old Town historic building survey*. Volume 1.

Zelinsky, W. 1990. The imprint of central authority. In *The making of the American landscape*, edited by Michael Conzen. London: HarperCollins.

Zelinsky, W. 1997. Seeing beyond the dominant culture. In *Understanding ordinary landscapes*, edited by Paul Groth and Todd Bressi. New Haven: Yale University Press.

0-595-27035-2